Pathways of Social Impact

Pathways of Social Impact

Higher Education for the Public Good

EDITED BY SEAN P. CROSSLAND
WITH ANNABEL WONG
AND THOMAS SCHNAUBELT

Campus Compact

BOSTON, MASSACHUSETTS
Distributed by Stylus Publishing, LCC.

Published by Campus Compact
89 South Street, Suite 103
Boston, MA 02111

Library of Congress Cataloging-in-Publication-Data
[to come]

13-digit ISBN: 978-1-945459-34-4 (cloth)
13-digit ISBN: 978-1-945459-33-7 (paperback)
13-digit ISBN: 978-1-945459-35-1 (library networkable e-edition)
13-digit ISBN: 978-1-945459-36-8 (consumer e-edition)

Printed in the United States of America

All first editions printed on acid free paper
that meets the American National Standards Institute
Z39-48 Standard.

Bulk Purchases

Quantity discounts are available for use in workshops
and for staff development.

Call 1-800-232-0223

First Edition, 2025

This book is dedicated to Gail Robinson, a steadfast champion of service learning, with or without the hyphen. And to our families for all your love and support.

CONTENTS

Note to Readers

*An Online Companion to this book can be accessed by scanning
the QR code that appears on the back cover of this book.*

INTRODUCTION

Pathways Framework and Tool

Thomas Schnaubelt, Sean P. Crossland, and Annabel Wong

D eveloped through iterative refinement over several years, the Pathways of Public Service and Civic Engagement ("pathways") offer a coherent framework for understanding how different but interconnected human actions and endeavors contribute to community capacity building and social change. By placing emphasis on a spectrum of strategies for addressing public challenges, the framework helps practitioners and students identify relevant academic disciplines to draw from, guiding informed action and the cocreation of knowledge and resources aimed at community impact.

It is crucial to recognize that the pathways are not rigidly defined categories but rather serve as a heuristic tool for examining how various approaches to social change intersect and diverge. They are explicitly designed to be intersectional, with flexible boundaries that acknowledge the complex root causes impacting local, national, and global communities.

The pathways are applicable to a range of professional roles in the public and private sectors. Furthermore, individuals whose career interests or roles closely align with a specific pathway can amplify their effectiveness as agents of social change by integrating insights drawn from other pathways. This underscores the notion that individuals can engage with each pathway regardless of their field, position, or status as a student or practitioner. Through shared language and tactics, the pathways emphasize a commitment to the common good.

Contributions in this volume build upon previous scholarship delineating pathways to careers as change agents. The community and civic engagement field often lacks common language and practices, making it difficult to meaningfully benchmark across institutions, and to conduct robust, cross-institution research or evaluation. We believe that the Pathways framework offers a valuable heuristic that can facilitate alignment and collaboration within the field and pave the way for more rigorous research.

Genesis and Evolution

The Pathways framework has a lineage that can be traced back to Minnesota Campus Compact's *Social Change Wheel*, BreakAway's *Active Citizen Continuum*, Joseph Kahne and Joel Westheimer's work on "What Kinds of Citizens?," and even the mantra "Change, not Charity." While various civic learning frameworks, including those mentioned, have played a role in shaping the pathways and advancing our field, none have gained widespread adoption. The use of the Pathways framework by numerous postsecondary institutions, schools, and programs, without external incentives, speaks to its resonance within the field. While the Pathways framework is built upon past efforts, its distinctive evolution has been shaped by thoughtful collaboration. In this section we will outline, to the best of our ability, the genesis and evolution of the Pathways framework and accompanying survey.

The pathways were first conceived as part of the development of a 5-year strategic plan for the Haas Center for Public Service at Stanford University. Around 2010, near the beginning of his tenure as the executive director of the Haas Center,[1] Tom Schnaubelt recognized some recurring patterns in his interactions with students. Two specific student examples—perhaps archetypes—illustrate a portion of the original motivation for the development of the Pathways framework (*Note*: The interactions were real, but the names are fictional).

Elaine the Eager Innovator: Many Stanford students arrive at the school knowing full well that the world is rapidly changing and faces monumental challenges. They bring with them optimism and eagerness to make positive change. During Admit Weekend, Elaine attended the Haas

Center's Open House and asked, "What social justice issue *isn't* being addressed at Stanford?" As the conversation progressed, it became clear that although Elaine had been involved in a wide array of community service initiatives as a high school student, she had not fully defined her own interests and passions. She simply wanted to *start* something.

Andy the Angular: Andy was a participant in a Design for America pitch session. Like Elaine, Andy had been encouraged to engage in social impact and public service projects by both his parents and educators during middle and high school. In fact, he and his family had already created a social venture through which he was selling bottled water domestically and donating all the proceeds to help provide access to clean water in underdeveloped communities in Africa.

As Andy described their venture, he explained that they had intentionally avoided structuring it as a nonprofit because they didn't "want to be beholden to donors" and that "nonprofits couldn't advertise or market products or services." Three things became obvious in the rest of the conversation with Andy. First, he had an unwavering devotion to the concept of social entrepreneurship. Second, his understanding of social entrepreneurship was at best limited, and at worst, highly misconstrued. Finally, he had been led to believe that other forms of engagement were inherently less optimal, sometimes even "bad." Andy had come to Stanford, as many students do, with a preconceived (and somewhat ill-formed) notion about a particular form of public service: in his case, social enterprises as the most effective mechanism for service and nonprofit organizations as inefficient. It is worth noting that while Andy's focus was on social entrepreneurship ("social-e"), this pattern also emerged in other areas, perhaps with the same frequency among students whose primary interest was in activism or policy. In other words, this phenomenon was not restricted to students interested in social-e.

Tom's observations about these interactions resonated with colleagues at the Haas Center and among peers at other postsecondary institutions. These trends were not exclusive to the students he was interacting with, nor were they isolated to Stanford University; they showed up among college and university students in many different contexts.

Another concerning pattern extends beyond students and pertains to a more widespread misunderstanding within the field of higher education community engagement. We use a dizzying array of terms to describe our work: service-learning, public service, civic engagement, social impact, social change, social justice, public scholarship, community-engaged [you fill in the blank], and so forth. Yet, irrespective of the language used locally, there often arises a need to explain how the focus of our work is different from mere volunteering, or some other misunderstanding stemming from assumptions. At the Haas Center for Public Service, the assumptions range from assuming that "public service" is synonymous with "government service, to thinking the center is the place that one should call when locked out of one's car ("public safety"), to believing it is where one makes a charitable donation, and, in fact students sometimes leave unwanted belongings at the doorstep as they move out of their dorm.

Each of these concerning patterns served as motivation to construct a framework that would allow us to both describe our work more accurately and complicate and deepen students' understanding of social change. In addition, we wanted to do it without implying or suggesting an established canon or hierarchy that positions some forms of social change as inherently better than others. While we may individually believe that some are better than others, there is no empirical or ethical consensus around this point.

The first iteration of the pathways emerged through strategic planning conversations with Haas Center staff and stakeholders. The center's 2010–2015 strategic plan, entitled *Linking Community and Student Development*, initially included the following five pathways for public service: Activism, Community-Engaged Learning and Research, Direct Service, Philanthropy, and Policy/Politics. Shortly thereafter, Social Entrepreneurship[2] was added as a sixth pathway.

Collaborations with other postsecondary institutions to refine the Pathways framework began around 2014. Tom Schnaubelt along with Kristy Lobo, a program director at the Haas Center who oversaw the Public Service Leadership Program, reached out to colleagues at University of California-Berkeley's Public Service Center and St. Mary's College of California's Catholic Institute for Lasallian Social Action to form a group with the intention of developing a shared language that might assist us in advising students. An underlying motive was to consider whether we might find potential differences in predispositions among students at our three institutions. Our group's work together generated some changes to the pathways language: Activism became Community Organizing and Activism, Policy/Politics became Policy and Governance, and Social Entrepreneurship became Social Entrepreneurship and Corporate Social Responsibility.[3]

Kristy Lobo developed an initial self-assessment survey tool that provided students an opportunity to reflect upon their experiences, interests, and predisposition toward each of the pathways. The initial working group then began to explore the development of a sophisticated psychometric tool similar to StrengthsQuest using the framework, but faced challenges in developing it without making the survey too long to implement practically. Instead, a brief self-assessment instrument was developed using the Qualtrics platform that included a graphic output that aptly became known as the "spider web" for its six prongs and interconnecting lines. The self-assessment instrument was piloted in 2014–2015 with several programs at Stanford University and St. Mary's College of California, and the initial analysis yielded interesting results. See Chapter 16, "Pathways Data: An Overview," for survey examples, results, and analysis over the years.

Between 2014 and 2016, a number of student workshops were piloted, deploying the initial survey instrument as an advising tool and exploring the language used by archetype student organizations (i.e., organizations that aligned themselves with one particular form of social change). The language used to define each of the pathways continued to evolve during this time, and modifications were made to the survey tool, which continued to be utilized primarily as an advising tool. Input was solicited from Campus Compact member institutions and through a series of workshops and webinars hosted by national organizations (e.g., American Association of Colleges and Universities, Campus Compact, the Community College National Center for Community Engagement, Coalition of Urban and Metropolitan Universities, International Association for Research on Service-Learning and Community Engagement, NASPA, the American Gap Association, the Building Bridges Coalition, and others).

Efforts to expand outreach to other postsecondary institutions ramped up in 2015 as Annabel Wong, Devanie Helman, and Gail Robinson, under the direction of Jo Wong (the Haas Center's director of evaluation and assessment), joined the Haas Center team. Annabel Wong started as a student intern from Stanford's Graduate School of Education during the 2015–2016 academic year, focusing her work on refining the survey instrument; distributing surveys to two community colleges, six public universities, and nine private universities across the United States; and then analyzing the data collected from more than 1,500 respondents. As a higher education consultant, Gail Robinson initially volunteered to assist with outreach to community and technical colleges to ensure the language and instruments were relevant in those contexts. In 2016, Gail became an official consultant at the Haas Center and in 2019 assumed the role of central organizer for the multi-institution Pathways of Public Service Working Group ("Working Group").

Under Gail's leadership, outreach began to expand the use of the framework and survey tool to other campuses. The members of the Working Group strongly influenced the evolution of the survey tool, exchanging information about advising and programming activities, and how the framework was being used at their respective campuses. Working Group members met quarterly via telephone conference calls, in-person at conferences and events, and eventually via Zoom meetings.

While a small financial contribution was solicited from each collaborating institution to support the Working Group, it was not a requirement for institutional participation. To ensure any campus could participate, efforts to organize and support the Working Group were largely funded by the Haas Center for Public Service. While the Working Group members came from a variety of types of institutions and professional backgrounds, they were interested in developing and implementing a shared framework and tool. With this motivation in common, they formed a learning community whose conversations offered broader insights into the scope and development of the Pathways framework. One important early insight from the group was that the examples that served as illustrations of each of the six pathways within the survey tool were just as important, if not more so, than the formal definitions that were generated.

It was during this period that Sean Crossland became actively involved with the pathways. While members of the Working Group joined from a variety of contexts, Sean's serves as illustrative of a common theme. When he joined, Sean was teaching a course on civic leadership and so was initially drawn to the Pathways framework for its strength in differentiating among various forms of social change. He conceived of the framework as a means of avoiding institutional reactiveness and concerns about the language of activism and organizing that was part of the material he emphasized in his teaching. He found the survey useful as a reflective tool for conversations with students, and through these interactions began to deepen his understanding of both flaws and value in each of the different pathways. What started as a "Trojan horse" for him became a tool for expanding his own views about, and sense of interconnection among, different forms of social change.

After numerous presentations at higher education conferences, the Haas Center team decided to host an institute designed to expose newcomers to the Pathways framework and the self-assessment tool and serve as a retreat for active members of the Working Group. The first Pathways institute and retreat took place in the fall of 2019 at Stanford University.

Among the major outcomes of the gatherings were a stronger learning community identity, an explicit focus on research to support the use of the pathways, the tacit endorsement of campuses' ability to "white label" the framework to suit their local context (while keeping the pathways themselves intact), and a conscious decoupling of the use of the framework from an expectation of participating in the joint survey project. There were also some major revisions to the survey and the way the survey results were displayed.

Although the COVID-19 pandemic hindered efforts to reconvene, additional Working Group retreats have been hosted by the University of Pittsburgh (2021), George Washington University (2022), and Utah Valley University (2023). Recognizing that Campus Compact would ultimately be a better long-term administrative home for the Working Group, a series of conversations led to the transition of the leadership of the Working Group to the Compact in 2022.

The Pathways framework itself is conceptually nonpartisan and devoid of ideological loyalties. In other words, the pathways could be utilized individually or collectively for regressive and authoritarian purposes, or toward liberational and democratic aims. Examples of engagement within each pathway exist across the political spectrum. Although students often choose (when given a choice) to participate in experiences that conform to their existing political perspective, care needs to be taken to ensure that involvement in pathways as educational opportunities do not exclusively promote, or put a thumb on the scale of, a particular political stance or ideology. Our work as educators should help in clarifying values but must not rob students of the hard work of determining what those values mean for themselves. These distinctions, and our ability to navigate them, are the most creative part of community engagement work—as well as the most fraught.

Pathways Working Group

By May 2023, 95 institutions and organizations had participated in the Pathways Working Group, with 17,225 students having taken the survey since 2015. Institutional participation has included:

- 73 four-year colleges and universities (both public and private)
- 14 community colleges (all public)

- four higher education consortia (National Campus Compact, two state Compacts, Philadelphia Higher Education Network for Neighborhood Development)
- one state commission on service (UServeUtah)
- four overseas universities (Qatar University, University of Western Australia, East China Normal University, and University of New South Wales)

Current participation includes a subset of this list.

The development of this work has been collaborative and cocreative, involving members of the Working Group and others with varying levels of exposure to the pathways. Our continuing work together on the Pathways framework is to ensure that it is meaningful and accessible for those not familiar with it and that it advances and informs the thoughtful, collective work underway within the Working Group.

Book Overview

Interest in the Pathways framework is growing nationally. This publication seeks to offer empirical and theoretical framings of the pathways for four related purposes: (1) to explore and synthesize literature focused on the knowledge, skills, and attributes within each pathway; (2) to offer an individual career profile for each pathway; (3) to provide exemplars of the diverse ways in which the pathways are being used across higher education institutions and within communities; and (4) to highlight practical and theoretical implications for future potential uses of the Pathways framework and tool.

Part One seeks to establish an empirical foundation of knowledge, skills, and attributes associated with each pathway. Systematic literature reviews were conducted to deepen and synthesize our current understanding of the unique and shared characteristics among practitioners within and across pathways. By delving deeper into the distinctive features of each pathway, our aim is to guide deliberative choices regarding which pathway(s) might make the most meaningful contributions to community capacity building. Additionally, we seek to further illuminate their interconnected potential.

Part Two elevates examples of pathway experimentation and usage across departmental, programmatic, and curricular approaches. At the department level, we share examples of how the pathways have shaped strategic visioning. At the cocurricular level, we feature examples of how the pathways have been effectively utilized to systematically transform students' passion into action. At the curricular level we include ways the pathways have complemented course- and discipline-level learning goals. Each example speaks to the successes and challenges in leveraging the Pathways framework.

Part Three offers generative possibilities for future practitioner scholarship and practical application concerning the pathways. We explore ways to enhance the utilization of and engagement with the pathways, encompassing both individual experiences and their potential impact on policy reform. The closing section serves as a call to action to realize the pathways' transformative potential for the community engagement field, and for advancing the public purpose of higher education.

This edited volume serves two primary purposes. First, it aims to offer foundational and empirical support of the Pathways framework, thereby enhancing its relevance to college student learning and career outcomes, social impact, and staff and faculty development. Secondly, it seeks to provoke critical reflection on the institutional commitment of higher education to democracy, emphasizing the ongoing necessity of examining and interrogating this relationship.

Generally, this book is for anyone looking for tools and ideas to help complicate binary thinking around social change and the public purpose of higher education. For those less familiar with the Pathways framework, this work will provide an accessible and in-depth review of its current and possible applications.

Faculty teaching courses related to social change will find value in the Pathways framework and this book as a resource to expand curricular and pedagogical innovations. Practitioners working in public service, civic engagement, and social change–oriented programming will find value in the articulation of the knowledge, skills, and attributes associated with each pathway. Additionally, practitioners and faculty with advisory capacity may find immediate application of the associated resources and examples to support advisees in framing their academic or professional goals around social change. The career profiles section will be relevant to anyone working with students exploring career options. The Pathways framework and associated work emphasize ways to integrate discussions of social change strategies into how students choose their majors and ultimately the careers they may opt to pursue. Graduate and undergraduate students can find value in the case studies as real-world examples of people engaging in one or more of the pathways, and the career profiles offer models that can inform students' choices about their academic and professional trajectories.

Community change organizations, including nonprofits, philanthropic entities, and state/local governments, may find value in imagining different ways to engage students and professional staff around the social issues that are the focus of their work. Specifically in Utah, the governor's Commission on Service and Volunteerism is using the Pathways framework as training for nonprofit organizations to craft meaningful volunteer opportunities for the community. To that end, they have developed an open-source version of the survey for members of the public seeking ways to become involved in their communities.

Ultimately, this volume should be viewed as a starting point from which scholar-practitioners and community engagement professionals can react, respond, adapt, critique, and innovate. We hope this work offers some insights about the interconnectedness of the pathways and how the convergence of multiple pathways fosters opportunities for enduring and systemic social change. Furthermore, this book is an invitation to practitioners, academics, and students to find their own ways to engage with the Pathways framework.

Notes

1. Tom also served as a resident fellow in Branner Hall, Stanford's public service and civic engagement theme dorm, from 2010 to 2022.

2. Social entrepreneurship was initially considered but rejected as a pathway by the Haas Center staff, due to concerns that social entrepreneurism, as often practiced, did not adequately attend to the center's principles of ethical and effective service. Eventually it was included as an attempt to influence the practice of social-e (at least at Stanford) with our principles.

3. With both social-e and activism, the decision to create a category using complementary concepts (as opposed to a single name) was in part due to the desire to avoid purely academic battles about the precise meaning of individual concepts that are widely debated.

Part One

PRACTITIONER PROFILES

Chapter 1

PRACTITIONER PROFILES INTRODUCTION

Sean P. Crossland and Annabel Wong

The Pathways of Public Service and Civic Engagement present a typology designed to highlight distinctions in ways to engage in social change without intending to sever the connections between them. Each pathway overlaps with multiple other pathways, so that activities falling within one pathway may also exist in another. Our interest to develop and share "Practitioner Profiles" emerged from a desire to translate findings from the literature reviews for each pathway into an accessible and concrete resource for advisors and students.

Phase I of the literature review processes began in January 2022. It was undertaken by a group of research fellows selected from a national call. In generating the reviews, we sought to use a similar methodology to that developed by Lina Dostilio (2017) in her seminal book, *The Community Engagement Professional in Higher Education: A Competency Model for an Emerging Field*. Our approach was to develop a preliminary competency model for each of the six pathways and frame our approach with caution and intention so as "not to promote a singular worldview or advance a singular valuation of success" (p. 29). In the same light, the Pathways Practitioner Profiles should be employed as a generative resource, and with care to avoid reductive or perspective application. Recognizing that this is the first published book on the Pathways framework, it is important to leave room for each of the profiles to grow and evolve as the utilization and understanding of the framework expands.

In an initial meeting with the research fellows, we set the goal of developing literature reviews around the knowledge, skills, and attributes associated with each pathway, as well as around how social change is described within each pathway. One challenge from the outset of the project was the inevitable overlap between the pathways when exploring them as distinct rather than overlapping and intersectional. However, for the sake of clarity in scope, research fellows sought to focus literature reviews on each pathway as much as possible. Over the following 6 months, research fellows met regularly and produced a first draft of literature reviews in the summer of 2022. Literature reviews are available in the Online Companion.

Phase II began in July 2022, with a peer review process of the literature reviews in which each research fellow read the literature reviews produced by others and provided collegial feedback. We hosted a group brainstorm session focused on how best to format the reviews and what would eventually become the first template for the Practitioner Profiles.

Once literature reviews were updated, research fellows began a community-checking process we called "practitioner advisor checks," or discussions. Practitioner advisors were identified based on their extensive experience and/or in-depth study within a specific pathway, as well as their comprehension of how these pathways intersect with social change.

Practitioner advisors' "expertise" was not predicated on their years of professional experience; instead, we were mindful to include voices from individuals in all stages of professional development and learning, including students and practitioners at early-career, mid-career, and advanced-career levels. In total, research fellows completed 69 practitioner advisor checks, five practitioner advisor focus groups, and four student focus groups. Three of the student focus groups were campus-based and made up of leadership groups and classes from Drake University, Juniata College, and Utah Valley University. The fourth focus group was an at-large group of students from four different U.S.-based colleges and universities. After incorporating feedback from practitioner advisor checks, drafts were shared with the Pathways Working Group for additional feedback.

Phase II was completed in May 2023, with the primary products being revised literature reviews and initial drafts of Practitioner Profiles. Final Practitioner Profiles were completed between August 2023 and March

2024, with two new authors stepping in for research fellows who were unable to complete the project. For a complete list of contributors to this project, see the Editors and Contributors section in this volume (Appendix A in the Online Companion).

Introducing the Pathways Practitioner Profiles

The Practitioner Profiles offered in the following section are intended to be used as starting places for ongoing development of the knowledge base of each of the pathways. We view this project as emergent rather than definitive. It is important to emphasize Practitioner Profiles are not intended to be reductive or prescriptive, nor are the pathways limited to a set of partisan views. The knowledge, skills, and attributes identified within each pathway are not necessarily distinctive, and some characteristics are shared across all pathways, as described in the next section. One ongoing challenge of developing examples within pathways is avoiding partisan political leaning as much as possible. As the body of work expands, we hope to identify interconnections among the knowledge, skills, and attributes across pathways and discern unique relationships between specific pathways.

Shared Characteristics

After the Pathways Practitioner Profiles were drafted, the following areas of knowledge, technical skill, relational skill, and attributes were identified as shared across of all the pathways.

Knowledge
- historical and contemporary context of the issue and larger field; lived experiences of the community; and especially power structures and relational dynamics among stakeholders, environments, and organizations
- personal positionality, identity, and biases, including core values, ethical limits, and perspectives on helping and "saving"
- systems thinking and social change theory
- policymaking, as well as political and nonprofit governance

Technical Skills

- written and spoken communication to multiple audiences, such as reporting, presenting, and providing feedback
- project management skills for time and resource allocation
- data and database management (collection, analysis, synthesis, summary, etc.)
- impact assessment

Relational Skills

- trust building, listening, and cross-cultural communication
- conflict resolution, facilitating dialogue, consensus building, and collaboration

Attributes

- openness and humility
- empathy and compassion
- flexibility and resilience
- sense of stewardship and responsibility

Pathways as Interrelated and Overlapping

Each pathway has potential to overlap and intersect with multiple other pathways, based on the desired impacts and approaches to social change. For example, calls for change within the Policy and Governance Pathway are often the focus of efforts from within the Community Organizing and Activism Pathway, whether that is organizing for police oversight through civilian review boards or advocating for establishing and enforcing guidelines for age-appropriate literature in schools. Initiatives within the Philanthropy Pathway often look to organizations aligned with the Direct Service Pathway to inform their decision making about financial support, such as using the number of volunteers and hours spent volunteering to demonstrate the deservingness and potential impacts of philanthropic support.

As another example, mutual aid offers an opportunity to explore how each of the pathways might converge within a single effort. Most mutual aid efforts tend to run entirely or primarily on volunteer labor (Direct

Service) and feature nonhierarchical organizational structure (Policy and Governance). Many include educational components for communities to learn (Community-Engaged Learning and Research) about a variety of topics, from community resources to structural exploitation (Policy and Governance). Grocery rescue programs often provide groceries and produce (Social Entrepreneurship and Corporate Social Responsibility). Donation drives and individual giving often supply needed items for community members (Philanthropy). Mutual aid is about building relationships to change social and political structures (Community Organizing and Activism).

The profiles in the following chapters of Part One are delineated out of necessity to define the scope of inquiry. We encourage readers to think about where the knowledge, skills, attributes, and activities might overlap. Like the framework itself, the profiles should be treated as heuristics rather than prescriptions. Countless questions persist about the ways in which the pathways converge, diverge, overlap, and intersect.

Profiles as Interdisciplinary

A previous iteration of the Pathways Profiles contained suggestions for students to explore majors and disciplines, depending on their particular pathway(s) of interests. However, these suggestions fell short in capturing the nuanced ways in which pathways could integrate seamlessly within any major. Instead of offering a restricted or overly general description of how students might consider the pathways in decisions about academic areas of study, it was decided to omit the section entirely. We encourage readers to consider how disciplines may be complemented by the Pathways framework and vice versa.

Using the Pathways Practitioner Profiles

The Pathways Practitioner Profiles can be used individually or in combination with each other. For example, if a learning experience is focused on Policy and Governance, it may be the only profile used. Alternatively, the Policy and Governance Profile may be centered while the other profiles serve to explore how other pathways might influence Policy and Governance.

The profiles were created primarily from existing literature and supported with practitioner advisor checks. The characteristics outlined in each pathway should be considered as key areas of emphasis rather than an exclusive list. In other words, there may be additional knowledge, skills, and attributes pertinent to each pathway that are not covered in the current profiles.

We hope that use of the profiles continues to evolve as an iterative process where practitioners share successes, challenges, and opportunities for growth moving forward.

Reference

Dostilio, L. (2017). *The community engagement professional in higher education: A competency model for an emerging field.* Campus Compact.

Chapter 2

PRACTITIONER PROFILE

Direct Service

Mike Moon

※

*D*irect service, as defined by the Stanford University Haas Center for Public Service, entails "working to address the immediate needs of individuals or a community, often involving contact with the people or places being served." It often serves as a gateway for students' lifelong civic engagement. Direct service allows students to intimately interact with community issues, fostering a deeper understanding of root causes and other pathways to address public concerns at the systemic level. Research has shown that participation in direct service positively affects students' commitment to their communities, their willingness to assist those in need, their promotion of racial understanding, and their influence on social values (Astin et al., 2000). Moreover, direct service offers students the opportunity to gain essential knowledge about community issues, needs, and desires; develop relevant skills; and understand the social context in which their service operates. These foundational elements serve as the bedrock for students' meaningful engagement in direct service activities, equipping them to contribute substantially to their communities while also shaping their values and choices. Additionally, such experiences allow students to explore the potential of pursuing direct service endeavors as a full-time career. For many current practitioners, an initial interaction with direct service in high school or college, as part of a community-engaged learning experience, led them to a full-time professional career in the Direct Service Pathway.

Direct service, sometimes perceived as a short-term remedy to pressing public concerns, is often situated within the broader debate about "charity vs. justice" models of service. The charity is represented as efforts to address the immediate needs of individuals, families, and communities, while justice encompasses a systemic, long-term approach to tackling the root causes of social issues. Although direct service is subject to critiques associated with the charity model—deficit thinking, saviorism, and failing to address root causes—it plays a vital role in responding to immediate needs and can serve as a form of harm reduction. Despite its perceived limitations, direct service remains a popular form of volunteerism due to its capacity to yield tangible outcomes in a relatively short time frame, providing volunteers with a sense of fulfillment. Furthermore, direct service, though often regarded as a short-term response to public issues, holds a crucial place within the broader landscape of civic engagement. It provides immediate relief, fosters personal connections to social challenges, and serves as a stepping stone for lifelong commitment to addressing societal needs. By equipping individuals with the necessary knowledge and skills, direct service empowers them to make a lasting impact on their communities while deepening their understanding of the multifaceted nature of public service. Therefore, it should be recognized and valued as an essential component of the diverse array of pathways to effecting positive social change.

Under the umbrella of the Direct Service Pathway, several engagement methods exist. Among them are ongoing engagement, event-based responses, and capacity building. Ongoing engagement refers to the continuous involvement of individuals in the planning, execution, and evaluation of services. This approach can foster a deep, sustained relationship between individuals providing service and the community, ensuring that interventions are responsive to evolving needs. Ongoing Direct Service opportunities can include participation on community boards, sustained involvement in volunteer programs, and developing long-term relationships and understanding within the community. Event-based responses as a form of direct service involve rapidly mobilizing volunteers and resources to address urgent needs during specific events or emergencies. These responses typically include activities such as organizing pop-up events, deploying rapid response teams, and distributing essential resources to those affected. The focus is on delivering immediate relief and support in a targeted, timely manner, often within a short timeframe. Capacity building in direct service emphasizes equipping individuals and organizations with the tools and knowledge they need to address community challenges effectively. This form of engagement includes providing coaching, offering advisory services, delivering instruction, and supporting logistical planning. The goal is to strengthen the overall capacity of volunteers and organizations, enabling them to respond more efficiently and sustainably to ongoing and future needs. By empowering a mix of these direct service methods, participants maximize their efforts, impact in the community, and individual growth. Each approach offers unique benefits, whether in building long-term relationships, responding to immediate needs, or empowering the community to take action.

Knowledge

Effective direct service work is grounded in a deep understanding of the community's needs, the root causes of social issues, and the broader systemic context in which these issues exist. This knowledge not only informs the approach and strategies employed by volunteers but also enhances their ability to contribute meaningfully to the communities they serve. Understanding the social, economic, and cultural factors at play is essential for making informed decisions and implementing solutions that address both immediate needs and long-term challenges:

- knowledge of the community being served, including their history, desires, cultures, and needs, as defined by the community
- knowledge of other pathways—how Direct Service serves as harm reduction and how other pathways can contribute to more long-term solutions
- awareness of organizations and initiatives that exist in the nonprofit, public, and for-profit sectors
- strategies to identify and best meet immediate needs
- knowledge of the history and context of root causes of the social issue being addressed
- understanding of the power of one's own personal actions
- knowledge of impact measurement
- knowledge of community engagement continuum—how a Direct Service volunteer can experience progression from a volunteer to an engaged/active contributor of social change
- self-awareness of individual perceptions, biases, power, and so on

Skills

Direct service, a hands-on approach to addressing community needs, necessitates a diverse set of skills for effective engagement and execution. Individuals involved in direct service must possess or develop a wide range of competencies, from interpersonal communication and empathy to logistical planning and problem solving. This multifaceted nature of direct service not only requires participants to bring a variety of skills to their work but also to cultivate new abilities through the challenges and experiences encountered in the field. Engaging in direct service offers a unique opportunity for personal and professional growth, as individuals learn to navigate complex social dynamics, adapt to changing environments, and respond to the immediate needs of communities. Thus, direct service allows for the utilization of diverse skills while also acting as a crucible and catalyst for the development of a broader skill set, thereby enriching the individual's capacity to make a meaningful impact while enhancing their overall competency portfolio (see Table 2.1).

Table 2.1. Skills That Can Be Exercised and Enhanced Through Direct Service Opportunities

Technical Skills	Relational Skills
• cross-cultural communication • verbal communication • data collection and analysis • effective assessment and allocation of available resources	• flexibility • reliability • consistency • cooperativeness • being teachable / willing to learn • decisiveness • ability to identify which personal and technical skills would be most helpful to the organization • compassion • being a team player • cultural awareness • ability to provide clear, constructive feedback

Attributes and Qualities

Beyond the essential skills and knowledge required for effective direct service, certain attributes and personal qualities play a crucial role in the success of these endeavors. Engaging in direct service often demands a unique combination of characteristics that enable individuals to navigate the complexities of community work, build trust, and maintain resilience in the face of challenges. In the context of public service and civic engagement, *attributes* refer to the inherent characteristics or personal traits that individuals bring to their service roles. These are often intrinsic qualities such as empathy, reliability, and adaptability, which influence how effectively one can engage with and support their community. *Qualities*, on the other hand, are the developed or cultivated traits that enhance an individual's effectiveness in service roles. These may include skills like resilience, problem solving, and leadership, which are shaped through experiences and training.

Table 2.2. List of Direct Service Attributes and Qualities

Attributes	*Qualities*
• *empathy*: understanding and connecting with individuals and communities being served • *adaptability*: adjusting approaches as circumstances evolve • *cultural competence*: understanding and appreciating different cultures and backgrounds • *patience*: staying committed and persistent in the face of setbacks • *community orientation*: a deep commitment to the well-being and prosperity of the community • *ethical and values-driven*: commitment to ethical principles and integrity	• *effective communicator*: verbal and nonverbal communication for building trust and collaboration • *problem-solving skills*: creative solutions and efficient issue resolution • *advocacy skills*: raising awareness, mobilizing resources, and influencing policies • *critical thinker*: analyzing situations and making informed decisions • *organization*: managing tasks, resources, schedules, and deadlines efficiently • *collaborative*: leveraging collective strengths and expertise for common goals • *resilience*: recovering from setbacks and maintaining commitments • *resourceful*: making the most of available resources and finding creative solutions • *self-reflective*: fostering continuous personal growth and improvement

Engaging in direct service not only requires individuals to possess certain foundational attributes but also encourages the development of additional qualities that are crucial for impactful service. These attributes and qualities enable individuals to navigate complex social dynamics, address community needs with sensitivity, and contribute meaningfully to their public service roles. As such, they are essential for anyone aiming to excel in the Pathways of Public Service and Civic Engagement (see Table 2.2).

Job Titles Associated With This Pathway

- nonprofit CEO or executive director
- volunteer/program coordinator
- community worker
- municipal parks and recreation coordinator
- public health community service director
- school teacher
- emergency first responder
- community-engaged learning professor
- state commission on service
- AmeriCorps administrator/staff/member
- higher education community engagement center/office
- social worker
- case manager
- counselor/therapist
- homeless shelter manager
- youth mentor
- public interest lawyer
- medical practitioner in underserved areas
- food bank manager
- housing advocate
- environmental activist
- elderly care worker
- domestic violence counselor
- youth service coordinator
- disaster relief worker
- veteran services officer
- faith-based worker
- community health worker

Activities

To cultivate a robust sense of working in the Direct Service Pathway, students have a multitude of engaging activities at their disposal. The following list shows some valuable options for students looking to embark on this meaningful journey:

- *Connect with the campus community engagement center*: Campus engagement centers are hubs for service opportunities, resources, and networking.
- *Enroll in community-engaged learning courses*: Enrolling in community-engaged learning courses integrates academic learning with practical service experiences.
- *Participate in AmeriCorps*: AmeriCorps offers structured service opportunities ranging from education and environmental conservation to disaster relief.
- *Join alternative spring break or study-abroad programs*: Many universities organize travel trips that provide intensive, hands-on experiences focused on service.
- *Engage in community-based research*: Collaborate with professors and community organizations on research projects that address local issues.
- *Offer mentorship and tutoring*: Provide mentorship or tutoring services to fellow students or local youth.
- *Participate in community events*: Attend community events, town hall meetings, and public forums to gain insight into local issues and connect with residents.
- *Form partnerships with nonprofits*: Collaborate with local nonprofit organizations, offering your time and expertise in areas such as marketing, fundraising, or technology to support their missions.
- *Create your own service project:* Identify a specific issue or need in your community and organize a service project or awareness campaign to address it.

Reference

Astin, A. W., Vogelgesang, L. J., Ikeda, E. K., & Yee, J. A. (2000). *How service learning affects students*. Higher Education Research Institute.

Chapter 3

PRACTITIONER PROFILE

Community-Engaged Learning and Research

Joanne Tien

Community-engaged learning and research are activities that integrate public service with academic goals. However, many people are not aware of the emerging field of community-engaged learning and research as a career pathway in higher education and elsewhere. As such, many practitioners enter the field by chance, or through exposure to it through a service-learning course in college. Many practitioners within community-engaged learning and research have transformative experiences when working with communities and aspire to continue having such a positive impact on a systemic level. At the same time, many community-engaged learning and research professionals have an interest in teaching, research, and evaluation, and many have earned PhDs. Some practitioners have even been drawn to leave traditional academic tenure-track positions in higher education in order to pursue community-engaged learning and research, seeing it as a more impactful way of doing research and teaching that is better aligned with their values. This is sometimes referred to as "Alt-Ac" for "Alternative Academic."

Practitioners in this field may participate in community-engaged *teaching* or community-engaged *research*.[1] Community-engaged teaching opportunities often occur within service-learning courses at universities or through community-based organizations, and may be cotaught by faculty, lecturers, staff, community partners, and others with community-based expertise. In these courses, instructors integrate academic coursework with field-based activities in which students work with community organizations on projects that ideally both support the needs of the organization while also advancing students' learning. Community-engaged teaching highlights the overlap and intersectional nature of the Pathways framework, as students can have an engaged learning experience through one or multiple pathways. The service-learning movement began with a direct service focus, meaning that instructors would incorporate some element of hands-on service designed to benefit a community. As the field evolved, so did the types and nature of activities in service-learning experiences. It is now a common occurrence at many institutions for students to participate in community-engaged research projects as part of their community-engaged learning experiences.

In addition to participating in a community-based project, students are typically asked to write papers and reflect on their learning in relation to academic content in the course. Therefore, instructors of these courses must have strong skills in teaching and curriculum development as well as the ability to develop partnerships and codesign projects with community organizations. In order to facilitate collaborative work in diverse community contexts, instructors must also have an awareness of systems of power and how their own and students' positionalities interact with these systems, *as well as* the ability to support students in understanding and reflecting on these systems, while they navigate them in practice.

Community-engaged research can take place in the context of a community-engaged course or outside of it. It typically involves researchers partnering with community organizations to better understand issues that impact communities and develop solutions. Community-engaged research involves collaborating with community members to codevelop research questions and codesign research projects in ways that involve community members in the collection, analysis, and publication of data. Community-engaged researchers often are able to see the real impacts of their research through policy and other systemic changes, and may produce white papers, publications for lay audiences, or other products of value to community organizations and their constituents. Practitioners in this field tend to have skills in, and a genuine enthusiasm for, research in addition to the interpersonal skills for building and sustaining community relationships.

Knowledge

- epistemological method that is community-based (drawing on the knowledges and experiences of those most impacted)
- asset-based framework, building upon asset-based community development as an alternative to deficit-based approaches
- valuation of community-generated knowledge and wisdom, decentering the idea that valid knowledge only comes from the academy
- understanding of the lived experiences of community members
- awareness of one's own positionality
  - understanding of one's own self, context of self, identity, and biases
  - acknowledgment of the power differential between members of the academic institution and members of the community, and willingness to disrupt and/or leverage that power
- knowledge of historical context
  - general knowledge of local history, specifically the relationship between the academic institution and local community (town–gown relationship)
  - understanding of historical contexts of privilege and power, specifically any power differentials between groups coming to work together
  - an understanding of relevant power dynamics such as those related to race, class, and gender

Skills

Table 3.1 outlines key skills, categorized as either technical or relational, along with specific examples and applications for each.

Table 3.1. Skills That Can Be Exercised and Enhanced Through Community-Engaged Learning and Research

Technical Skills	Relational Skills
<ul><li>teaching<ul><li>knowledge of both the theory and practice of engaged-learning pedagogy</li><li>ability to build curriculum</li><li>understanding of the theory and practice of social justice and diversity, equity, and inclusion, particularly as they relate to classroom teaching</li></ul></li><li>research<ul><li>ability to perform evaluation and assessment to meet community partner needs</li><li>ability to write and publish for multiple audiences—both academic publications and public scholarship pieces</li><li>knowledge of and ability to practice participatory data-collection and analysis methods collaboratively with community partners</li></ul></li><li>project management<ul><li>administrative skills to manage the research project, including scheduling meetings, interviews, focus groups, and so on</li><li>ability to coordinate and communicate between different stakeholders involved in the project, including members of the research team, community partners, and constituents</li></ul></li></ul>	<ul><li>trust and relationship building<ul><li>cross-cultural communication: an understanding of how people from differing backgrounds communicate and the ability to understand and communicate across difference</li><li>ability to be a good listener</li><li>showing up for community partner needs and events</li><li>accountability: setting clear expectations across all stakeholders and following through on those expectations</li></ul></li><li>emotional intelligence<ul><li>understanding of the five components of self-awareness, self-regulation, motivation, empathy, and effective communication</li><li>clear and compassionate communication</li><li>consensus building</li></ul></li><li>ability to work with diverse groups of people<ul><li>ability to understand another's point of view</li><li>systems thinking mindset: understanding of the root causes of the social inequalities that community-engaged research and teaching aim to address</li></ul></li></ul>

Attributes and Qualities

- *cultural humility*: an awareness of the limitations of one's own worldview and ability to understand the backgrounds and experiences of others, in combination with an openness to understanding others' cultural backgrounds and worldviews; cultural humility prioritizes mutual respect and partnerships with others
- *curiosity*: holding off from assumptions and approaching new situations with an openness to various outcomes and willingness to learn
- *reciprocity*: centering interdependence in the community-partner relationship, which involves a consideration of the strengths, knowledges, and capacities of all those involved in the partnership, a shared responsibility to work toward mutual benefit, and collaboration in all parts of the project to ensure value and relevance to all those involved
- *flexibility*: ability to adapt to shifting circumstances and understand the potentially changing needs of community partners and all stakeholders involved in the project
- *resiliency*: ability to respond effectively to difficult and unpredictable situations, which can come up in community-engaged work and in addressing social inequalities
- *compassion*: ability to understand, empathize with, and respond effectively to the experiences of others
- *critical thinking*: ability to analyze arguments, make inferences and decisions, and think on one's own; this involves a continuous questioning of the status quo and an analysis of existing systems of power

Job Titles Associated With This Pathway

- director of community-engaged research
- professor
- lecturer
- program manager
- researcher
- evaluator
- curriculum developer
- data scientist
- data analyst
- geographer/cartographer

- partnerships manager
- partnerships coordinator
- director of programs

Most jobs are found within community organizations, nonprofits, universities, or research institutes. Practitioners typically pair skills in teaching and research with skills from other pathways, especially community organizing, policy, and direct service.

Activities

There are many ways for students to develop the foundational knowledge and skills needed to be successful as a community-engaged learning and research professional. Notably, many of these skills students have already developed through their college coursework, such as those related to writing, analysis, and research methods. It can be useful to take a variety of research methods courses across a wide range of qualitative and quantitative approaches in order to broaden one's toolkit to meet an array of community needs. Many practitioners also find service-learning courses to be particularly helpful in learning how to do research with communities.

In addition to "hard" technical research skills, "soft" skills are often more crucial for success in this field. These skills, such as communication, emotional intelligence, and the ability to collaborate with diverse groups of people, are typically honed through experience and on-the-job training. Many of these soft skills, coupled with courses in engaged pedagogy, also prepare practitioners for roles as community-engaged learning instructors. Many successful practitioners have noted that they developed these skills through participation in community-engaged teaching and research activities, and the more experience they had, the more effective they became in this field.

Note

1. Depending on the field, community-engaged research can take many different names, including but not exclusive to "community-based participatory research," "participatory action research," "community-based research," etc. In general, these different names hold similar principles around creating nonhierarchical relationships in the research process and examining and seeking to alter larger systems of power.

Chapter 4

PRACTITIONER PROFILE

Social Entrepreneurship and Corporate Social Responsibility

Renee Sedlacek Lee

Social entrepreneurship and corporate social responsibility (SECSR) are both concepts that blend business acumen with a commitment to societal and environmental impact. Together, these approaches fall under the broader umbrella of corporate citizenship, which emphasizes a company's role in contributing positively to society. One way to distinguish between these two concepts is to view social entrepreneurship as a proactive approach to social issues through the creation of new businesses, while corporate social responsibility is often a reactive response to existing business practices. The SECSR Pathway is growing in popularity with students due to its ability to foster both financial and social returns (Nabi et al., 2017; Papi-Thornton, 2016), making it essential to understand the distinct roles of these approaches and how they address the complex challenges facing society.

Social entrepreneurship (SE) is the practice of using commercial strategies to create and run financially sustainable organizations (i.e., social enterprises) that address a specific social and/or environmental challenge (Bornstein & Davis, 2010; Dees, 1998; Roberts & Woods, 2005). Unlike traditional entrepreneurs who are most interested in maximizing profits for themselves and their investors, the "socialpreneur" is focused first and foremost on driving social value and reinvesting the profits toward achieving that goal. Some exemplar social entrepreneurs include

- Muhammad Yunus, who founded microlending organization Grameen Bank (now the Grameen Foundation) to provide small loans to women entrepreneurs in developing countries who otherwise wouldn't qualify for financing;
- Zachary Quinn and Brian Keller, who started their company Love Your Melon in an entrepreneurship class at the University of St. Thomas to improve the lives of children battling cancer; and
- Yve-Car Momperousse, whose beauty product company Kreyol Essence supports Haitian farm workers by sourcing their key ingredient, Haitian Black Castor Oil, from the crops they grow.

In comparison, *corporate social responsibility* (CSR) is the integration of ethical practices and community-oriented initiatives into existing business operations or the contribution of corporate resources for the public good (Chang et al., 2014). CSR encompasses a wide range of activities from charitable donations and employee volunteering to ethical material sourcing and the decarbonization of business activities. Environmental, social, and governance (ESG) factors are integral to CSR by providing a structured framework for evaluating and reporting a company's impact and practices in these three key areas. According to the Boston College Center for Corporate Citizenship,[1] CSR encompasses the activities that a company undertakes and ESG is the taxonomy that categorizes those activities. Furthermore, companies who want to take their CSR commitments even further can opt to pursue B-Corp certification, which demonstrates their ability to meet rigorous social and environmental performance standards, legal accountability, and transparency.

CSR extends far beyond the confines of social enterprises and large corporations; it thrives within a diverse ecosystem of organizations dedicated to promoting responsible practices. This ecosystem encompasses a variety of entities that play crucial roles in supporting CSR initiatives, each contributing in unique ways to foster positive social and environmental impacts. Types of organizations that illustrate this dynamic landscape include

- *businesses or nonprofits that independently certify impact and sustainability*, like industry-specific fair trade or sustainability certifications;
- *independent advocacy groups* that lobby corporations directly to change their practices;
- *think tanks and academic groups* that research and share best practices in corporate social responsibility and/or social entrepreneurship;
- *global foundations and impact funds* built to support and fund social entrepreneurs who may have difficulty accessing funding through traditional banking and financial institutions;
- *impact investing* arms of traditional banks or philanthropic enterprises;
- *cooperative development centers*, often nonprofits, that help launch and scale small, community-minded cooperatives;
- *social venture incubators, residencies, or fellowships* that help coach and/or fund founders launching social enterprises;
- *government agencies* that regulate corporate reporting standards for sustainability;
- *crowdfunding platforms* that help purpose-driven businesses and real estate projects capitalize through groups of unaccredited investors.

Knowledge

- *impact measurement*
  - understand the role that quantitative and qualitative data play in conveying the stories behind the *what* and *why* of social impact
  - become familiar with tools and frameworks such as social return on investment, return on sustainability investment, and the United Nations sustainable development goals
  - become familiar with global standard-setting organizations such as the International Organization for Standardization, Global Reporting Initiative, International Sustainability Standards Board, and Carbon Disclosure Project
  - understand the negative impact of "greenwashing," "green hushing," and other tactics used to avoid stakeholder scrutiny

- *civic and social*
  - take a nuanced perspective on the issue area being impacted, including its historical and contemporary context, the complexity of the problem, power dynamics of any interrelationships, and the ripple effects of the solution, including unintended impacts and trade-offs; Daniela Papi-Thorton coined the phrase "apprenticing with the problem"[2]
  - understand the local to global policies and regulations related to the business and issue area being addressed
  - recognize how power and privilege influence the narratives that are told and accepted and be willing to elevate the voices that rarely have power over their own stories

- *ethics and economics*
  - cultivate insights into the history of money and capitalism, including the cultural values embedded in modern economic theory and business practice
  - enhance awareness of how one's socioeconomic class impacts life experiences
  - become familiar with market tools such as impact investing and conscious consumerism
  - understand the relationship between business, wealth centralization, and the unequal impacts of development both locally and globally
  - recognize how different finance strategies impact businesses' ability to fulfill impact

Skills

Table 4.1 outlines key skills, categorized as either technical or relational, along with specific examples and applications for each.

Table 4.1. Skills That Can Be Exercised and Enhanced Through Social Entrepreneurship and Corporate Social Responsibility

Technical Skills	Relational Skills
impact measurement • analysis of qualitative and quantitative data for strategic decision making • conducting materiality assessments and developing a theory of change • using global standards and frameworks to measure and report outcomes *problem solving* • human-centered design • systems thinking *business and marketing* • building a pitch deck • market analysis • genuine networking • cold calling + emailing • project management *accounting* • management of day-to-day cash flow and recordkeeping • ability to balance tax favorability with corporate responsibility to the public • ability to evaluate the nonfinancial risks and opportunities that could affect the enterprise cash flow, access to finance, or cost of capital *finance and start-up strategy (SE)* • pro forma and discounted cash flow analysis with emphasis on equity, debt, and public finance sourcing	*collaboration and negotiation* • conflict resolution • active and reflexive listening • expectation management *public speaking* • storytelling • (SE) understanding that many social businesses are the first of their kind in the modern economy, resulting in comfort interrogating present systems publicly while presenting alternatives • (CSR) embracing intrapreneurship, or transforming an existing business by introducing new ideas, values, and processes *cultural competence* • valuing diversity, researching other knowledge, and developing approaches based on cultural considerations of the communities served • involving those impacted by integrating cultural contexts into policymaking, administration, service delivery, and structures that enable effective cross-cultural work

Attributes and Qualities

- *risk tolerance*: willingness to take *measured* risks, knowing that at least some innovations are bound to fail and being able to pivot to new strategies after a failure
- *growth mindset*: belief that individuals—particularly oneself—are not limited by fixed traits but can continuously learn and evolve
- *business-mindedness*: strategic understanding of the business's motivations, processes, and goals in order to successfully make the case for change within business contexts
- *perseverance*: understanding that small, incremental victories stack up to long-term transformational impact; not letting the perfect be the enemy of the good
- *proactivity*: for SE, a willingness to approach others to ask for funding, feedback, and other assistance; for CSR, proactivity that pushes you to seek for, pitch, and operationalize new, impact-minded ideas and processes within your organization
- *systemic imagination and creativity*: a capacity to reimagine finance and other market structures as tools of solidarity alongside a commitment to teaching others how to approach problem solving in current systems from different value sets and new vantage points

Job Titles Associated With This Pathway

Nearly any role in a traditional company could also exist within a social business, so in this pathway it can be more important to pay attention to the impact mission of the company or organization than to the job title itself. Moreover, impact roles in business often constitute just one dimension of a job or arise from personal passion, so there are numerous opportunities to shape one's work in support of causes they care about, regardless of an official title. There are a variety of job boards, such as the one hosted by the Association of Corporate Citizenship Professionals, that curate lists of ESG and CSR jobs. Some job titles associated with this pathway include the following:

- affordable housing developer
- chief sustainability officer
- community engagement and giving campaign manager
- community impact or philanthropy director

- community relations manager
- cooperative development specialist
- corporate programs senior manager
- corporate responsibility consultant
- CSR manager/analyst
- DEI specialist
- ESG controller
- stakeholder engagement manager
- ethics and compliance manager/officer
- fair trade coordinator
- head of foundation
- impact investing analyst
- nonprofit CEO/founder
- social impact reporting analyst
- sustainable procurement manager
- sustainability associate/manager

Activities

There are a variety of ways to test out interest and knack for work in SE and CSR during undergraduate years. Many universities have centers for social impact, social innovation, or social entrepreneurship located within their business schools, where they likely host courses, internship programs, social venture competitions, speaking events, and more. Internships can be in social impact roles, or if not, may still offer meaningful learning in business contexts. An internship can be a great way to get a feel for working within a large business to create change. For social entrepreneurship, interning for a start-up can support understanding the process of building and scaling a business. Many universities have mentorship programs and grants available for student social entrepreneurs. Business schools often have many opportunities to network with industry and business leaders; informational interviews with founders and other leaders provide an excellent opportunity to hear about their work and get advice.

Notes

1. Boston College Center for Corporate Citizenship, based under the Carroll School of Management, is a membership-supported organization dedicated to

advancing CSR, alongside ESG performance and disclosure. They offer monthly research and regulatory bulletins, regular webinars on emerging ESG issues, a quarterly CSR magazine, and an annual Corporate Citizenship Conference. For more information visit https://ccc.bc.edu/content/ccc.html.

2. Papi-Thornton (2016) stresses the need for higher education to strike a balance between fostering the skills needed for successful social venture creation and understanding the societal contexts that drive the problems. In *Tackling Heropreneurship*, Papi-Thornton urges educators to counter the "obsession with becoming a founder" with experiences that help students "apprentice with the problems they care about": https://tacklingheropreneurship.com/tackling-heropreneurship-report/.

References

Bornstein, D., & Davis, S. (2010). *Social entrepreneurship: What everyone needs to know*. Oxford University Press.

Chang, Y. J., Chen, Y. R., Wang, F. T. Y., Chen, S. F., & Liao, R. H. (2014). Enriching service learning by its diversity: Combining university service learning and corporate social responsibility to help the NGOs adapt technology to their needs. *Systemic Practice and Action Research, 27*(2), 185–193.

Dees, G. (1998). *The meaning of social entrepreneurship*. Kauffman Foundation & Stanford University. https://community-wealth.org/content/meaning-social-entrepreneurship

Nabi, G., Linan, F., Fayolle, A., Krueger, N., & Walmsley, A. (2017). The impact of entrepreneurship education in higher education: A systematic review and research agenda. *Academy of Management Learning & Education, 16*(2), 277–299.

Papi-Thornton, D. (2016, February 23). Tackling heropreneurship. *Stanford Social Innovation Review*. https://ssir.org/articles/entry/tackling_heropreneurship

Roberts, D., & Woods, C. (2005). Changing the world on a shoestring: The concept of social entrepreneurship. *University of Auckland Business Review, 7*(1), 45–51.

Chapter 5

PRACTITIONER PROFILE

Policy and Governance

Lisa Morde

olicy and Governance as a Pathway is defined as "participating in political processes, public governance, and policymaking" (Stanford Haas Center, n.d., para. 4). Like most pathways, elements of this one can be integrated into everyday life in a variety of ways, from a lifelong career to participation in short-term campaigns, and everything in between. Student engagement in policy and governance is supported by both literature and legislation advocating that postsecondary education has a responsibility to support student civic participation (Camacho, 2022; U.S. Department of Education, 2022).

This pathway includes maintaining or changing democratic society through institutions, organizations, and communities that engage in a range of decision-making processes, from more formal processes such as advocating for legislative action and becoming involved in civic associations to more informal processes such as mutual aid. It involves making the laws, rules, and policies that we live by, in addition to engaging with various governance structures and practices. This is a distinct type of community and civic involvement defined by its

> systemic dimension and various forms of engagement with public policy issues, as well as electoral politics at all levels. A key

criterion is that political activities are driven by systemic-level goals, a desire to affect the shared values, practices, and policies that shape collective life. (Colby, 2008, p. 4)

This section is written from a U.S. perspective, which is just one context to consider and does not imply it is the only or best one. Pathways in policy and governance are applicable worldwide but may vary depending on the context.

Structure: Public Governance

Public governance is a structure in which groups of people make the rules, laws, and polices that impact their communities. This structure includes formal processes to include community members in the decision-making processes, either through direct input or delegating a representative to make the decisions on a group's behalf. Work in this pathway can take place at many different levels. The following are a few examples:

- *national*: Congress
- *state*: state-level house of representatives and state-level senate
- *local*: city council, select board
- *university level*: student government association, faculty council
- *hyper local*: homeowners association, parent–teacher association

Process: Political Process

Within the structure of public governance, the political process refers to the way decisions are made and implemented. Engaging in the political process can take many different forms, as in the following examples:

- voting in local, state, and national elections
- registering, mobilizing, and educating other voters
- advocating for a specific cause
- attending or organizing community meetings
- volunteering to join a decision-making committee
- working on a campaign to elect a candidate
- running for an elected position

Another way to engage in the political process is through election administration, from maintaining voter registration records to managing election logistics to counting ballots and more.

Action: Policymaking

Policymaking occurs in some form within most institutions, including corporations, churches, universities, nonprofit organizations, and more. Within public governance, there are many ways to engage meaningfully in policymaking. Some examples include

- drafting legislation or policies to propose to governing bodies;
- analyzing proposed legislation or policies and developing a policy memo;
- advising elected officials regarding a specific subject in your area of expertise, which includes lived experience;
- lobbying lawmakers on particular issue areas or legislation; and
- offering testimony at public meetings to inform policymakers as well as the general public.

Advocating for and influencing policy can also take place through other pathways, such as Community Organizing and Activism. Some examples include

- sharing your input with decision-makers through letters, phone calls, emails, attendance and participation at public meetings, or in-person visits to offices; and
- attending or organizing public demonstrations such as rallies or protests to communicate en masse with elected officials and other policymakers; and
- Work in coalition with others who care about a cause to produce an advocacy and organizing strategy and plan of action that might include either of the items noted previously and more.

Knowledge

Knowledge in these areas is particularly relevant to the Policy and Governance Pathway:

- civic knowledge
  - understanding of democratic decision making, including its strengths and weaknesses
  - awareness of how policies and decisions are made within the relevant context (i.e., local government, nation, corporation, non-profit, or other institution)
  - general understanding of the structures of power, including how power can be gained or lost
  - general understanding of the systems and institutions that structure how residents engage with government or how members of a specific community engage with those in power
- knowledge of the issue area
  - historical and contemporary context of the issue area, as well as an appreciation for the complexities of history and its present-day effects that can include multiple and conflicting truths
  - awareness of the many factors that affect and influence the issue
  - knowledge of the key stakeholders who affect and are affected by the issue
- understanding of inequities in the system
  - awareness of the gap between the ideals and realities of the democratic process
  - understanding of the inequities between those with the power to make policy and those who are most affected by the policies

Skills[1]

Table 5.1 outlines key skills, categorized as either technical or relational, along with specific examples and applications for each.

Table 5.1. Skills That Can Be Exercised and Enhanced Through Policy and Governance

Technical Skills	Relational Skills

• decision making
  ○ assessment-based decision making: analyzing multiple types of data
  ○ shared governance
  ○ ethics and social responsibility
  ○ radical change and incremental reform
  ○ ability to work creatively and with a constrained budget
• communication skills
  ○ intercultural communication
  ○ facilitation
  ○ public speaking
  ○ marketing and messaging
  ○ advocacy and persuasion
• research
  ○ applied research methods—employed for social, political, and organizational analysis as well as problem solving
  ○ understanding of when and how to apply research methods appropriate to the issue at hand
	• coalition building and public engagement
	  ○ designing effective processes for public engagement and cross-sector collaboration
	  ○ mapping community or organizational assets; leveraging community knowledge, skills, abilities, and interests
	  ○ forming strategic partnerships and alliances
	• teamwork
	  ○ building positive working relationships
	  ○ assessing team members' skills and knowledge
	  ○ fostering collaboration; avoiding groupthink
	  ○ managing difficult group dynamics
	• conflict management
	  ○ intergroup dialogue
	  ○ community mediation
	  ○ stakeholder negotiating
	• identifying, analyzing, framing, and resolving ethical tensions
	  ○ structural, human, political, and symbolic frames of organizational development
	  ○ managing trade-offs in process, relationship building, and desired outcomes
	  ○ stakeholder analysis

Attributes and Qualities

Attributes and qualities in these categories are especially valuable for the Policy and Governance Pathway:

- *community-oriented*
  - genuine interest in the common good
  - a sense of responsibility for your community

- belief that everyone has something to contribute toward the common good
- value building and maintaining trust with those in your community
- readiness to contribute what you can when it matters
- *democratic ideology*
  - belief that you can make a difference, you belong, and your voice matters
  - belief that others in the community belong and their voices matter
- *patience*
  - ability to listen deeply to opposing viewpoints
  - tolerance for slow processes, compromise, and consensus building
  - resilience

Job Titles Associated With This Pathway

Public Governance

People in government roles can be elected, appointed, or hired. Positions can be paid or unpaid.

- *elected officials*: mayor, attorney general, senator
- *appointed advisors*: climate and clean energy innovation and implementation, political affairs strategic planning policy, chief medical advisor to the president
- *hired positions*: political campaign manager, government aide, lobbyist, policy analyst, traffic engineer, social worker, property manager

Political Process

Local, regional, national, and international organizations hire part-time, temporary/contract, and full-time staff specifically dedicated to these efforts.

- campaign manager
- city clerk

- data analyst
- director, impact and state networks
- elections commissioner
- poll worker
- senior director, strategic initiatives
- speechwriter
- ward chair

Policymaking

Policymaking occurs within almost all institutions, from corporations to universities to nonprofit organizations.

- *government*: city council, school board members, Congress
- *corporations*: human resources, chief executive officer
- *nonprofit organizations*: student government association (SGA), board members, executive director

Other Ways to Engage

In addition to formal jobs, anyone can engage in this pathway through a variety of methods, such as the following:

- advocating and raising awareness of the general public on particular issue areas
- participating in public demonstrations such as rallies or protests
- making your ideas known to public officials through letters, phone calls, emails, or in-person visits
- producing, participating in, and supporting public art focused on a specific topic
- volunteering with your local civic association or with a community organization

Activities

Students can engage in a variety of activities to explore and grow their experience in the Policy and Governance Pathway. Perhaps some of the most obvious activities include joining the Student Government Association

(SGA) and similar governing bodies on campus. Ask to serve as the student representative on other governing bodies on campus such as the President's Council, Faculty Council, Staff Council, or special committees. Many campuses also have voter engagement initiatives. There are often regional and national organizations to support students in this work such as Ask Every Student and Every Vote Counts.

Beyond campus, engage in local government by attending local committee meetings, contacting representatives, and joining demonstrations or advocacy initiatives. Other opportunities include interning for a political campaign, working as an election poll official, or serving as a protest marshal.

An impactful route into this work is through your passion. Join a student organization or volunteer, intern, or work at an organization addressing topics of interest. Working alongside established organizations is a good way to learn about work that has already been done, current initiatives taking place, and the challenges faced in the work.

Note

1. See Appendix B (Online Companion) for reference to the work of Nancy Thomas.

References

Camacho, S. (2022). The praxis of realizing election imperatives in Trump's America. *eJournal of Public Affairs, 11*(1), 157–175.

Colby, A. (2008). The place of political learning in college. *Peer Review, 10*(2–3), 4–9.

Stanford Haas Center. (n.d.). *Pathways: Public service and civic engagement.* Haas Center for Public Service. https://haas.stanford.edu/about/our-approach/pathways-public-service-and-civic-engagement

U.S. Department of Education. (2022, April 21). *Requirements for the distribution of voter registration forms.* Federal Student Aid. https://fsapartners.ed.gov/knowledge-center/library/dear-colleague-letters/2022-04-21/requirements-distribution-voter-registration-forms

Chapter 6

PRACTITIONER PROFILE

Community Organizing and Activism

Shamili Ajgaonkar

The Community Organizing and Activism Pathway entails addressing issues of public concern by "involving, educating, and mobilizing individual or collective action to influence or persuade others" (Stanford Haas Center, n.d., para 5). Further, as Marshall Ganz explains, organizing and activism is "leadership that enables people to turn the resources they have into the power they need to make the change they want" (Sinnott & Gibbs, 2014, p. 4). But underlying these commonalities, there are differences in the approaches of organizing versus activism. Community organizing takes a long-term strategic approach focused on building structures, networks, and relationships. In contrast, activism tends to be more immediate and direct, aimed at raising awareness and challenging the existing power structures and narratives.

Organizing brings people together around shared interests, builds relationships, and establishes frameworks for pooling resources, knowledge, or skills. It enables the development of strategies to address complex social, political, or environmental issues that require collective action. Organizing can take numerous forms, but in most cases the underlying goal is to create a sense of belonging and solidarity among individuals in ways that empower communities to become change agents. Organizing creates a platform for marginalized voices to be amplified and establishes a structure for communities to advocate for their rights beyond the scope of any specific issue campaign.

Activism usually has a sense of urgency, aiming to raise awareness of pressing issues and mobilizing others to demand immediate change that addresses systemic injustices. Activists use their voices through such means as protests and public campaigns to draw attention to and rally support for their causes. By shining a light on inconvenient truths, activism brings attention to issues that may otherwise be overlooked, creating momentum for broader change. Like organizing, activism can be a potent tool for augmenting the voices of marginalized communities and advocating for justice and equality.

Interviews with practitioners in this pathway suggest that some see themselves as educators, others as activists, and some as community organizers. However, they unanimously agreed that the defining characteristic of practitioners in this pathway is their role as change agents dedicated to promoting positive social change in their communities. Most discovered this pathway as a result of wanting to make a difference related to an issue they personally cared about. To be effective in this pathway requires a deep understanding of systemic and power structures in order to strategize effectively, coupled with the skill to use storytelling to build movements that shift policy.

Knowledge

A job profile report by the Community Learning Partnership, a national network of community change studies programs based in community colleges, acknowledges that "the traditional path to professional community organizing could proceed with or without a college degree," but the report also recognizes that "this is rapidly changing as the social, economic and political challenges [that] organizers face become more complex, and as a degree becomes a credential that employers, including community organizations, more frequently require" (Community Learning Partnership, 2013, p. 3).

Combining literature review findings with the practitioner interviews, the following list outlines key competencies for the pathway:

- *knowledge of the field (theoretical framework)*
  - history of social movements and organizing
  - craft of community organizing

- pedagogy of participatory education
- understanding global justice movements for reform and liberation and what makes a movement a movement
- models/theories of social change
- *civic education*
  - basic understanding of relevant social, economic, and political concepts
  - structure and roles of government and nongovernmental organizations
  - understanding the political system and policymaking process (local, state, national)
- *knowledge about the issue/struggle*
  - understanding the issue (five *w*'s—who, what, where, when, why)
  - some technical knowledge based on the field (environment, food, housing, etc.)
  - understanding intersectional dynamics
  - understanding interconnections to the other civic engagement pathways
- *knowledge about personal identity, the community, and relationships*
  - know who you are—owning one's own history and struggles
  - knowledge about the community, its systems, and its problems (with the recognition that some of the knowledge might be dependent on the discipline)
  - knowledge of institutional and community structures and how to connect to them
  - understanding power, privilege, and oppression

Skills

Table 6.1 outlines key skills, categorized as either technical or relational, along with specific examples and applications for each.

Table 6.1. Skills That Can Be Exercised and Enhanced Through Community Organizing and Activism

Technical Skills	Relational Skills
strategic analysis: understanding the community and engaging in strategic analysis of social structures within the community	*power analysis*: engaging in power analysis of personal and interpersonal dynamics
customer relationship management: managing lists of potential organizers, people to participate in events, and so on	*communication skills*: listening and dialoguing across difference (engaging, deliberating, and reframing the conversation)
database management: collecting, analyzing, evaluating, distilling, and summarizing both quantitative and qualitative data	*relationship building*: achieving proficiency in various aspects of building community relations, including
communication skills: achieving proficiency in various communication modalities	• cultural competence and openness to learning
• reading and writing reports	• connecting what one learns from the community to strategies to make a change
• making public presentations	• building a base
• facilitating intergroup dialogue	• guiding people and being able to identify and develop leaders
• democratic deliberation practices	• building solidarity and deep relationships (no lonely heroes)
• advocacy skills	• building "coalitions of support" within and among communities, organizations, and stakeholders
critical and creative thinking	• building a sense of agency
• ability to understand the context of the problem/issue	• acting as conveners in creating a collaborative environment
• ability to identify a problem/issue and determine whether the solution to the problem requires preventing or creating change	• helping the community find leverage points for systemic change
• ability to develop constructive solutions to problems/issues through deliberation and active participation	*systems thinking*: becoming proficient in various aspects of building community relations, including
• knowing how to struggle (when and why to struggle, who to struggle with, what to struggle toward)	• being able to see the connection between personal experience and public policy
organizational, planning, and time-management skills	• being able to understand the interconnections between various issues
• using resources (time, energy, and workplace) efficiently and effectively	
• prioritizing, setting goals, and maintaining a clear picture of what needs to be accomplished and when	
• taking initiative, working strategically, and making decisions	
• problem-solving and delegating tasks and responsibilities	

Attributes and Qualities

- *committed to social justice and the collective good*
  - view and embrace social justice as a lifestyle
  - able to.envision a different (more just and fair) world
  - possess an intentional and sustained commitment to the collective good
- *interested in collective action*
  - always use the lens of a grassroots organizer
  - find value in being together with people who are willing to put their bodies on the line
- *creative problem solving*
  - willing to challenge oneself to take initiative
  - able to work toward resolving issues effectively
  - willingness to be intentional yet flexible
  - able to make the most of available resources
- *organized*
  - emphasize accountability
  - demonstrate follow-through
  - manage tasks and schedules
- *capacity for self-reflection*
  - cultivate continuous personal growth
  - be willing to learn and be open to change
  - nurture a sense of purpose
- *culturally competent*
  - have cultural humility
  - be appreciative of different cultures and backgrounds
  - develop a deep understanding of different backgrounds
  - be receptive to alternative viewpoints
  - believe that everyone's voice matters
- *collaborative*
  - able to work both independently and as part of a team
  - able to leverage the collective assets and expertise of the team to achieve common goals
- *resilient*
  - be tenacious and willing to take risks
  - possess ability to cope with setbacks
  - able to adjust approach as circumstances change

Job Titles Associated With This Pathway

Practitioners are unified by a commitment to social justice wherein they see their role as change agents within their professional sphere of influence. They perceive community organizing and activism as an operational framework for how they approach their work. Thus, the sectors that community organizers work in are highly varied and diverse. Rather than focusing solely on job titles, the following are examples of various types of organizations with which community organizers and activists are engaged:

- labor and community organizations
- educational institutions (K–12, community colleges, and universities)
- community/economic development organizations
- policy advocacy organizations
- arts and culture organizations
- city and county government
- social service agencies

Activities

Becoming a change agent is best approached as a developmental process, in which students should actively seek out scaffolded experiences. The benefit of a developmental approach "is that students are not bifurcated into nonactivist/activist dichotomy; rather, all students are seen to have the potential to become more participatory members of their communities" (Hemer & Reason, 2021, p. 40). Additionally, students' sociopolitical development benefits from both structured curricular and cocurricular experiences that cultivate an activist mindset, supported by a campus climate that nurtures community activism and participatory democracy.

The types of experiences/organizations that facilitate the activist mindset include the following:

- college-wide organizations such as student council and student clubs that provide opportunities to participate in and lead issue-focused activism efforts on campus
- direct service participation either independently or with cohort-based peer groups, in such organizations as Honors Society,

leadership programs, or other reputable organizations to better understand social issues and needs on a systemic level

- thoughtfully structured activities like an alternative spring break or study-abroad program that provide opportunities to develop a robust understanding of social injustices without reinforcing stereotypes or perpetuating ideas of "us" helping "them" ("savior ideology"), experiences that can underscore the complexity of civic work and help clarify a future path for civic engagement through opportunities for formal and informal reflection
- multidimensional and advanced civic experiences embedded in coursework and programs of study that provide a supportive peer network (cohort) and mentors as well as opportunities for sustained reflection
- academic majors that allow for the integration of civic identity (which can be thought of as an identity category comprising one's knowledge, attitudes, values, and actions regarding civic engagement) with postcollege careers
- internships, fellowships, and other preprofessional engagements that allow the development of specific skills associated with community organizing and connect students to professionals and mentors in the field

References

Community Learning Partnership. (2013). *Listening—building—making change: Job profile of a community organizer.* https://drive.google.com/file/d/123Dn hiZzstbN2YFiq6hD-MOCjMNCiPPI/view

Hemer, K. M., & Reason, R. D. (2021). Civic learning for dissent: Developing students' activist orientation. *Journal of College Student Development, 62*(1), 37–54. https://doi.org/10.1353/csd.2021.0003

Sinnot, S., & Gibbs, P. (2014). *Organizing: People, power, change.* https://common-slibrary.org/wp-content/uploads/Organizers_Handbook.pdf

Stanford Haas Center. (n.d.). *Pathways of Public Service and Civic Engagement.* https://haas.stanford.edu/about/our-approach/pathways-public-service-and-civic-engagement

Chapter 7

PRACTITIONER PROFILE

Philanthropy

Nairuti Shastry

Compared to the other pathways, philanthropy—in its current consolidated and professionalized form[1]—is one of the relatively newer ways in which students are being encouraged to contribute to social change. Broadly speaking, philanthropy, defined as "donating or using private funds or charitable contributions from individuals or institutions to contribute to the public good," (Stanford Haas Center, n.d., para. 4) is a vital component of a much larger ecosystem of funding that fuels social change in the United States and abroad.

The philanthropic sector today consists of

- large, private multinational foundations with endowments ranging from $2 billion to $50 billion, often founded by wealthy individuals;
- smaller, public community foundations and movement-led funds that are often place-based and hyperlocal (though some operate nationally, regionally, or globally), with much smaller, publicly collected endowments;
- collaborative funds that serve as intermediaries between financial capital and grassroots social movements;
- local, Global South–originated funds that serve as "'self-financing arms of their own movements and communities . . . [that] feel their role is more of a bridge that enables part of their society to

benefit from philanthropic support they would otherwise not access" (Souza, 2018, para. 4);

- national and international agencies—financed by governments and multilateral organizations—with a grant-making arm;
- private corporate philanthropy, often a part of corporate social responsibility programs at large companies;
- entrepreneur support organizations that provide catalytic financial support as well as leadership development and technical assistance to individuals using next economy principles and sustainable business models to address the world's most pressing issues;
- integrated capital funds that blend philanthropy with loans and impact investments;
- small- to medium-sized family foundations, many of which have less than $10 million in assets and were created in the past 30 years, with a strategic geographic- or issue-based focus (National Center for Family Philanthropy, 2020);
- donor-advised funds maintained and operated by a separate sponsoring organization;
- financial and wealth management services with a philanthropic arm;
- philanthropy-serving organizations (including university centers, advisors, and consultants/consulting groups) that provide research and assessment on the sector and/or training and networking for philanthropy professionals;
- accountability structures for the industry (governmental or not)—watchdogs that ensure that philanthropy is most responsive to its beneficiaries;
- high–net worth individuals (and their respective family offices and staff who support with planned giving [i.e., wills, estate planning], donor education, and advising) that donate privately to causes in which they are interested;
- donor networks for wealthy individuals to learn from, connect with, organize alongside, and give collectively with their peers;
- place- and affinity-based giving circles; and
- large numbers of low–high net worth individuals who contribute small sums of money and other resources, including time, talent, ties, and testimony, also known as the "4Ts of philanthropy" (Bernholz, 2021; Milken Institute, 2020) to causes, campaigns, or projects for the social good.

Philanthropy practitioners often say they arrived at their profession by chance. As undergraduates, most of them were generally interested in a particular social issue (e.g., housing, abortion access, health, disability justice, education, climate change, etc.) and wanted to effect change within that field. They pursued areas of study as divergent as economics and English literature but, ultimately, spent much of their time on and off campus reflecting on their positionality and cultivating their skills as a dedicated problem-solver and strong advocate.

Today, as professionals within the sector, they work in a variety of capacities with diverse teams but are all fundamentally motivated by connecting communities—especially those presently and historically minoritized—with the resources they need to thrive.

Knowledge

- epistemological stance toward inner work—moving from scarcity to abundance
  - consciously letting go of knowledge that overrepresents saviors and subject matter expertise
  - foundational understanding and practice of critical consciousness
  - language skills and international travel for global work
  - commitment to a practice of decolonization
  - interrogating personal and ancestral relationships with money, class, income, and wealth
- knowledge of the nonprofit sector and/or social justice issue(s)
  - awareness of local, state, and regional politics and policy and the broader funding ecosystem
  - firsthand experience in communities that are the target of grant-making efforts
- appreciation for and partnership with nonprofit leadership and management
  - accountability to communities served
  - nonprofit governance and leadership
- a systems-thinking mindset—how capital shapes social change
  - acknowledgment of the structural racism, sexism, ableism, homophobia, and other barriers that shape the current landscape
  - shift from a mindset of shifting capital to shifting power

Skills

Table 7.1 outlines key skills, categorized as either technical or relational, along with specific examples and applications for each.

Table 7.1. Skills That Can Be Exercised and Enhanced Through Philanthropy

Technical Skills	*Relational Skills*
• financial and business acumen, including understanding an organization's operating budget, conducting/reading the risk profile of an organization, and general awareness of tax code and policy • experience with database management, including grants or donor databases and customer relationship management systems • comfort with collecting, summarizing, distilling, analyzing, and evaluating large amounts of both quantitative and qualitative data • reading and writing reports and the overarching ability to distill nuanced ideas into various presentation modalities (e.g., PowerPoint, Jamboard, Miro, etc.) • familiarity with geographic information systems and other mapping technology • experience conducting social network analysis	• a global, structural, and power-conscious analysis of (financial) risk • being able to make a case (i.e., a healthy mix of code switching, advocacy, allyship) by marrying data to what matters: grassroots impact • decision making (including humanely saying no to nonprofit leadership and/or fundraising and development professionals—i.e., conflict literacy, nonviolent communication) • various modalities of in-person and e-communication, particularly across lines of difference • practicing radical candor (Scott, 2019) and speaking truth to power (especially with high-net-worth individuals) • openness to learning (i.e., cultural competence and humility) • ability to practice deep listening and openness to feedback (especially for white folks in the industry) • taking space, making space (especially for white folks in the industry) • effective and thoughtful collaboration (including network and coalition building) • comfort with ambiguity and ability to juggle multiple tasks at once

Attributes and Qualities

- creative problem solving
  - critical thinking
  - imagination abundance
  - acknowledging that change is ambiguous, complicated, and challenging

- an ethic of stewardship and care
  - being good → being whole
  - interest in helping others
  - increased sense of responsibility or obligation to local geographies
- individual (and community) transformation
  - a dramatic, positive shift in beliefs and values, interests, and intentions related to civic engagement and social responsibility
  - self-reflection
  - leadership
  - increasing awareness of one's positionality
  - cultivating a sense of belonging and purpose

Job Titles Associated With This Pathway

Many foundations have the following teams and associated job titles:

- leadership (executive director / chief executive officer)
- programs (program officer—director, senior, associate, assistant)
- monitoring and evaluation or impact assessment (director, senior, associate, assistant)
- communications (president or vice president, director, manager, associate, assistant)
- development and fundraising (vice president, director, development officer, major gifts officer, manager, associate, and assistant; can also include volunteer coordinators or program managers)
- grants administration (often cross-cutting and team-based)
- finance and operations (president or vice president, chief operating officer, chief financial officer, director, manager, associate, assistant)
- human resources (president or vice president, director, manager, associate, assistant)

Most philanthropic institutions also have boards (or steering committees) and executive directors (and other members of the leadership team) who are typically responsible for board communications and governance. Other job functions across nonfoundation philanthropic entities might include research, consulting, facilitation, organizing, grant making, donor organizing, or program development/management.

Activities

While there are many activities in which students can engage to culti-vate the foundational knowledge and skills needed for the Philanthropy Pathway, many of our practitioners began their journey well before their undergraduate studies. In reflecting on their upbringing, many philan-thropy professionals point to their family or faith traditions as critical to their orientation to the field: "I was raised to give back," they share. A few even had the opportunity to be philanthropists, either with their families of origin or after receiving an inheritance.

For all practitioners, social identity—particularly race—from a young age played a foundational role in shaping the kinds of activities they chose to pursue as students. For example, many BIPOC practitioners found their way to philanthropy through participating in and leading student orga-nizing efforts and issue-focused activism on their campuses. These expe-riences enabled them to place themselves, and the issues about which they cared, within the larger ecosystem of social change. For white profession-als, many of them point to domestic volunteer experiences or traveling abroad to a different cultural context as pivotal moments that prompted reflection and lead them to confront their own positionality, privilege, and savior complexes.

Beyond on-campus engagements, internships, fellowships, and other preprofessional engagements—in the philanthropy field or elsewhere—were particularly useful for those interested in engaging in the pathway. Not only did these experiences allow undergraduates to develop a variety of technical skills, from research to fundraising to program management, they also connected students to professionals and mentors in the field.

Note

1. See a brief history of the industry at https://www.historyofgiving.org/.

References

Bernholz, L. (2021). *How we give now: A philanthropic guide for the rest of us*. The MIT Press.

Milken Institute. (2020, September 23). *Considering your philanthropy holistically*. https://milkeninstitute.org/article/considering-your-philanthropy-holistically

National Center for Family Philanthropy. (2020, November 19). *Trends 2020: Foundation identity.* https://www.ncfp.org/knowledge/trends-2020-foundation-identity/

Scott, K. (2019). *Radical Candor: Fully revised & updated edition: Be a kick-ass boss without losing your humanity.* Pan Books.

Souza, M. A. (2018, September 19). *How Global South funds are evolving the field of international philanthropy.* Human Rights Funders Network. https://www.hrfn.org/resources/how-global-south-funds-are-evolving-the-field-of-international-philanthropy/Stanford Haas Center. (n.d.). *Pathways: Public service and civic engagement.* https://haas.stanford.edu/about/our-approach/pathways-public-service-and-civic-engagement

Part Two
CURRENT USES

Chapter 8

OUR STARTING POINT

Using the Pathways to Develop a Comprehensive Social Impact Education Model

Cassie Bingham and Summer Valente

T he mission of the Utah Valley University (UVU) Center for Social Impact (CSI) is to develop compassionate community advocates who collaborate on strategic social impact. Our approach to this mission utilizes our innovative strategic impact continuum, which includes relational care, our integrated strategies, and the Pathways framework that provide students with a range of meaningful social impact learning experiences and skills that are relevant to their personal and professional lives. This chapter will focus on how the pathways were our starting point to develop this comprehensive social impact education model.

UVU is an integrated university and community college that educates every student for success in work and life through excellence in engaged teaching, services, and scholarship. UVU is the largest public university in the state and is located in Orem, Utah—a politically and socially conservative community in one of the most politically and socially conservative states. The school has a deeply rooted and long-standing commitment to serving the needs of the community. UVU's emphasis on engaged teaching and learning earned the institution the Carnegie Elective Classification for Community Engagement in 2015.

The CSI has been a cornerstone of community engagement at UVU for 30 years, starting in 1993 as Volunteer Services. In 2001, the department established a formal partnership with an Academic Affairs unit and became the Volunteer and Service-Learning Center. Over the years, additional resources and programming were added as more and more students were involved in its activities. After discovering the Pathways framework in 2016, departmental leadership began to envision an expanded mission and made a formal proposal to this end. In June of 2018, the department received approval to expand its mission and became the Center for Social Impact in August 2018.

Strategic Framework

Utah is consistently ranked as the number-one state for volunteerism rates. The ideals of charity and service are deeply engrained traditions stemming from the state's historical founding by a religious organization. However, there is a strong resistance to concepts such as social justice/change/progress in the community. In fact, when we told our in-state higher education colleagues about our strategic shift and the new names we were considering for the center to mark that shift, they told us we would never get any of those names approved. And they were almost right. It was our focus on the Pathways framework that allowed the Board of Trustees to approve our proposal.

Pathways of Social Impact

When we started making the case to stakeholders on campus and in the community, we focused on the significance of our role in teaching the "how" of building strong communities. The Pathways framework was easy for stakeholders to understand, particularly when we could point out that we were already integrating two of the pathways—Direct Service and Community-Engaged Learning and Research—into our work and intended to add the four additional pathways of the framework. We committed to the design of programs, initiatives, and collaborations that would move students from pathway entry points to more substantial community learning experiences.

As we engaged in conversations across campus, we emphasized the following characteristics of the Pathways framework, depending on our audience.

The Pathways Framework Is Interdisciplinary

Social impact is an inherently interdisciplinary field with a rigorous, but dispersed, academic history. With few spaces to dive into focused social impact thought, theory, and practice, students often falsely believe they can only be involved in this work through the nonprofit or social work sectors. With the Pathways framework, students in any major can see themselves in the work and gain the knowledge and skills necessary to create the social impact they desire in their field. For example, business and economics students are often left out of social impact spaces, but by including Social Entrepreneurship and Corporate Social Responsibility as a pathway, students in those fields can envision how to contribute their knowledge and skills to making social impact. In addition, in an increasingly globalized and interconnected world, having cross-sector knowledge and skills, which can be developed through experience in multiple pathways, is desirable.

The Pathways Framework Is Inclusive of More Identities

By adopting the Pathways framework, we offer more opportunities for people of diverse backgrounds to see themselves represented in the work we are promoting. For many people of color, community organizing and activism is a legacy among their families and communities. By including this pathway in the framework, it allows them to see that work and themselves as part of the larger ecosystem of social impact. They are also exposed to other forms of social impact where their lived experience is critically important, but often ignored, such as policy and governance. Since we have adopted the Pathways framework, we have seen a dramatic increase in the number of diverse students participating in CSI programming.

The Pathways Framework Is Not Inherently Partisan

This was probably one of the more important points of our discussions, given the community in which we live. One of the biggest concerns we repeatedly confronted, and wished to challenge, was about the CSI developing and advocating for a particular political agenda. While nearly anything can be weaponized as a political agenda, we repeatedly demonstrated how the pathways themselves are not inherently partisan. For example, we showed how the Policy and Governance Pathway is about form and process, not the beliefs of a particular political party. We assured stakeholders that our goal was not to dictate which issues students should care about or prioritize, but to educate them on effective ways they can make an impact in their community. This alleviated the concerns we were facing at the time.

Integrated Social Impact Strategies

In 2018, the newly adopted Pathways framework was already beginning to resonate with students, many of whom were younger millennials and Generation Z, known for their eagerness to learn how to make social impact a part of their day-to-day lives and, for some, a foundation for developing meaningful careers (O'Boyle, 2023; Vesty, 2016). Many students who engaged with the CSI had a desire to address social issues but often felt insecure about taking action. We knew that our responsibility as educators was to provide students not only with the pathways forward but also with the tools to help them act within the pathways as strategically, effectively, and ethically as possible.

While researching best-practice strategies for social impact work, we found that many tools fall roughly into three phases: (1) the research and familiarization phase, when approaching a social issue and the communities it affects; (2) the planning phase, when courses of action are considered, chosen, and strategized; and (3) the execution and evaluation phase, when an intervention occurs and is measured to assess its effectiveness. We intentionally looked for language and tools that are interdisciplinary, backed by credible sources, and in the upswing toward mainstream use in the field. We also sought tools that aligned with our relational and decolonizing values of (1) rejecting saviorism and supremacy complexes and (2) letting those with lived experience lead (Cole, 2021).

These boundaries eventually led us to recognizing the holistic value of design thinking, a multistep process that includes several other strategies we were starting to consider. As we drove deeper into understanding design thinking, we found a multiday workshop offered by the Creative Reaction Lab (n.d.), a Black woman–owned community design organization that adapted design thinking to become Equity-Centered Community Design (ECCD)™. ECCD incorporates values of equity and social justice into each of the six steps of the design process and overlays them with the need to understand historical context and dismantle power constructs (Creative Reaction Lab, n.d.). After participating in the workshop in 2019, the CSI modeled our equity-centered design framework on what we learned.

Simultaneously, the CSI began to participate in Map the System, a global competition held by the Skoll Centre for Social Entrepreneurship at the University of Oxford (n.d.). This required our staff members to become well versed in systems thinking, a strategy that is quickly transitioning from the field of engineering to an additional use in the field of social impact. This transition was advanced to a great extent by the writings of the late MIT professor Donella Meadows, who detailed how the interconnectedness of social problems requires an analysis of systems rather than the symptoms of social problems alone (Academy for Systems Change, 2014).

The CSI began to officially teach equity-centered design and systems thinking to students as thorough, rigorous, and actionable strategies to help them both understand and strategize through the social issues they care about. Meanwhile our staff recognized the importance of employing theory of change and impact measurement—strategies crucial in the

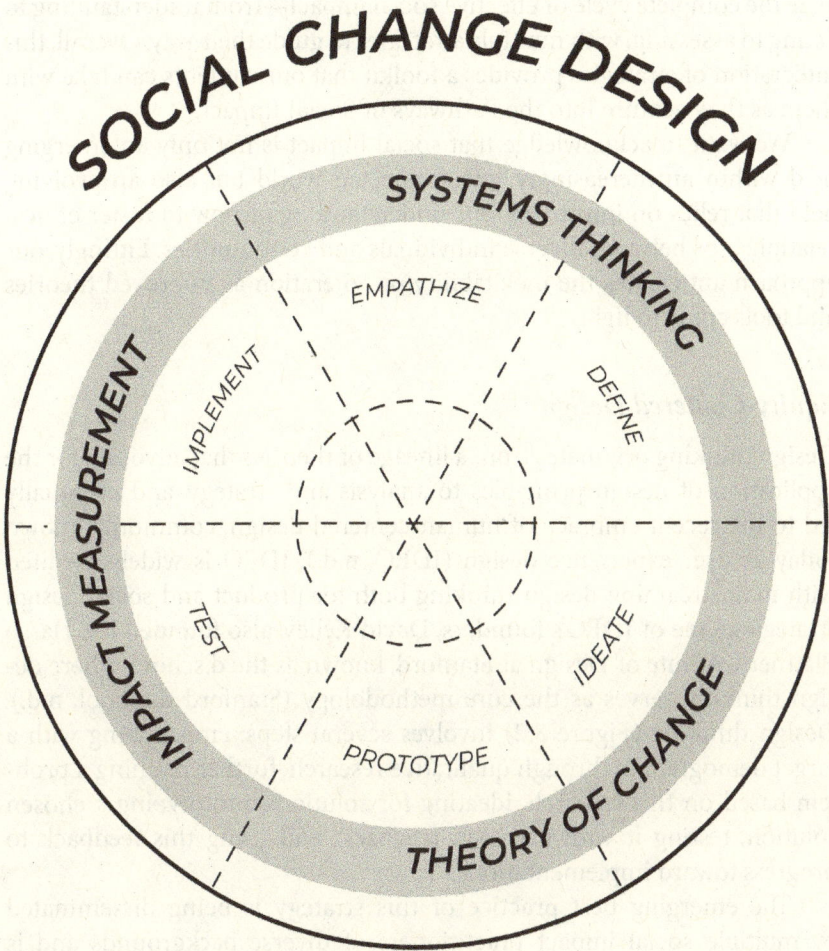

Figure 8.1. Integrated social impact strategies.
Original image, Kate Gallacher. Reprinted with permission.

nonprofit and NGO aid sectors—for effective implementation and assessment of social impact. We drew further inspiration for articulating an easily understood framework of impact measurement from a graphic developed by the Sorenson Impact Center at neighboring University of Utah (Reynolds et al., 2018).

In 2022, as CSI staff sought more intuitive methods for teaching these identified social impact strategies, we discovered that systems thinking, theory of change, and impact measurement each mapped to pairs of steps within the six steps of design thinking. This led to our current integrated strategies approach (Figure 8.1), which we designed to help students visualize the complete cycle of effective social impact—from understanding to acting to assessing, with multiple strategies to guide their way. Overall, this integration of strategies provides a toolkit that our students can take with them as they venture into the Pathways of Social Impact.

We want to acknowledge that social impact is not only an emerging field within an increasingly interconnected world but also an evolving field that relies on improving our understanding of how to foster ethical relationships between diverse individuals and communities. Fittingly, our approach anticipates the inevitability of reiteration as improved theories and tools come to light.

Equity-Centered Design

Design thinking originates from a lineage of theories that advocate for the application of design principles to analysis and strategy, and eventually led to the recent embrace of human-centered design, commonly known today as user experience design (IDEO, n.d.). IDEO is widely credited with mainstreaming design thinking both for product and social design strategies. One of IDEO's founders, David Kelley, also founded the Hasso Plattner Institute of Design at Stanford, known as the d.school, where design thinking serves as the core methodology (Stanford d.school, n.d.). Design thinking (Figure 8.2) involves several steps: empathizing with a target demographic through qualitative research, further defining a problem based on this research, ideating for solutions, prototyping a chosen solution, testing it with gathered feedback, and using this feedback to progress toward implementation.

The emerging best practice of this strategy is being disseminated by multiple social impact practitioners of diverse backgrounds and is

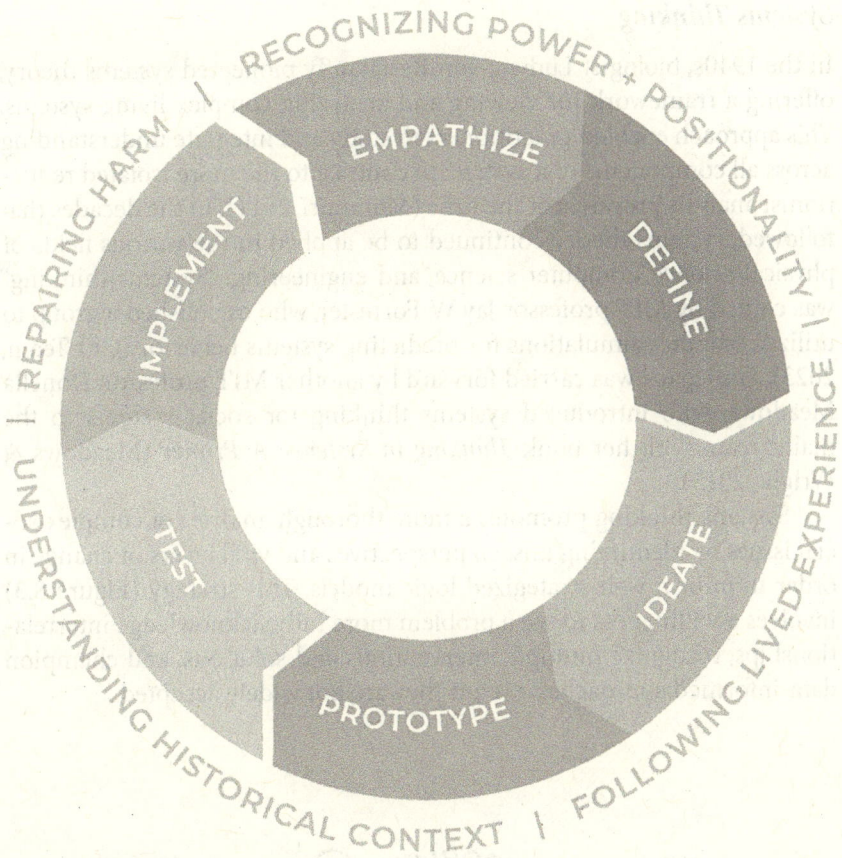

Figure 8.2. Equity-centered design.
Original image, Kate Gallacher. Reprinted with permission.

frequently referred to as equity-centered, or liberatory, design (Equity Design Collaborative, n.d.). Pioneers of this evolution of design thinking include the Creative Reaction Lab (n.d.) and the National Equity Project (n.d.). Equity-centered design preserves the original steps of design thinking while adding elements for fostering equitable community and social impact design, such as incorporating lived experience in every step of the process, recognizing power and positionality, understanding historical context, and repairing harm.

Systems Thinking

In the 1940s, biologist Ludwig von Bertalanffy pioneered systems theory, offering a framework for viewing and analyzing complex living systems. This approach enabled practitioners to study and integrate understanding across all components of a system, in contrast to the more isolated reductionist analysis prevalent at the time (Montuori, 2011). In the decades that followed, systems theory continued to be applied in the various fields of physical science, computer science, and engineering. "Systems thinking" was coined by MIT professor Jay W. Forrester, who established a group to utilize computer simulations for predicting systems behavior (CFI Team, 2023). His legacy was carried forward by another MIT professor, Donella Meadows, who introduced systems thinking for social systems to the mainstream with her book *Thinking in Systems: A Primer* (Meadows & Wright, 2015).

Systems thinking promotes a more thorough analysis of complex social issues by identifying unseen perspectives and vital levers of change in order to inform well-strategized logic models. This strategy (Figure 8.3) involves a willingness to see a problem more fully, acknowledge interrelationships, recognize multiple interventions and solutions, and champion data-informed approaches, even if they are not widely accepted.

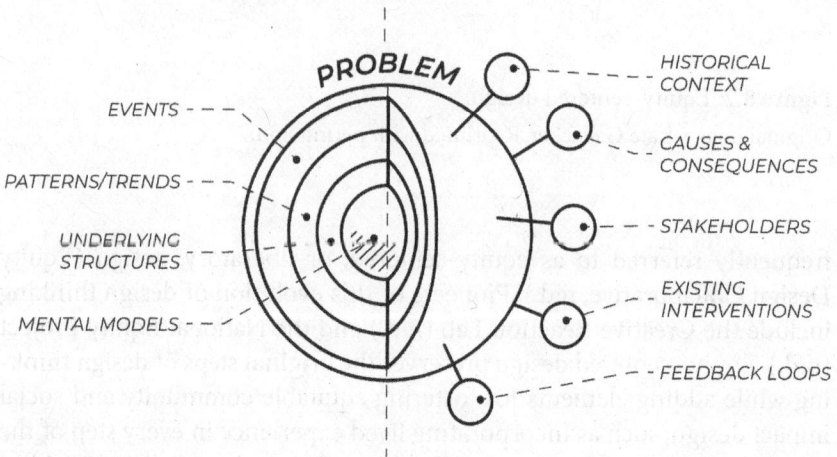

Figure 8.3. Systems thinking and mapping.
Original image, Kate Gallacher. Reprinted with permission.

Due to the complexity of systems, this strategy requires visual story-telling rather than textual information alone. Systems mapping includes creating hybrid visual and written depictions of a system that convey its narrative, players, and gaps in ways that are simple enough to be accessible to a broader audience. If done well, systems mapping can illuminate critical levers of change and generate greater buy-in and consensus for comprehensive and sustainable social impact strategies.

Theory of Change

Theory of change (Figure 8.4) comes out of the field of program evaluation, which rapidly developed in the 1990s, facilitated by the formation of the Aspen Institution of Research's Roundtable of Community Change in 1995 (Fulbright-Anderson & Auspos, 2006). This group analyzed various forms of community intervention planning and assessment and produced scholars like Carol Weiss, who wrote a seminal article that helped popularize the phrase "theory of change" (Weiss & Connell, 1995).

Today, a theory of change is known as the description of actions and goals that can be expected to lead to a specific change. It is often visually presented as a flowchart depicting what will be invested and what actions

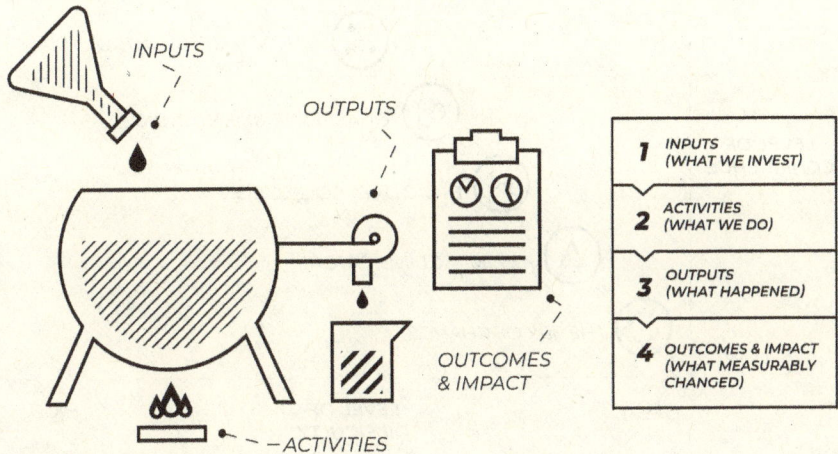

Figure 8.4. Theory of change.
Original image, Kate Gallacher. Reprinted with permission.

will be taken to address a social problem, what will happen because of those investments and actions, and what will measurably change. It serves as a planning tool to outline the details of an intervention to identify effective methods, potential gaps, and key indicators of success.

Impact Measurement

Social impact assessment and program evaluation are fields that involve identifying the necessary data to be collected to gauge the effectiveness of interventions. Evaluation requires measuring baseline and comparative metrics to make an assessment. Impact measurement, therefore, entails tracking key impact indicators through qualitative and quantitative research methods to confirm if a social intervention is producing positive, sustainable, and scalable impact. This process ensures interveners are held accountable for their results. As detailed by the Sorenson Impact Center, impact measurement (Figure 8.5) can include developing a theory of change, identifying key performance indicators, collecting data, and executing quasi-experimentation and randomized control trials (David Eccles School of Business, n.d.). However, each form of measurement increases in difficulty and resource needs (Reynolds et al., 2018).

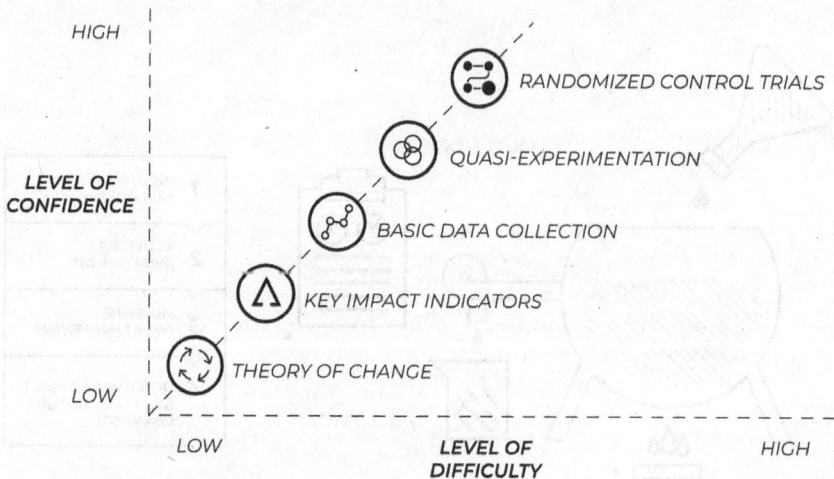

Figure 8.5. Impact measurement.
Original image, Kate Gallacher. Reprinted with permission.

Learning Experiences

At UVU, the programming offered through the CSI aims to inspire students to transition away from apathy and toward compassion, empowering them as engaged community advocates through a variety of meaningful social impact learning experiences and skill-building opportunities. These opportunities are centered on the Pathways of Social Impact and our integrated social impact strategies. Some examples of explicit pathways in instruction and programming include our Social Impact Seminar course and our Pathways 101 and Impact Speaker Series monthly events. In the following sections we provide short case studies of specific applied student learning experiences we offer in the pathways at a beginning, intermediate, and advanced level.

Beginning—Alternative Breaks

Alternative breaks offer opportunities for learning and community engagement, replacing traditional seasonal student break activities. The CSI's Alternative Break Program is an immersive learning opportunity carefully crafted to help students develop compassion, examine their assumptions, learn specifically about each pathway, and consider how they want to develop patterns of involvement in their own communities.

When planning alternative break trips, we examine community-identified social issues in our selected travel locations and collaborate with local community members who are actively addressing those issues through actions that fall within the Pathways framework. Participating community partners serve as educators and guides to students, offering insights into local perspectives on selected social issues through one or more pathways. For example, one trip examined gentrification in Salt Lake City and partnered with an affordable housing development firm specializing in social entrepreneurship. Most recently, students learned about community organizing and activism from Black organizers in Los Angeles who facilitated community gatherings at a local bookstore. They also contributed to direct service by volunteering with a local organization that sends letters and books to incarcerated individuals.

Each alternative break trip begins with an orientation training on the Pathways framework and systems thinking. This equips students with the mindset to analyze the systemic causes of the problems they are learning about while also highlighting how local community partners utilize the pathways as engaged stakeholders. At the end of the trip, students are trained on equity-centered design, helping them to ideate based on the insights they've gathered.

Many students are deeply affected by the pathways knowledge they gain through their collaboration with community partners and the tools acquired from systems and design thinking trainings. One student who attended an alternative break trip to Santa Fe, New Mexico, had this to say about her experience:

> I learned that it is important to understand the historical side of a marginalized community in order to create meaningful change. It is also key to recognize one's positionality and what kind of privileges [we] might have. . . . From now on I will try to see things through a different lens. —Estrella Farias

Intermediate—Podcast

The CSI's student-produced podcast, *Critical Mass*, features regular episodes that center lived experience to illuminate challenges and systemic impacts on communities (UVU Center for Social Impact, 2020–present). Students research compelling social impact topics, recording discussions between the hosts or interviewing relevant guests for the podcast.

In its first 3 years, the podcast has been led by the CSI's community-engaged learning and research fellow. The program relies on community-engaged research, incorporating literature reviews and qualitative interviews to facilitate community-engaged learning by exposing students to diverse community perspectives. Additionally, episodes often touch on discussions across various pathways, providing valuable insights for many listeners. Season 1 coincided with an election year, and several episodes highlighted policy and governance topics, including perspectives on the two-party political system. The most recent season spotlighted community organizing and activism, featuring diverse forms of student organizing in each episode such as protest movements and journalistic resistance among queer, Indigenous, Latine/o/a, and housing-insecure students. In their scriptwriting, students apply systems thinking skills by situating social problems within historical contexts and power constructs.

The podcast also amplifies marginalized identities that lack opportunities to share their stories and perspectives. In the last year alone, the program elevated the voices of Latine/o/a students from UVU's

Undocumented Student Group, queer students who participated in the Strike Out Queerphobia protest at Brigham Young University, student leaders of the Student Housing Coalition at UC Santa Cruz who protested unsustainable housing costs, and student contributors to the countercultural media collective Prodigal Press in Provo, Utah (Baron, 2022; Harris, 2022).

Advanced—Map the System

Map the System is a global competition founded by the Skoll Centre for Social Entrepreneurship at the Saïd Business School at the University of Oxford. University students around the world form teams to engage in research on social problems and create visual maps to depict the surrounding systems. Teams initially compete at their own universities, with winning teams advancing to the global intercollegiate competition hosted by Oxford. To support the program at UVU, the CSI holds an instructive workshop series on systems thinking and mapping, followed by a competition during which teams present their research and visual representations to a panel of judges.

Part of the project deliverables include identifying existing interventions for the selected social problem and assessing their effectiveness (UVU Center for Social Impact, n.d.). Students are equipped with concepts from the integrated social impact strategies, including the basics of theory of change and impact measurement. Moreover, as students identify gaps and opportunities through their systems analysis, they can explore opportunities for additional interventions through the lens of each pathway.

Regardless of winning the UVU or Oxford competitions, multiple student teams continue to use the social impact strategy skills they developed to push their research forward. In recent years, a student team that studied sexual assault against women in the military earned the opportunity to present their research at a national conference. In other cases, the student lead for a project about mental health disparity among Black Utahans was offered a job at a premiere therapy clinic after presenting to off-campus community stakeholders, students who presented on the wage gap for American women won a research award under another department at UVU, and the student lead for the winning UVU team in 2021 went on to become a CSI impact fellow and eventually was accepted into a PhD program at MIT. This student reflected on their experience in the following way:

The research we conducted opened my eyes to many systemic inequities and taught me the value of lived experience in systemic
analyses. In my role as a . . . Fellow, I co-instructed workshops
that taught systems thinking and equity-centered design to undergraduate researchers. [Through the CSI] participants investi-
gate defined issues with tangible consequences, often leading to
transformative realizations and an increased capacity for social
impact work. Few programs present undergrads with this type of
opportunity. —Jo Hickman

Future Integrations of the Pathways

From the outset, the Pathways framework allowed us a clear vision of
numerous ways to integrate the pathways into not only our current and
emerging initiatives at the CSI but also other campus offerings, and even
our own internal governance structure.

In the following section, we outline further potential applications for
our own work and hope that it may serve as a launching point for others to
consider applications of the pathways at their own institutions.

Mapping Existing Campus Offerings

One future integration we are considering involves mapping existing campus offerings to the Pathways framework. This effort aims to establish our
center as an institutional hub, facilitating students' connections to opportunities aligned with their interest and experience. This comprehensive approach will encompass courses, campus events, and campus resources that
can deepen students' understanding and application of the pathways. This
might include programming hosted by academic departments or other
campus centers, such as the Entrepreneurship Institute in the business
school, Multicultural Student Services, the Center for Constitutional Studies, or resources made available by the sustainability and basic needs offices.

Offering Future Social Impact Credentials

With few spaces to dive into focused social impact thought, theory, and
practice, students often incorrectly assume that involvement in this work
is restricted to nonprofit or social work sectors. To address this, we are

Foundation	Methods	Application	
Foundations of Social Impact (3 credits)	Strategies of Social Impact (3 credits)	Pathways of Social Impact Courses (3 credits each)	Elective (3 credits) upper-division, field-specific classes across campus

Social Impact Certificate (18 credits - 3 pathway courses required)

Minor/Integrated Studies Major Emphasis in Social Impact (21 credits - 4 pathway courses required)

Social Impact Major (27 credits - 6 pathway courses required)

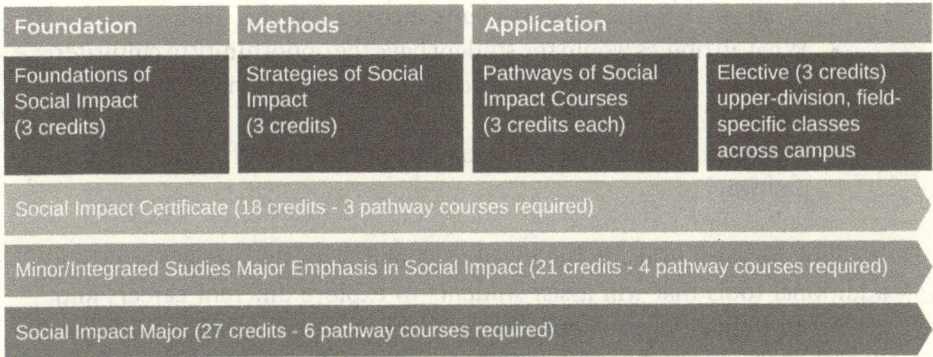

Figure 8.6. Social impact curriculum diagram.
Original image, Summer Valente. Reprinted with permission.

developing a comprehensive suite of offerings—a social impact certificate, minor, and major—aligned to the pathways and our integrated strategies, as seen in Figure 8.6.

The Foundations of Social Impact course would include an introduction to our strategic impact continuum, including relational care, our integrated strategies model, and the Pathways framework. It would also cover the historical context of social impact, key figures, best practices, and current discourse in the field. The Strategies and Pathways of Social Impact courses would provide deeper explorations, including critiques, ethical considerations, and detailed case studies of their applications. A list of approved electives would be available and include courses such as macro social work, political theory, economic systems, and others.

Providing Internship/Career Guidance

In our efforts to enhance students' career development in social impact, we started with the pathways as a guide to develop internship and career guidance. Our earliest conceptualizations led to the development of a 2-year faculty fellow project called the Pathways Practitioner Profiles Research Project, which serves as a foundation for several submissions in this publication. The project explored the following questions:

- What foundational knowledge would students pursue in this pathway?

- What skills would make students successful in this field?
- What attributes would the student have the opportunity to cultivate?
- What are the ways in which social impact is described within this pathway?
- How will students have the opportunity to effect change in this pathway?

We look forward to using the insights gained from this project to create additional tools that will assist students to explore different careers and sectors in which they can apply their social impact knowledge and skills.

Expanding Internal Governance Structures

We are exploring a deeper integration that would involve establishing an advisory board for the CSI, built around the pathways. This board would include a student, faculty member, practitioner, and staff member representing each pathway who would collaborate to enhance and advise on CSI offerings within their respective pathways. Additionally, the advisory board could play a crucial role in developing career paths, providing internship guidance, and advising on graduate school opportunities (see Figure 8.7).

Figure 8.7. Internal governance model.
Original image, Summer Valente. Reprinted with permission.

Summary

This chapter has explored how the pathways serve as a foundational framework for our comprehensive social impact education programming. With its emphasis on interdisciplinarity, inclusivity, and inherent nonpartisanship, the Pathways framework has proven invaluable. Combining the framework with our integrated social impact strategies provides students with tools that enhance their community engagement along each pathway as strategically, effectively, and ethically as possible. This rigorous education framework not only expands students' capacity to engage with diverse pathways that go beyond their initial interest but also encourages critical analysis and constructive critique. This engagement has already spurred meaningful refinements to the framework, paving the way for improved refinement and greater impact in our educational mission.

References

Academy for Systems Change. (2014, April 1). *Dana's writing.* https://donella meadows.org/donella-meadows-legacy/danas-writing/

Baron, E. (2022, May 21). UCSC students list housing demands in on-campus protest. *Santa Cruz Sentinel.* https://www.santacruzsentinel.com/2022/05/20/ucsc-students-list-housing-demands-in-on-campus-protest/

Cole, T. (2021, June 6). The white-savior industrial complex. *The Atlantic.* https://www.theatlantic.com/international/archive/2012/03/the-white-savior-industrial-complex/254843/

Corporate Finance Institute Team. (2023, May 9). *Systems thinking.* Corporate Finance Institute. https://corporatefinanceinstitute.com/resources/management/systems-thinking/

Creative Reaction Lab. (n.d.). *A method for co-creating equitable outcomes.* https://crxlab.org/our-approach

David Eccles School of Business. (n.d.). *Impact measurement and management.* https://sorensonimpactinstitute.com/impact-measurement-and-reporting/

Equity Design Collaborative. (n.d.). Equity Design Collaborative. https://equitydesigncollaborative.com/about/

Fulbright-Anderson, K., & Auspos, P. (2006). *Community change: Theories, practice, and evidence.* Aspen Institute Roundtable on Community Change. https://www.aspeninstitute.org/wp-content/uploads/files/content/docs/rcc/COMMUNITYCHANGE-FINAL.PDF

Harris, M. (2022, October 11). *BYU students join nationwide walkout against "Queerphobia" at religious schools.* KUER. https://www.kuer.org/education/2022-10-11/byu-students-join-nationwide-walkout-against-queerphobia-at-religious-schools

IDEO. (n.d.). *About IDEO: Our story, who we are, how we work.* https://www.ideo.com/about

Meadows, D. H., & Wright, D. (2015). *Thinking in systems: A primer.* Chelsea Green Publishing.

Montuori, A. (2011). Systems approach. In Mark A. Runco & Steven R. Pritzker (Eds.), *Encyclopedia of creativity* (2nd ed., pp. 414–421). Academic Press. https://www.sciencedirect.com/referencework/9780123750389/encyclopedia-of-creativity

National Equity Project. (n.d.). *Introduction to liberatory design.* https://www .nationalequityproject.org/frameworks/liberatory-design

O'Boyle, E. (2023, July 21). *4 things gen Z and millennials expect from their workplace.* Gallup. https://www.gallup.com/workplace/336275/things-gen-millennials-expect-workplace.aspx

Reynolds, G., Cox, L. C., Fritz, N., Hadley, D., & Zadra, J. R. (2018, December 21). A playbook for designing Social Impact Measurement (SSIR). *Stanford Social Innovation Review: Informing and Inspiring Leaders of Social Change.* https://ssir .org/articles/entry/a_playbook_for_designing_social_impact_measurement

Stanford d.school. (n.d.). *Liberatory design is an approach to addressing complex equity + design challenges.* https://dschool.stanford.edu/tools/liberatory-design

University of Oxford. (n.d.). *Map the system.* https://mapthesystem.sbs.ox.ac.uk/ home

Utah Valley University Center for Social Impact. (n.d.). *Map the System presentations.* https://uvu.contentdm.oclc.org/digital/collection/p17182coll25

Utah Valley University Center for Social Impact. (Producer). (2020–present). *Critical Mass* [Audio podcast]. https://podcasters.spotify.com/pod/show/ critical-mass-pod

Vesty, L. (2016, September 14). Millennials want purpose over paychecks. So why can't we find it at work? *The Guardian.* https://www.theguardian.com/ sustainable-business/2016/sep/14/millennials-work-purpose-linkedin-survey#:~:text=Achieving%20a%20low%20score%20doesn,creating%20 meaningful%20work%20a%20priority

Weiss, C. H., & Connell, J. P. (1995). Nothing as practical as good theory: Exploring theory-based evaluation for comprehensive community initiatives for children and families. In J. P. Connell, A. C. Kubisch, L. B. Schorr, & C. H. Weiss (Eds.), *New approaches to evaluating community initiatives: Concepts, methods, and contexts* (pp. 65–92). The Aspen Institute.

Chapter 9

USING THE PATHWAYS FOR PUBLIC SERVICE AND CIVIC ENGAGEMENT FOR CAMPUS STRATEGIC PLANNING

Ryan W. Flynn and Alyssa Wiseman

A s colleges and universities continue to focus more on career exploration, we have a unique opportunity to embed civic education into this process. With so many possible career options represented in the six Pathways of Public Service and Civic Engagement, the framework has the potential to recontextualize our work and better prepare students for careers of service and leadership. While making connections to coursework is valuable, integrating cocurricular experiential learning opportunities can provide essential hands-on practice for students going into public service fields. While larger universities may offer professionalized academic programs that help students navigate these fields, smaller institutions like Illinois College, which may lack the resources to launch new academic programs for each pathway, can utilize a combination of curricular and cocurricular strategies to effectively prepare students.

Illinois College's Office of Civic Engagement and Student Leadership set out to utilize institutional data collected from the Pathways survey tool to develop scaffolded programming that supports students in achieving their career goals. This work, begun in 2022, involved a multistep process integrating student and staff feedback, a literature review, and an analysis of existing curricular and cocurricular programming. The result is a strategic plan detailed in this chapter.

The strategic plan was developed to fit the needs and capacities of Illinois College, a private liberal arts college with an undergraduate population of around 1,000 students. The college has a rich history of graduating students who pursue careers in public service and has prided itself as an institution that focuses on service as a core student experience. While this strategic plan may be a useful starting point for administrators and faculty at other colleges and universities, adjustments are recommended to better account for the needs and capacity of larger institutions.

Literature Review

Many colleges offer programs dedicated to civic education and preparing students for careers in service to the public. However, these programs often solely rely on curriculum-based approaches and may not always integrate cocurricular programming and experiential learning opportunities specifically focused on public service. While students at Illinois College are accustomed to experiential learning and integrating service with learning, organizing opportunities in relation to specific public service pathways is a newer concept. The Pathways of Public Service and Civic Engagement represent an opportunity to pull together several threads—experiential learning, service-learning, and career exploration.

The practice of experiential learning has become deeply integrated into a broad array of disciplines, producing desirable outcomes for both higher education and student career development. In *Democracy and Education*, Dewey (1916) argued that students should be engaged in both thought and action in order to fulfill the lofty goals of education within a democracy, offering an early exploration of experiential learning and its connection to civic education. In *Experience and Nature*, Dewey (1925) asserted that by combining "noncognitive" experiences and reflective experiences, we are able to develop a deeper understanding of various subjects. Expanding on the insights of Dewey, as well as Kurt Lewin (1946) and

Jean Piaget (1952), David Kolb (1984) developed an experiential learning theory that further contextualizes and elaborates on the "noncognitive" experiences.

The emphasis on experiential learning has influenced the evolution of civic education over the last few decades. This emphasis on action and reflection in learning aligns closely with service-learning pedagogy, a practice that balances learning goals and volunteer service outcomes while encouraging learners to reflect on their experience (Jacoby, 1996). The development of the service-learning field has since been shaped by several influential frameworks: Porter-Honnet and Poulsen's (1989) "Wingspread principles," Kretzmann and McKnight's (1993) asset-based community development approach, Morton's (1995) paradigms of service-learning, and Freire's (1968/2016) critical pedagogy emphasizing explicit social justice goals.

The movement toward new forms of instruction for democratic engagement beyond just community service marks a pivotal moment in higher education's contribution to democracy. As Ronald J. Daniels (2021) asserts, American higher education has four distinct functions: social mobility, citizenship education, the discovery and communication of knowledge, and the cultivation of a pluralistic society. Strategies that address these four functions look different at every college and university, and we know this work occurs both inside and outside the classroom. While democratic principles have been discussed in the classroom for centuries, adding an explicit experiential learning component to encourage students to actively practice their civic skills is now essential.

This shift toward civic-focused experiential learning may stem from the diminishing divide between curricular and cocurricular experiences, but we might optimistically attribute it to generational proactivity on social issues. The last two generations have been more politically engaged, specifically on issues of human rights and social justice, and higher education is responding to this trend. With this in mind, there is still work to do (Parker et al., 2019). While many institutions are implementing programs conducive to civic education and more critical forms of engagement, a significant number of these programs still struggle with siloing. As David Matthews (2009) asserts, democratic engagement efforts within higher education institutions are often "ships passing in the night," highlighting the significant challenges still to be overcome.

As higher education embraces more critical forms of engagement, the Pathways of Public Service and Civic Engagement offer a framework to organize and structure programs around shared language. They also provide valuable data directly from student feedback that enables colleges and universities to better meet the civic education needs of students. The research outlined in this chapter focuses on Illinois College's progress toward a strategic plan that emphasizes this engagement.

Data Collection and Analysis

The distribution of the Pathways survey tool began in November 2022 with a trial involving several student organizations, including Alpha Phi Omega (APO) and Student Senate. This initial phase allowed us to refine our methods for promoting and distributing the survey to collect meaningful data. After the trial run, we distributed the survey to the first-year class during a prescheduled event featuring a promotional giveaway and were able to see emerging trends in the data. After developing a broader distribution plan, we launched the survey during April 2023 as part of our Global Volunteer Month programming, offering gift cards as an incentive for students' participation. After removing any incomplete responses, we ended with 93 responses, representing approximately 9% of Illinois College's student population.

Using data collected through the Pathways tool nationally between 2018–2021, we were able to do a comparative analysis with our institutional data. Our comparison focused on questions 9–14 on the Pathways tool, which asked students about their prior experience in each of the public service pathways, their interest in learning more and engaging in each pathway, their personal strength in engaging in each pathway, and how much impact they believe each pathway has on society. Figures 9.1–9.4 illustrate these four data points from the Pathways tool using 2022–2023 Illinois College–specific data.

Compared to the national data, we found two notable deviations with our data: (1) Illinois College students reported lower interest in participating in the Direct Service Pathway compared to the national data set, and (2) Illinois College students reported higher levels of experience engaging with the Social Entrepreneurship and Corporate Social Responsibility Pathway compared to the national data set. The reasons for the latter differences are not yet fully understood and require further analysis in the future.

To effectively interpret the data collected via the Pathways tool, we first needed to assess what the institution was already doing in each of the six pathways, including both curricular and cocurricular initiatives. To

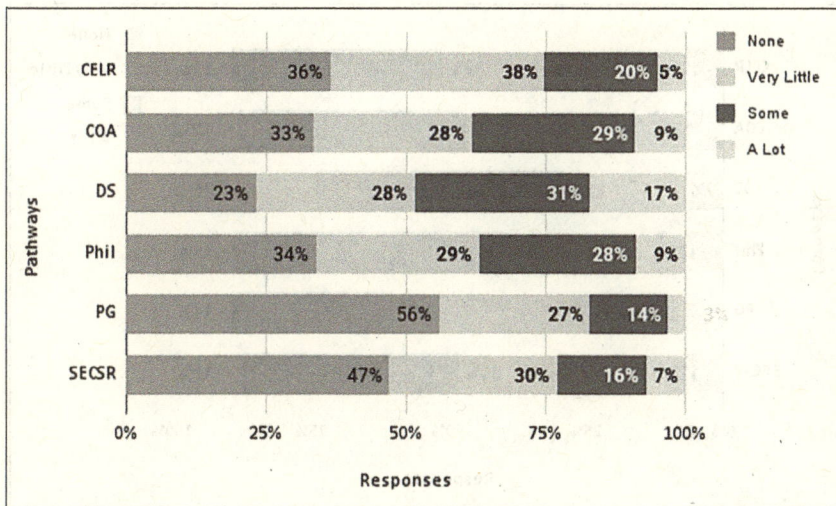

Figure 9.1. Respondents' experience in the pathway prior to taking the survey.

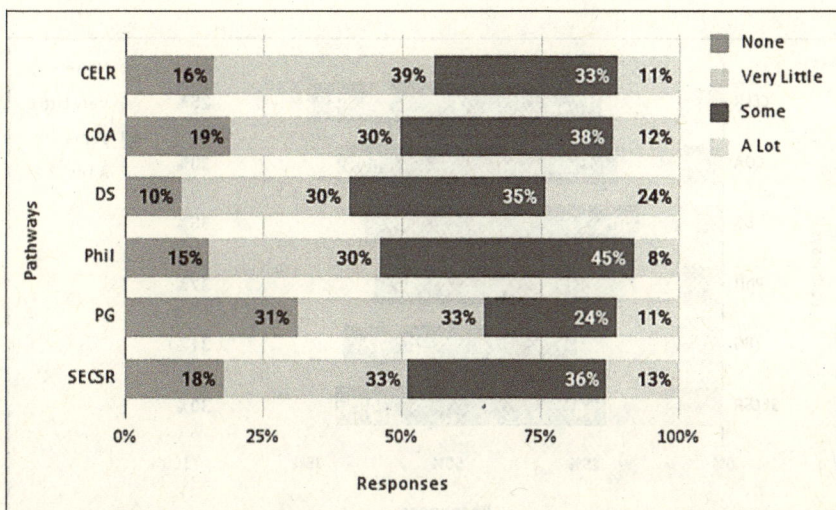

Figure 9.2. Respondents' interest in that pathway.

gain insight from a curricular perspective, we analyzed syllabi language from the academic year 2022–2023 and categorized the data based on the six pathways. For the cocurricular perspective, we analyzed available event data and similarly categorized it using the six pathways. Our cocurricular

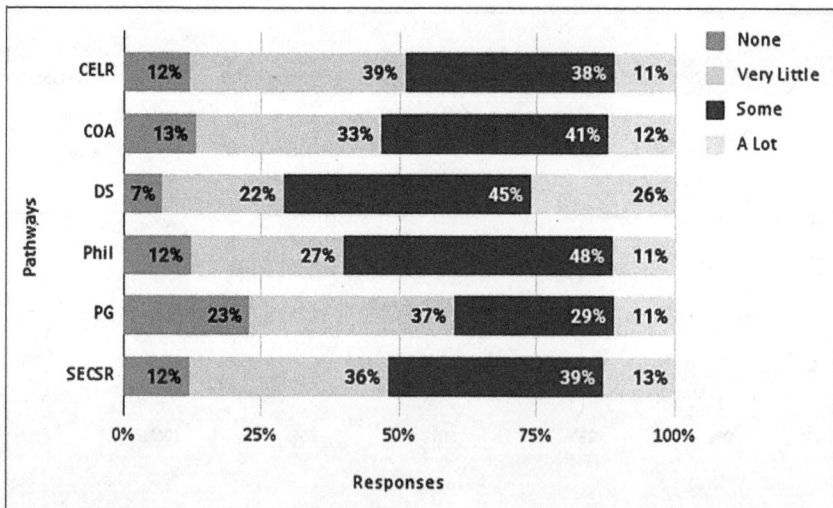

Figure 9.3. Respondents' view of their own personal strength to have an influence on the pathway.

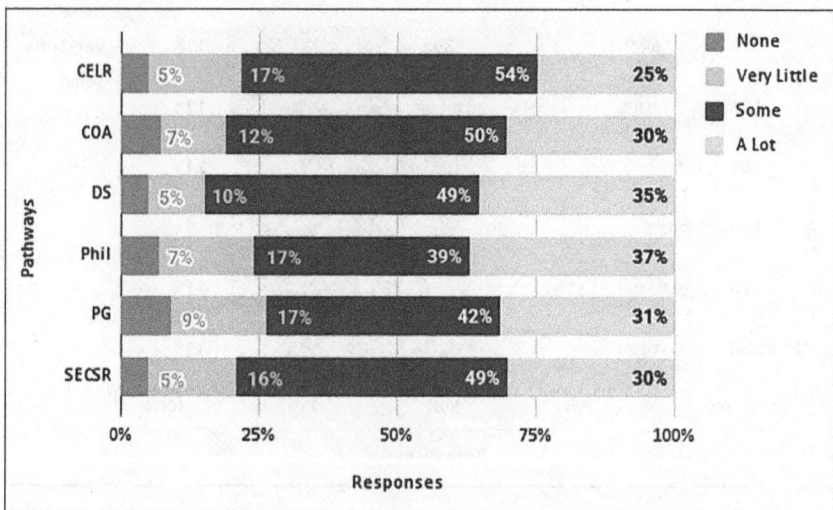

Figure 9.4. Respondents' opinion on whether each pathway has any impact on social issues.

assessment included a subjective review of event data from our Presence database (a Modern Campus event-tracking platform). For this review, we focused on the academic year 2022–2023 data only, focusing primarily on events planned and implemented by student organizations or college offices, programs, and departments. Based on this review, we found that while there has been a significant focus on direct service activities, particularly within our student organizations, every other pathway was either dramatically underrepresented or not represented at all. Initially, this led us to believe that Illinois College lacked programming for these other five pathways. To dig deeper into the data, we conducted additional analysis looking at events not labeled "direct service" and discovered that a variety of staff-led and student-led events could potentially align with the other pathways if reframed slightly. With this additional insight, we realized we could adapt existing programming to align with our needs as we integrate the pathways language moving forward, which represents a cost-neutral adjustment.

For the curricular assessment, we analyzed all syllabi submitted by faculty for the academic year 2022–2023 and separated those from the fall and spring semesters. The fall 2022 semester contained 220 unique syllabi, and spring 2023 contained 231 unique syllabi. Using these syllabi, we conducted a qualitative review of assignments, controlling for each of the six pathways. Specifically, we were looking for any assignments that contained phrasing that would indicate at least some discussion on one of the pathways. Our findings contained several important takeaways: (1) No pathway was represented by more than 10% of courses in either

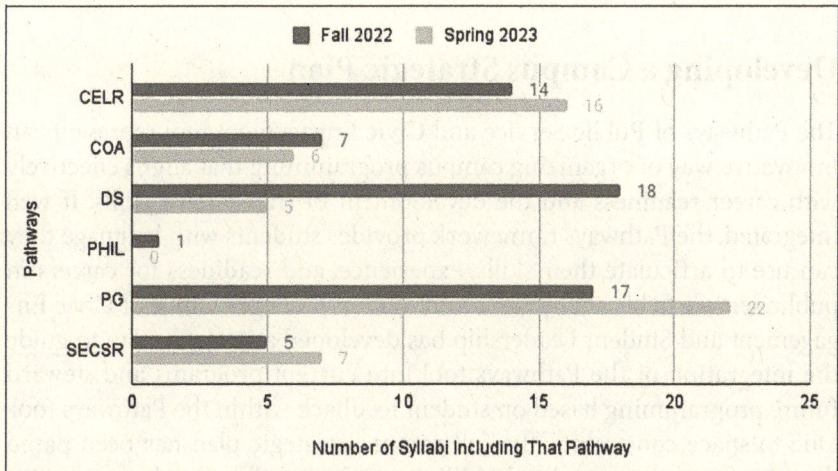

Figure 9.5. Pathways representation in AY2022–2023 syllabi.

Note: The total number of classes found for each of the six pathways, controlling per semester.

semester; (2) the language of "policy and governance" was represented in syllabi more than that of any other pathway; (3) "direct service" had greater representation in the fall semester, primarily because our first-year service program requires each first-year seminar course to perform a weekend of volunteer service; and (4) "philanthropy" was found in only one syllabus, in the fall semester.

Analyzing our curricular and cocurricular programming along-side student responses for the 2022–2023 Pathways survey reveals three insights that help inform the campus strategic plan resulting from this research. The first is that, while most respondents have experience with direct service, their exposure to the other five pathways is minimal. Our second takeaway is that many respondents chose "Very Little" or "Some" in their responses to a variety of questions in the categories of "experience," "interest," and "personal strength," which illustrates a potential lack of awareness about the six pathways and their connection to future career prospects. Our final takeaway is that while many respondents might not be confident in their experience related to a pathway, or express a specific interest in pursuing certain pathways, they are confident that each of the six pathways is having "Some" or "A Lot" of social impact. This underscores that students perceive value in each of the pathways. These three take-aways are useful, if not surprising. The data collected in this inaugural year of using the survey offers valuable insight into how to proceed with fully integrating the framework into our campus programming.

Developing a Campus Strategic Plan

The Pathways of Public Service and Civic Engagement tool represents an innovative way of organizing campus programming that aligns effectively with career readiness and the development of transferable skills. If well integrated, the Pathways framework provides students with language they can use to articulate their skills, experience, and readiness for careers in public service fields after graduation. Illinois College's Office of Civic Engagement and Student Leadership has developed a strategic plan to guide the integration of the Pathways tool into current programs and steward future programming based on student feedback within the Pathways tool. Due to space constraints, the full campus strategic plan has been pared down to four key strategies that Illinois College will be implementing incrementally starting in fall 2023.

Strategy 1: Integration Into the First Year Experience

Illinois College has a scaffolded First Year Experience Program that guides students' transition to college and includes several major programs. One is the Hilltop Service Program, which includes a class service project, a preservice workshop that contextualizes the service experience, and a postservice lesson plan that faculty can utilize to round out the student volunteer experience. Beginning in fall 2023, the Pathways tool will be embedded into the preservice workshop to expose first-year students to new areas of public service. During the workshop, which is facilitated by the Office of Civic Engagement and Student Leadership, students will reflect on their survey results using two printed articles showcasing the breadth and depth of opportunities available to serve the public and the common good. One article provides an example of throwing starfish back into the ocean as a simple act of service, whereas the second article highlights an attempt at reforesting streets in Detroit and how complex that act of service can become. These two articles allow us to discuss volunteer motivation and engage in a conversation about why each student is participating, which in turn provides an opportunity to discuss other forms of public service. The goal is to expose students to additional models of civic engagement beyond direct service, which offers a meaningful counterbalance to the direct service–heavy Hilltop Service Program projects. This initial strategy sets the stage for strategy 2, which aims to further capitalize on the survey results to explore career possibilities.

Strategy 2: The Pathways Tool Results for Career Exploration

As the college continues to move toward a career exploration focus with the First Year Experience, the Pathways tool will yield a valuable dataset both for students and for the Office of Civic Engagement and Student Leadership. While student responses are anonymous within the Qualtrics system, we have budgeted for extra incentives and giveaways for students if they are willing to send a screenshot of their results and/or meet with staff to process their results. This allows us to build a database of results that can be referred to during future career coaching meetings with students. Integrating the Pathways tool into the Hilltop Service Program allows us to leverage these data over the next 4 years to help counsel and connect students to opportunities that align with their preferred method of civic engagement. Additionally, should students decide to pursue a career that has a public service focus, these data could prove valuable for exploring career opportunities, especially if collected annually until graduation.

Strategy 3: Ensure Programming Coverage in All Six Pathways

In analyzing the data collected during academic year 2022-2023, we found that while there are many opportunities for direct service participation, fewer opportunities exist for engagement in the other five pathways. Based on the data, we will be building out additional opportunities for engagement to ensure that there is at least one cocurricular program offering in each pathway. Table 9.1 includes current and planned programming to meet each pathway. Any new programming launched in academic year 2023-2024 or planned to be launched in the future is listed in italics. While this list of programming is not exhaustive, it may provide a starting point for other colleges facing similar situations and seeking to expand their programming opportunities.

Table 9.1. Current and Planned Programming by Pathway

Pathway	Cocurricular Programming (new offerings in *italics*)
Community-Engaged Learning and Research	• summer student–faculty research offerings with the Office of Civic Engagement and Student Leadership • independent research in social science disciplines • internship opportunities with regional nonprofits
Community Organizing and Activism	• MLK Commemoration Week • social justice–themed speaker series • *community organizing student leadership workshops*
Direct Service	• Hilltop Service Program • student organizing volunteer projects • alternative breaks
Philanthropy	• *National Philanthropy Day Penny Wars Competition with Illinois College Greek letter organizations* • *convocation with regional philanthropic foundations*
Policy and Governance	• Constitution Day commemorative events • voter registration and education events • Newman Civic Fellowship through Campus Compact • *rebuilt student leadership training for Student Senate*
Social Entrepreneurship and Corporate Social Responsibility	• *National Entrepreneurship Week—Student Small Business Showcase (social media promotions and "craft fair"-style event; delayed for next academic year)*

In both the Philanthropy Pathway and the Social Entrepreneurship and Corporate Social Responsibility Pathway, we plan to utilize existing celebration days/weeks to seamlessly introduce new programming. Although the college has not traditionally commemorated National Philanthropy Day or National Entrepreneurship Week, these occasions provide ideal opportunities to pilot innovative programming around these themes.

Another notable initiative involves revamping a student leadership training for Illinois College's Student Senate. This program, tailored to empower students in student government, will incorporate additional training and context focused on the Policy and Governance Pathway. Based on our survey data, the Policy and Governance Pathway has low levels of reported experience and interest, but a high level of reported impact. This presents an opportunity to reshape student perspectives through guided training. In the hopes of giving students more of a voice on our campus, allowing them to experience what governance can look like on a systemic level, we hope that leadership training will foster a deeper understanding and urgency for contributing to positive change within our campus community.

Strategy 4: Leverage Regional Partnerships

In coordination with strategy 3, there is a considerable opportunity to leverage the pathways to expand and diversify regional partnerships. While our college possesses certain expertise, we recognize that we are not always the best source for specialists in all six pathways. However, we can connect students to regional organizations and community leaders who hold this expertise. Partnerships can come in many different forms, and we plan to focus on experiential learning and speakers.

Experiential learning can be integrated across all six pathways. At Illinois College, we have actively expanded experiential learning opportunities with a focus on civic engagement in recent years. The Pathways framework further emphasizes this commitment. Suggestions to expand these opportunities include developing additional internships with local nonprofit agencies that encourage students to reflect on their pathway connections, expanding our volunteer programs to include new partners, and rebranding our community-based student work program to align more closely with the pathways' objectives.

Additionally, we will be expanding our pool of potential speakers for campus-wide events and classroom visits, focusing on pathways for which programming is currently limited. One initiative we plan to pursue involves developing partnerships with local philanthropic foundations to host speakers that can demonstrate the economics behind fundraising for social causes. While Illinois College is in a rural area, we are fortunate to have several family foundations and community foundations within a short drive. This presents an opportunity to collaborate with campus-based partners to identify speakers, a strategy we intend to leverage and expand on in the future. This collaborative effort is crucial moving forward.

Conclusion

The development of experiential, student-focused programming, both curricular and cocurricular, is an iterative process with continual revisions. While we have highlighted strategies utilized or planned by Illinois College's Office of Civic Engagement and Student Leadership, we recognize that our initiatives are continually evolving based on feedback from student, faculty, staff, and community partners. The Pathways for Public Service and Civic Engagement have proven invaluable for collecting feedback from students and promptly translating it into actionable improvements. As we continue to integrate the Pathways tool into our programming, we anticipate finding novel ways to analyze the data and further enhance our programs. This chapter outlines the foundational steps we have taken at Illinois College to advance our civic education approach with the Pathways survey tool, and we hope it offers insights for other institutions seeking to adapt to the evolving landscape of civic education.

References

Daniels, R. (2021). *What universities owe democracy.* Johns Hopkins University Press.

Dewey, J. (1916). *Democracy and education.* Macmillan.

Dewey, J. (1925). *Experience and nature.* Dover.

Freire, P. (1968/2018). *Pedagogy of the oppressed* (M. B. Ramos, Trans.; 50th anniv. ed.). Bloomsbury Academic. (Original work published 1968)

Jacoby, B. (1996). *Service-learning in higher education: Concepts and practices.* Jossey-Bass.

Kolb, D. (1984). *Experiential learning: Experience as the source of learning and development.* Prentice-Hall.

Kretzman, J., & McKnight, J. (1993). *Building communities from the inside out: A path toward finding and mobilizing a community's assets.* ACTA Publications.

Lewin, K. (1946). Action research and minority problems. *Journal of Social Issues,* *2*(4), 34–46. https://doi.org/10.1111/j.1540-4560.1946.tb02295.x

Matthews, D. (2009). Ships passing in the night? *Journal of Higher Education Outreach and Engagement, 13*(3), 5–16. https://doi.org/10.54656/YBJA4431

Morton, K. (1995). "The irony of service": Charity, project, and social change in service-learning. *Michigan Journal of Community Service Learning, 2,* 19–32.

Parker, K., Graf, N., & Igielnik, R. (2019, January 17). *Generation Z looks a lot like Millennials on key social and political issues.* Pew Research Center. https://www.pewresearch.org/social-trends/2019/01/17/generation-z-looks-a-lot-like-millennials-on-key-social-and-political-issues/

Piaget, J. (1952). *The origins of intelligence in children.* International University Press.

Porter-Honnet, E., & Poulsen, S. J. (1989). *Principles of good practices for combining service and learning.* Johnson Foundation.

Chapter 10

"TO SET THEIR OWN PATHS"

Using the Pathways to Help Students Self-Identify Their Unique Roles in Shaping a More Just and Compassionate World

Katie L. Price

A s part of my role as senior associate director at the Eugene M. Lang Center for Civic and Social Responsibility at Swarthmore College, I am charged with helping students "set their own paths" toward creating a more just and compassionate world. This chapter discusses how Swarthmore's Lang Center is using the Pathways tool to help students learn about different avenues of engagement and better articulate how their personal approach fits into a larger tapestry of engagement possibilities. In particular, this chapter discusses how we use the Pathways tool to prepare Swarthmore College students for ethical engagement in the context of summer internships through our Social Impact Summer Scholarship program. We have found that the Pathways framework and tool offer an excellent foundation for students to identify their strengths and interests as they begin to chart their own paths. We then build upon the tool results with additional educational offerings and revisit the Pathways framework to help students reflect on their summer experiences. This process enables them to articulate their impact on the world around them, both for themselves and broader audiences.

Institutional Context

Swarthmore College is a small liberal arts college located near Chester, Pennsylvania, and just outside of Philadelphia. Swarthmore has a central commitment to "peace, equity, and social responsibility, rooted in our founding as a coeducational Quaker institution" (Swarthmore College, 2003, para. 2). This commitment attracts students who have either participated in civic engagement and social justice work or have an interest in pursuing these activities during their college years.

The Eugene M. Lang Center for Civic and Social Responsibility at Swarthmore College

Endowed in 2001, the Lang Center provides "vision, leadership and support for the College's central commitment to educate students for civic and social responsibility" (Lang Center for Civic and Social Responsibility, 2003, para. 1). More specifically, the center's charge is to "prepare and motivate" students to "set their own paths toward shaping a more just and compassionate world" (para. 1). In order for students to chart their own paths in an informed way, they must first understand the options available to them and consider those approaches within a broader context of social change.

Under the leadership of Executive Director Benjamin Berger, the Lang Center has adopted Ernest Boyer's notion of "engaged scholarship" to describe our general approach to civic and social responsibility. While we often rely on the practical definition of *engaged scholarship* as research and teaching that "connect the rich resources of the university to our most pressing social, civic, and ethical problems," we recognize that Boyer (2016) thought more capaciously about "a special climate in which the academic and civic cultures communicate more continuously and more creatively with each other" (p. 27). The Lang Center sees our role on campus as dual in the sense that we support engaged research and teaching and also contribute to a "special climate" of engagement through a range of cocurricular programs and initiatives. For example, our Chester-Swarthmore Fellows

Council—which consists of residents with deep roots in the nearby city of Chester—meets quarterly with Swarthmore faculty and staff. Together, they shape student training programs, consult on place-based initiatives, explore the feasibility of potential projects, and strategize on long-term, transformational collaborations.

At the Lang Center, we frequently encounter students with strong backgrounds in civic engagement. However, during my 8 years with the college, I have found that students often arrive with direct service or community organizing/activism experience, but are less familiar with other pathways, particularly community-engaged learning and research and social entrepreneurship. Given that, our center focuses on engaged scholarship and deepening students' understanding of the ethics in *how* we, as representatives of higher education institutions, address contemporary public and ethical issues. Supporting community-engaged learning and research along with cocurricular programming is integral to our mission. These opportunities enable students not only to participate in and deepen their understanding of each of the six pathways but also to consider the role of each of these pathways in fostering larger social, structural, and systemic change. Our approach includes multiyear funding for students to undertake social impact projects with community partners (e.g., Lang Opportunity Scholarship, Engaged Humanities Studio, Project Pericles Fund); courses and modules that are cotaught by Lang Center staff, faculty, and community partners (including Introduction to Engaged Scholarship, Systems Thinking for Social Change, and Preparing Students for Ethical Engagement); and courses with cocurricular components such as internships or embedded study (the President's Sustainability Research Fellowship, Chester Semester). The Lang Center also houses the Co-Lab, a hub for cocurricular learning opportunities that introduces students to social innovation and systems thinking approaches to civic engagement that are often new to them.

Social Impact Summer Scholarship Program

Each summer, the Lang Center funds over 100 students to undertake engaged scholarship opportunities, whether through internships, faculty-led engaged research, or projects with community partners. Working closely with colleagues Jennifer Magee and Ashley Henry to administer these various programs, I oversee our Social Impact Summer Scholarship (SISS) Program. SISS supports approximately 70 students each year, spanning across class years. Through internships with organizations and corporations with social good as a core mission, students are able to add further dimension to their coursework by exploring complexity, applying and testing theories, and gaining valuable real-world experience.

This program offers a wraparound cocurricular experience for students. While the main focus is supporting students in community-based internships over the summer, Swarthmore provides a series of predeparture workshops in the spring; reflection exercises during the summer that include academic readings; and, in the fall, opportunities to synthesize their learning and share back with their peers. Additionally, the following spring, students participate in evaluating applications for the next cycle. It is the Lang Center's most popular summer grant program and the second-largest group of summer-funded students on campus.

Development of Civic Identity in a Liberal Arts Context

Young adulthood can be characterized as a developmental phase during which individuals transition from inward-looking adolescence to an outward-looking sense of self in the context of society (Gaudet, 2007). One of the Lang Center's stated learning goals is that students will be able to participate in community engagement activities that reinforce or clarify their sense of civic identity and social responsibilities. We further articulate this learning goal by emphasizing that students should be able to answer two fundamental questions: Who am I in relation to others in society/this community? What are my roles and responsibilities? The SISS program plays a pivotal role in helping students meet this learning goal. It provides financial support for students to undertake community engagement activities and offers a cocurricular experience that prepares them for engagement with community partners. Through the program, students engage in critical reflection during their experiences and share their learning back with their peers.

We also view this program as essential to meeting two of Swarthmore's four learning goals for students. "Students will engage with different cultures, ideas, institutions, and means of expression to enable the critical examination of their own perspectives." "Students will have the opportunity to engage in activities that support personal development, encourage interaction with off-campus communities, and build interpersonal and leadership skills" (Swarthmore College, 2003, para. 9). Engagement is crucial to both of these learning goals, and we see the Lang Center's emphasis on engaged scholarship as integral for delivering this type of engaged liberal arts education. Through our programs, students actively collaborate with community partners to cocreate solutions to social problems in ways that enhance their understandings of themselves and society.

Description of Pathway Usage

For the past 2 years, the Lang Center has used the Pathways of Public Service and Civic Engagement tool as the first step in our annual training for student grantees who engage in summer internships, faculty-led research, or independent projects that link their academics to social good. Students first complete the survey independently, and then share and reflect on their results at two points: immediately following completion of their preexperience requirements (which includes readings, workshops, and training on ethical engagement) and again after their summer experience.

Why Do We Start With the Pathways Tool?

Asking students to complete the Pathways tool as a first step in our "Preparing Students for Ethical Engagement" series before they embark on their summer opportunities offers them a chance to explore different approaches to civic engagement and social responsibility, and to identify areas of personal interest. It helps students achieve our center's learning goals, which includes having students develop an understanding and approach to responsible community engagement that is consistent with their own personal values, ethics, skills, and time constraints. Participating in the Pathways survey provides students with vocabulary that they continue to use in a series of reflections they participate in during their summer experience.

What Do Students Get Out of Doing the Survey?

We have found that completing the tool is often an eye-opening experience for students who may never have considered the broader spectrum of ways they might engage in the world around them. Students also value reflecting on how their skills and interests can best contribute, and they appreciate learning about the diverse ways their peers choose to engage.

In other words, the survey serves as a tool of both self-reflection and self-imagination. For instance, a student shared, "It was interesting to see the results and compare that to my preconception of what my strengths and interests were." Additionally, we find the tool challenges the idea that some ways of engagement are inherently better or more ethical than others. Instead, the tool offers several viable and valid paths to engagement—spanning different approaches, issues, and levels of commitment—and encourages students to consider how they might combine multiple approaches. One student shared, "These results can inform my summer experience by reminding me that these are the areas of work in which I am passionate and where I have some previous experience. This summer, I will be connecting my top two pathways."

How Do We Build on the Pathways Tool?

We find the Pathways tool functions best when paired with other training in engaged scholarship. While the survey is a first step in our presummer training, it primarily serves as a foundation on which to build. In summer 2023, students

- completed the Pathways tool as an opportunity to learn about different approaches to civic engagement and social responsibility, and to self-identify areas of particular interest;
- participated in a place-based workshop to contextualize their summer experience, either with off-campus study (if traveling internationally) or with social sciences and data librarian Simon Elichko through an April workshop entitled, "Places, Data, and Understanding: Doing Place-Based Research";
- attended an all-day retreat that covers practical matters such as budgeting, health, and well-being, and adjusting to a new internship as well as required readings and workshops led by faculty on core concepts of ethical community engagement, including empathy, inclusion, objectivity, and justice; and
- engaged in a peer-led workshop during which students work in groups to discuss how they would address ethical dilemmas that might arise during their summer experiences.

Once students have completed this series, we assess their understanding through a quiz designed to encourage reflection and synthesize learning. In summer 2023, we asked, "What were the results of your Pathways of Public Service and Engagement survey? How can these results inform your summer experience?" A primary benefit of asking students to reflect on how their results might influence their summer experience is that it encourages many to start thinking about conversations with their future supervisors, such as being able to ask for and articulate specific projects they might want to work on. As one student wrote, "These results can be used to help shape the individual project that I will create during my internship." Others expressed that taking the survey gave them more confidence going into their internship because it confirmed that their strengths and interests were well aligned with the internship that they were pursuing.

In the fall, we revisit the Pathways framework during a reflection luncheon that brings together all students who participated in a Lang Center–funded summer experience. During this session, students reflect on which pathways they found themselves using during their summer experience and engage in small-group discussion about the limitations and opportunities associated with each pathway. Was the pathway they named the same one they identified when completing the Pathways tool preexperience? Would they pursue this same pathway again? What others might they want to try? Which are best suited to their aims? Did students tend to gravitate to some approaches over others? This reflection and conversation further helps students contextualize their learning and experience in relation to their peers and provides them an opportunity to reconsider what their own path to civic and social responsibility might look like. In summer 2023, the majority of students said that their summer experience best embodied the Community-Engaged Learning and Research Pathway, suggesting that our programs are succeeding in their intention to expand students' notions of civic engagement beyond direct service and community organizing and activism.

Challenges/Accomplishments and Recommendations

One challenge we face is encouraging students to critically assess how the Pathways framework applies to the work that they are doing during their summer experiences and beyond. Some students do not fully embrace the opportunity to reflect on the Pathways framework in a broader context of how it could complement other approaches or intersect with different pathways to enhance the impact of their chosen path, particularly in relation to social and structural change. As part of their presummer training, all students read Eve Tuck's "Suspending Damage: A Letter to Communities" (2009) and the first chapter of Paulo Freire's *Pedagogy of the Oppressed* (2005). Given the complicated histories between communities and academic researchers (and harms that have resulted), we view these texts as crucial touchstones. They allow students to consider these histories and imagine alternatives in which campus–community relationships are based on mutual understanding and respect, a shared recognition of assets and contributions, and a conscious effort to work against preexisting structures of oppression. It would be interesting to see students reflect on which pathways might best lend themselves to working *with*, not *for* or *on behalf* of people, and in ways that resist dehumanization (Freire) or how the Pathways tool may or may not perpetuate ways of thinking about community that are damage-centered (Tuck).

Future Directions

In recent feedback from students about completing the Pathways tool, they expressed that the survey was helpful not only in identifying activities that they already engage in but also in providing them "words that [they] can put on a résumé." This prompted the idea to further explore how we might revisit the Pathways tool, after summer, in a practical résumé-updating workshop, which we plan to integrate for summer 2024 grantees.

While the Lang Center uses the Pathways tool with its summer grantees, these students represent a small percentage of the student body and may be self-selected as students already more familiar with the approaches presented in the tool. Could expanding the use of the tool benefit other Swarthmore students who might not initially self-identify as civically engaged? What insights might emerge if we were to administer the Pathways tool to the entire student body, similar to the approach taken by Juniata College as described in the following chapter? Given Swarthmore's environment, which attracts civically engaged students, how might the Pathways framework help students better understand themselves and their connections to each other in our collective effort to work toward a more just and compassionate world?

Conclusion

Exposing students to the Pathways framework early on in a cocurricular learning experience, and revisiting it afterward, can be a useful way for students to identify their place and "set their own path" in civic and social responsibility. Recognizing one's unique skills, preferences, and ability to contribute to positive social change is critical in young adulthood, and the Pathways framework offers students a tool to begin to articulate their vision for how they want to make meaningful contributions to the world.

References

Boyer, E. (1996). The scholarship of engagement. *Journal of Public Service & Outreach, 1*(1), 11–20.

Freire, P. (2005). *Pedagogy of the oppressed.* Continuum.

Gaudet, S. (2007). How the ethical experience defines adulthood: A sociological analysis. *Advances in Life Course Research, 12,* 335–357.

Lang Center for Civic and Social Responsibility. (2003, June). *About.* https://www.swarthmore.edu/lang-center/about-lang-center

Swarthmore College. (2003, June). *College mission, goals, and planning.* https://www.swarthmore.edu/assessment/college-mission-goals-and-planning

Tuck, E. (2009). Suspending damage: A letter to communities. *Harvard Educational Review, 79*(3), 409–427.

Chapter 11

ENGAGEMENT BECOMES CURRICULAR POLICY

Creating a General Education Requirement to "Inspire Citizens of Consequence"

Sarah C. Worley and Lillian Case

Introduction

Juniata College's introduction to the "Pathways of Public Service and Civic Engagement" at Campus Compact's 2016 national conference could not have come at a better time. Fortuitously, the introduction coincided with a pivotal moment in our college's history. The support of a relatively new provost helped validate and galvanize an existing group of faculty and staff already engaged in service-learning pedagogy and practice, and which had previously operated with limited visibility or institutional awareness. Moreover, the priorities outlined in the college's newly passed strategic plan included community engagement and the articulation of a vision for Juniata College to be a place that "inspires citizens of consequence." Around this same time, and with the support of a grant from the Mellon Foundation, faculty undertook a complete revision of the general education curriculum that, when passed in 2018, included a "Local Engagement" requirement for every student at Juniata. Accompanying this curricular change was a decision to rename the Community Service Office the Center for Community Engagement and resituate it within Academic Affairs (from Student Affairs) under a newly appointed faculty director who would report directly to the provost. This new model came with a half-time teaching load reduction for the Center's faculty director and adjustment from a nine-month to a ten-month contract.

During this period of momentum, it became clear that there was a lack of shared, interdisciplinary terms and definitions that could facilitate understanding among administrators, faculty, and students regarding the diverse array of potential opportunities for community engagement on campus. We sought a way to generate a sense of cohesion that might help name, explain, and capture what people were doing across campus. The Pathways framework and tool proved instrumental in moving us toward this goal. The convergence of these institutional factors, coupled with the integration of the Pathways framework and membership in the Pathways Working Group, made an institutional transformation toward community engagement possible at Juniata.

Institution Context

Founded by members of the Church of the Brethren in 1876 as a coeducational normal school, Juniata College is a small, 4-year, independent, private, residential, liberal arts college. It is a predominately White institution that in spring 2023 had 1,226 students enrolled, 24 of whom were graduate students. While the majority of students are from Pennsylvania, over 100 are international students from 24 countries. The mission statement reads, "At Juniata College, our mission is to provide an engaging, personalized educational experience empowering our students to develop the skills, knowledge and values that lead to a fulfilling life of service and ethical leadership in the global community" (Juniata College, 2025, para. 1). Juniata is a college with a tradition of social justice and peacemaking and is intent on providing a personalized academic experience, experiential learning (including community engagement), global education, mentored research, and inclusive excellence for students across all disciplines. A new strategic plan was passed in 2023 that reinforces this commitment to inspiring citizens of consequence and outlines experiential learning and equity-minded culture as key priorities.

Although Juniata's community engagement efforts can happen through various pathways both regionally and globally, it is important to contextualize the college in its local community. Huntingdon County is located in rural central Pennsylvania, nestled within Appalachian foothills and valleys. Our region is rather isolated, with small towns scattered among farms and forests. Approximately 70% of people in the region have access to broadband, and there is no integrated public transportation system. Huntingdon Borough, where Juniata's campus is situated, comprises approximately 100 of the county's 895 square miles. Pennsylvania's June 2023 *Workstats* reports Huntingdon's population at 44,458 people, with a population density of 50.4 per square mile, according to the 2020 Census. There is little racial, religious, or cultural diversity. The most recent U.S. Census estimates the county's racial makeup as 92.3% White, 5.3% Black/ African American, and 2.1% Hispanic. The median age in Huntingdon County is 43.4. These statistics include the predominantly young, male, African American inmates in two state correctional institutions located 2 miles from campus.

Huntingdon's top employment sectors are government, health care, manufacturing, retail, and tourism. The median household income is $57,055, and 13.9% live in poverty. Voter registration data reflect Huntingdon's conservative nature: Of 27,185 registered voters, 66% (18,021) are registered Republican. Many residents here fundamentally distrust institutions, and stereotypes about both college people and rural communities sometimes challenge relationships between these groups. The people of Huntingdon County can be described as proud, generous, conservative, Christian, patriotic, outdoorsy, settled, and loyal to place and family. These geographic and demographic characteristics help contextualize the unique opportunities and logistical challenges that colleges in rural areas face when implementing community engagement and outreach initiatives in partnership with the local community.

Through a community-wide deliberation process, Institutional Learning Outcomes (ILOs) were created in 2016 that outline goals in five areas. The first four are Knowledge and Skills, Intellectual Engagement, Interdisciplinarity, and Ethical Behavior. The fifth area is "Engagement With the Self and the World," which outlines the following specific objectives: collaborative work in cultural settings from local to global, engaged citizenship and respectful interactions, and understanding of how a holistic and intentional approach to life fosters well-being. Based on these ILOs, the faculty set out to design a new curriculum to facilitate these outcomes.

In 2018, a new general education curriculum was passed by faculty that was implemented in fall 2019. That new curriculum included a "Local Engagement (LE)" requirement for all students under the "Engagement

With Self and World" ILO. Regarding the language of LE, it is important to note that "local" does not necessarily mean Huntingdon. Instead, it refers to a highly contextualized, place-based learning experience that is rooted in mutually beneficial partnerships with communities and is infused with the values of reciprocity and asset-based thinking. This approach acknowledges that students may have that type of learning opportunity anywhere in the world.

A learning community made up of faculty, staff, students, and community partners was tasked with designing the requirements for this new addition to the curriculum. Ultimately, the LE requirement includes three components:

1. A preparatory module is provided during the First-Year Foundations course, including the Pathways to Community and Civic Engagement diagnostic survey and associated activities.
2. Students take part in a semester-long (at least 15-hour) local-engagement experience:
    a. curricular option—students taking a designated LE course
    b. cocurricular option—a student experience approved by justifying that it aligns with at least one of the pathways and then concurrently pairs it with the LE seminar
3. Finally, a two-part e-portfolio contribution will provide documentation of the experience and a response to a standardized prompt for critical guided reflection on the experience.

The learning outcomes for LE apply to all options available for fulfilling the requirement. LE courses are taught by faculty from at least 12 different departments, representing a variety of disciplinary perspectives. Additionally, students can fulfill the requirement through a cocurricular engagement option paired with an academic seminar. Through critical guided reflection paired with the community-engaged learning experience, students, regardless of instructor or department, learn to work collaboratively in local cultural settings, engage in citizenship through respectful interactions, and articulate how LE fosters individual and collective well-being.

For a course to receive the LE designation, it must be approved by the General Education Committee and the director of Community-Engaged Teaching and Learning. They evaluate the proposed course to ensure that it reflects the learning objectives of LE as outlined in the syllabus, includes the required signature assignment, and indicates that students will receive the minimum 15 hours of required engagement with a community. Each student's signature assignment must be uploaded to an e-portfolio network, allowing for sampling and evaluation to ensure that learning outcomes are being met.

Relevant Literature and Resources

What follows is an overview of the specific literature and resources that were pivotal in generating buy-in from faculty and administration. These resources provided the conceptual foundation that informed the design and implementation of our curricular requirement and integration of the Pathways framework. Several resources were also key to informing our learning community's approach to developing the learning objectives and expectations of Juniata's general education requirement. Among them were resources from the American Association of Colleges and Universities and Campus Compact.

In the past decade, civic engagement in higher education has gained significant attention for its potential to increase college access and success while fostering democratic values and active citizenship. Saltmarsh and Hartley (2011) advocate for a "democratic-centered" (p. 23) framework of engagement in higher education that actively involves students, faculty, and communities in collaborative and reciprocal partnerships, arguing that to achieve this paradigm shift, institutions must prioritize civic and community engagement as a means to promote social justice, civic responsibility, and democratic values. This can be achieved by integrating engagement into a college's core mission and ensuring that it influences policies and practices in teaching and research, as well as decision making at all levels. Liberal arts colleges seem particularly well suited to make this paradigmatic shift since, as Nussbaum (2007) argues, liberal education "cultivates the whole human being for the functions of citizenship and life in general" (p. 38). Saltmarsh and Hartley (2011) contend that engagement defined by "democratic purposes and processes," referring to the enhancement of a culture of democracy and the processes of engagement with off-campus communities, moves us beyond traditional models of education focused solely on knowledge transfer and academic research and leads to "epistemological, curricular, pedagogical, research, policy, and culture implications" (pp. 17–18). They acknowledge a variety of challenges and barriers to implementing engagement in higher education, which have "undermined the democratic purposes of colleges and universities" (p. 15). These range from resource limitations and lack of faculty development to the "corporatization of the university," the narrowing of faculty "disciplinary specialization," and the trend of "decontextualized learning" (p. 15). However, that does not mean higher education is doomed to perpetuate the status quo. It is possible to creatively leverage resources like faculty time, curriculum, and institutional alignment of priorities, values, and resources to overcome some of these barriers when there is "conceptual and ideological coherence" (p. 14), the characteristics suggested by Saltmarsh and Hartley as necessary to launch a movement.

Research has shown a connection between civic engagement and college outcomes, including access, learning, skill development, and completion rates (Cress et al., 2010). For example, in one such study, a meta-analysis of nine studies comparing courses with a service-learning component to those without one found that the addition of a service-learning component increases learning outcomes by 53% (Novak et al., 2007; Warren, 2012). Despite these findings, a report submitted to the U.S. Department of Education by AAC&U in 2012, entitled *A Crucible Moment: College Learning and Democracy's Future*, identified that these types of learning opportunities were for the most part "random, unconnected, uneven, optional, and available only to some students" (McTighe Musil, 2015, p. 3; National Task Force on Civic Learning and Democratic Engagement, 2012). Liberal arts colleges are particularly well suited to take the type of multidisciplinary approach outlined in *Making Civic Learning Routine Across Disciplines*, as Juniata did, to ensure equitable access to and distribution of engagement opportunities (McTighe Musil, 2015). The findings outlined in *A Promising Connection* and the recommendations of the National Task Force on Civic Learning and Democratic Engagement in *A Crucible Moment*, paired with the body of literature on high-impact practices, helped to make the case at Juniata for the creation of a general education requirement that would ensure that all students, regardless of major, would have the opportunity to benefit from these learning experiences (Cress et al., 2010; National Task Force on Civic Learning and Democratic Engagement, 2012).

High-impact experiential learning practices are characterized by key attributes that significantly enhance student learning, engagement, and success. Participation may be especially beneficial for underserved students (Brownell & Swaner, 2010; Kuh, 2008). AAC&U recognizes 11 specific practices, at least five of which were built into the general education requirements at Juniata, including first-year seminars, capstone courses/projects, global learning, e-portfolios, and community-based learning. Characteristics of high-impact practices specifically captured in Juniata's LE requirement include integrating community-engaged learning into the curriculum, where by students actively engage and interact with course material through partnerships with the community. Through these partnerships, instructors create opportunities for real-world application and ensure that students engage in guided critical reflection to help make the connections explicit.

By establishing shared language and criteria, frameworks such as AAC&U's (2009) *Civic Engagement VALUE Rubric* and the Pathways to Public Service and Civic Engagement enable the assessment of learning outcomes in this area. Following the graduation of the first cohort under the new general education curriculum in spring 2023, assessment efforts were underway to assess for evidence of students meeting learning objectives through a sampling of reflective portfolio contributions on their general education experiences.

Description of Pathways Usage

Integrating high-impact practices, such as community-engaged learning, into the general education requirements ensures that every student, regardless of major, has at least one community-engaged learning experience that aligns with at least one of the pathways during their time at Juniata. This has become an area for distinction in our National Survey of Student Engagement results. The Pathways diagnostic survey and framework have been implemented at an institutional level at Juniata, helping to effectively align this work across departments and divisions and make this type of learning experience more visible to students. The pathways are initially introduced to all students in the First-Year Foundations course to encourage them to consider which pathway best aligns with their skills, values, and interests as they explore which LE option to pursue. This also allows Juniata to track, to some degree, what students report about their level of experience with the pathways as they enter college and what issues they are most concerned about.

The framework has also been integrated into the approval process for a cocurricular experience to fulfill the LE requirement. During this process, students are asked to familiarize themselves with each pathway and provide a rationale for how the experience they are proposing aligns with at least one of them. The seminar course paired with the cocurricular experience is designed based on the Pathways survey and framework. Some students encounter the pathways when they log their hours in our tracking system, and again if they choose the option of taking the Local Engagement Seminar course. Beyond the First-Year Foundations course, the Pathways tool is used in the GE 101 Local Engagement Seminar, as well as in other select classes. Seniors are also asked to complete the survey as part of their exit interview before graduation. Realigning institutional understanding and language to the terms and definitions provided by the Pathways framework has been transformative in shifting the way we talk about and implement these curricular goals and priorities.

While the majority of data collected at our institution using this survey represents the experiences and opinions of first-year students, there are also data from other class years that enable comparison of responses across different class cohorts. This comparison has yielded some interesting findings. Comparing aggregated student responses to the Pathways survey from students in their first-year, sophomore, and junior years with those from seniors provides insight into how students' perceptions of and attitudes toward specific pathways may evolve through their time at Juniata. Having compiled Juniata-specific data collected using the Pathways survey from 2018–2023 and comparing seniors to everyone else, we observe that all students at Juniata report having the highest interest in exploring the Direct Service Pathway during college, which seems to remain consistent across all 4 years. However, seniors report more interest than underclass students in the Community-Engaged Learning and Research Pathway, and underclass students report more interest in exploring the Philanthropy Pathway than do seniors. Seniors also report more interest in the Policy and Governance Pathway than all other class cohorts do, and they perceive it as having more impact on social issues than all other student cohorts combined. We cannot definitively prove a direct correlation between exposure to the general education curriculum, or specifically to the LE requirement, and a change in interest to explore specific pathways. However, it does suggest that students' experiences at Juniata influence their understanding and perception of different pathways and which ones they might wish to further explore in the future.

Assessment of student reflections submitted to their e-portfolios allows us to gauge the extent to which the LE learning outcomes are being met and how the pathways might be useful in helping students reflect on their experiences. Our work is just beginning, but a preliminary qualitative analysis of assignments uploaded to date shows that when reflecting on the pathways, some students note that being introduced to the concept of six pathways to community engagement helped broaden their understanding of the diverse range of options available to them. Also noteworthy were students who indicated that understanding the pathways, in combination with the community-engaged learning experience, expanded their understanding of potential career options. The majority of assignments analyzed have been coded as students having an "overall positive" assessment of their LE experience, some specifically mentioning changes in their sense of connection and belonging to the community. Others mentioned having their stereotypes challenged in association with the experience.

Furthermore, we have implemented a system using Qualtrics for students at Juniata to use to log their community engagement hours according to the Pathways framework. Students can earn a transcript notation honor for exemplary community engagement if they log 120 or more hours aligning with at least one of the pathways. Between 2020 and 2023, a total of 24,192 community engagement hours were logged by the 19.5% of the student body that participated in the Qualtrics log. Students reported work with over 200 different community partner organizations. The top two pathways reported were Direct Service (62.6%) and Community-Engaged Learning and Research (34%), followed by Policy and Governance, Community Organizing and Activism, and Philanthropy, respectively. Twenty-five percent of entries reported a specific experience as aligning with more than one pathway. Of those entries, 76% paired Direct Service with another pathway, most commonly Community-Engaged Learning and Research.

While the diagnostic tool and framework have been crucial in creating and implementing this new curricular policy, as well as tracking and assessing student experiences, membership in the national Working Group described in this book's introduction has also been influential. This group of thoughtful, committed, and equity-minded people has been instrumental in pushing the pathways forward and supporting each other in an effort to contribute to the field and the implementation of community-engaged work across higher education. Personally, the relationships I have built with colleagues across the country, representing a diverse network of institutions, have been among the most meaningful experiences of my 20-year career in higher education. Membership in this group has inspired and stimulated fresh ideas and new strategies for introducing students to the pathways, inspired activities that reinforce the framework, and opened up possibilities for further research.

Accomplishments and Challenges

The implementation of the Pathways tool and the framework on campus through the general education curricular requirements has enabled us to systematically track and document the degree to which institutional learning outcomes are being achieved. This initiative has also elevated community engagement as a distinct and integral aspect of the academic experience at Juniata. As a result, we were successful in obtaining the Carnegie Classification in 2020, observed improvements in students reporting multiple experiences with high-impact practices in our National Survey of Student Engagement data, and received recognition for community-engaged learning as a curricular strength by our Middle States reviewers during the re-accreditation process. We have also achieved success in obtaining grants aimed at using the curricular requirement as a platform to create experiential learning opportunities for students aligned with grant objectives.

A significant challenge has been the need for consistent reinforcement and repeated communication across various channels to ensure that the understanding and language become rooted and widely understood by students, faculty, administration, and donors. We have encountered resistance from some faculty and students. Faculty resistance appears to be driven by a perception that efforts to implement standardized practices and track community-engaged learning are akin to "policing," rather than fostering institutional consistency and cohesion. Additionally, some students have expressed resistance, viewing the LE requirement as a barrier to taking other classes required for their major, without realizing that the requirement can complement most majors and that the learning is relevant across majors and disciplines. These challenges present opportunities for conversation and better messaging.

Recommendations for Implementation

For a college or university to succeed at implementing a curricular requirement for community-engaged learning, it is important to first assess campus climate and align decisions with mission and institutional learning objectives. In our case, the creation of a learning community comprising faculty, staff, students, and community partners was instrumental in developing the curricular requirement and helped surface the kinds of perceptual and logistical barriers we might face in the effort to implement the initiative. The learning community also played a crucial role in establishing a shared language and list of resources for people interested in advancing this work through their roles. We plan to reengage the learning community in the formal assessment process for the LE requirement as well. Of value in the ongoing design, implementation, and assessment processes are staff and administrators whose work intersects with, or is adjacent to, that of community engagement. Working collaboratively and taking a grassroots approach to understanding campus climate can help to identify allies across campus who will actively contribute to building capacity and generating the buy-in for the successful implementation of a curricular requirement. Through this process, we can identify gaps in knowledge, skills, and resources and develop strategies to build capacity or creatively leverage existing resources to address these gaps.

Conclusion

The decision to include community-engaged learning as a general education requirement, and to make it an academic curricular priority, represents a mission- and vision-driven decision based on evidence that supports its effectiveness in improving student learning outcomes, retention rates, and relationships between colleges and communities. The Pathways tool, framework, and Working Group have been pivotal in our successful implementation of the new curricular requirement. Together, they have enabled us to bring coherence and consistency to our institutional language and understanding of community engagement beyond direct service. This approach can integrate various pathways as high-impact learning experiences across disciplines and help to garner support and resources from administrators and donors. In our initial efforts to assess data related to the implementation of the LE requirement, we see early evidence that learning objectives are being achieved. Looking ahead, our challenge will be to sustain the momentum and growth we have experienced in recent years, ensuring that we can continue to strengthen and improve our institutional implementation of this high-impact practice.

References

Association of American Colleges and Universities. (2009). *Civic engagement VALUE rubric*. https://www.aacu.org/initiatives/value-initiative/value-rubrics/value-rubrics-inquiry-and-analysis

Brownell, J., & Swaner, L. (2010). *Five high-impact practices: Research on learning outcomes, completion, and quality*. American Association of Colleges and Universities. https://www.aacu.org/publication/five-high-impact-practices-research-on-learning-outcomes-completion-and-quality

Cress, C., Burack, C., Giles, D., Elkins, J., & Carnes Stevens, M. (2010). *A promising connection: Increasing college access and success through civic engagement*. Campus Compact. https://compact.org/resources/a-promising-connection-increasing-college-access-and-success-through-civic-engagement

Juniata College. (2025). *Mission statement*. https://www.juniata.edu/about/mission.php

Kuh, G. (2008). *High-impact educational practices: What are they, who has access to them, and why they matter*. American Association of Colleges and Universities. http://provost.tufts.edu/celt/files/High-Impact-Ed-Practices1.pdf

McTighe Musil, C. (2015). *Making civic learning routine across disciplines*. American Association of Colleges and Universities. https://www.aacu.org/publication/civic-prompts-making-civic-learning-routine-across-the-disciplines

National Task Force on Civic Learning and Democratic Engagement. (2012). *A crucible moment: College learning & democracy's future, a national call to action*. Association of American Colleges and Universities. https://www.aacu.org/publication/a-crucible-moment-college-learning-democracys-future

Novak, J., Markey, V., & Allen, M. (2007). Evaluating cognitive outcomes of service learning in higher education: A meta-analysis, *Communication Research Reports, 24*(2), 149–157. https://doi.org/10.1080/08824090701304881

Nussbaum, M. (2007). Cultivating humanity and world citizenship. *Forum Futures*, 37–40.

Saltmarsh, J., & Hartley, M. (Eds.). (2011). *"To serve a larger purpose": Engagement for democracy and the transformation of higher education*. Temple University Press. http://www.jstor.org/stable/j.ctt14bt6rz

Warren, J. (2012). Does service-learning increase student learning?: A meta-analysis. *Michigan Journal of Community Service Learning, 18*(2), 56–61.

Chapter 12

ENHANCING EXISTING FRAMEWORKS, THEORY, AND PROGRAM TRADITIONS

An Example of How Implementing the Pathways of Public Service and Civic Engagement Strengthened a 40-Year-Old Program at Georgetown University

Melissa Bernard and Ray Shiu

A t Georgetown University, we have utilized the Pathways to Public Service and Community Engagement framework to guide incoming students in their discernment of vocation, career, and social justice work. Use of the framework has both strengthened the designs of long-running programs and informed strategic planning for future growth. In this chapter, we share how we have integrated the Pathways framework in our work with students at Georgetown University's Center for Social Justice Research, Teaching & Service (CSJ). We explore the ways we have connected the framework to existing programs and community partnerships, and we reflect on the lessons learned. These insights will

117

guide our future efforts to infuse and implement the pathways in ways that enhance student learning opportunities and effectively respond to community needs.

In 2021, CSJ joined the Pathways Working Group on behalf of Georgetown University. After a year of learning from fellow practitioners about how pathways enhanced their programmatic offerings and courses, the CSJ team used the summer of 2022 to rethink and reframe a nearly 40-year-old program at Georgetown: the First-Year Orientation to Community Involvement (FOCI). FOCI is a preorientation program that introduces new undergraduate Hoyas, both first-year and transfer students, to community engagement and service work in Washington, DC. It aims to establish a student community committed to social justice. It has long served as a springboard for dozens of incoming students who commit to social justice engagement throughout their time at Georgetown.

One of the reasons we were drawn to pathways is because it aligns closely with the Jesuit Catholic values and mission that guide our university. At Georgetown, we educate our students in a tradition of academic excellence that enhances students' growth ethically and spiritually. This approach ensures that they carry with them a "Faith That Does Justice" throughout their undergraduate years at the university and beyond. In the Jesuit tradition, an "authentic following of the Gospel of Jesus [requires] an obligation to address the social realities of poverty, oppression, and injustice in our world" (Georgetown University, n.d., para. 9). This commitment applies to students' future lives as well as the current moment. CSJ takes this charge seriously, serving as a hub and a catalyst for undergraduates to engage in the creation of a more just world through research, academic courses, and service. The addition of the Pathways framework, both implicitly within program design and explicitly explained and explored with students, enhances their understanding of how to use their talents, strengths, and gifts to enact a faith that does justice throughout their undergraduate careers, as well as in vocational and personal endeavors throughout their lives.

Connecting FOCI and Pathways

For nearly 40 years, FOCI has introduced incoming students to Georgetown's traditions of service, social justice, and community engagement. The program employs an immersion and experiential learning pedagogical approach, providing students opportunities to connect with diverse communities, nonprofit leaders, and organizations throughout Washington, DC. The program has a long history of meeting its learning objectives. Participants arrive 1 week prior to new student orientation in a smaller, focused program experience. The program includes 40–50 student participants and a team of 12–14 peer student leaders. During a typical preorientation week, students participate in four to six site visits to organizations addressing various social justice issues with DC communities. Daily reflection sessions are incorporated to advance the learning cycle and meaning making (Kolb, 2015). Our program evaluations indicate an increase in students' social justice leadership skills, and participants maintain interest in continued community engagement throughout their undergraduate years (see Figure 12.1).

FOCI Program Outcomes √ = contributes independently to meeting the learning outcome √+ = enhances and improves existing frameworks in meeting the learning outcome	*Existing Frameworks and Theories*	*Pathways to Public Service and Community Engagement Framework*
Students will explore leadership development and avenues for social change.	√	√ +
Students will challenge their understanding and broaden their perspectives of the community.	√	√
Students will understand power relationships related to community engagement.	√	
Students will understand how to access resources, people, and information to learn about social justice issues.		√
Students will continue their engagement in social justice issues and immersion experiences after the program.		√
Students will build knowledge of self.	√	√+
Students will reflect on their personal responsibility and obligation for advancing social justice.	√	√+
Students will understand ways in which their actions can affect change.	√	√+
Students will learn, live, and love DC.	√	√+

Figure 12.1. FOCI program outcomes with frameworks and theories.

FOCI serves as a community service and engagement program for our incoming first-year and transfer students and a leadership development program for the upperclassmen student leader team. Leader team members begin meeting between 6 to 9 months in advance of the 1-week immersion experience, participating in weekly training sessions and workshops designed to enhance their leadership skills, self-awareness, and capacity to work for social change.

While FOCI's framework incorporates several learning models and pedagogies (see next section), our program aligns closely with our Jesuit and Catholic roots by utilizing a "Two Feet of Service"[1] framework, a concept promoted and embodied by the Catholic Church and related faith-based organizations (U.S. Conference of Catholic Bishops, n.d.). This framework suggests that to "walk the path of love," or strive toward a more just world, requires two "feet," or approaches, coupled together: social justice and charitable works. The framework explains that while it is imperative to work for social justice, to remove the systemic and structural root causes of inequity in the world, it is equally as important to address the immediate needs of people affected by inequity. In this metaphor, an individual focusing solely on one foot would not be balanced when moving forward. With the Two Feet framework, the same unbalance applies to social change.

While this Two Feet framework has strengths in effectively encouraging students to integrate action, critical reflection, and learning beyond acts of charity, in practice, it limits approaches to working for justice to only two simultaneous methods. The Pathways framework enables students to develop a more nuanced understanding of more diverse approaches to effecting social change. While the message of the Two Feet framework is valuable—stressing the importance of both direct and indirect service for comprehensive social change across different issues and communities—it leads to an expectation that students should be working with "both feet" regardless of their passion, skills, or experience. This expectation of the Two Feet framework led our students to feel stretched thin when attempting to maintain the balance of the Two Feet. The Pathways framework retains the foundational principles of the Two Feet framework while also encouraging exploration of the different pathways. For us at Georgetown, expanding beyond the Two Feet framework allowed us to honor our Catholic mission and values while updating our program planning and curriculum.

Program Model of Theories

Prior to integrating the Pathways framework into our program, FOCI was organized around theories, pedagogies, and best practices of Ignatian pedagogy, experiential learning, the social change model of leadership development, community-engaged learning, and racial justice. Ignatian pedagogy is informed by the spiritual exercises of St. Ignatius of Loyola, the founder of the Jesuit order, emphasizing an iterative, transformative learning process for students that encourages them to regularly reflect upon and revisit their learning in order to uncover more complex understandings of a subject. This iterative process follows the learning cycle of context, experience, reflection, action, and evaluation (International Commission on the Apostolate of Jesuit Education, 1993). In many ways, Ignatian pedagogy shares similarities with Kolb's (2015) theory of experiential learning, yet it incorporates additional steps in the learning process that reflect the values and aims of Jesuit Catholic higher education. In the case of FOCI, program directors and the leader team look at the *context* of who our program participants are and incorporate it into our programming. The FOCI program week, with site visits, speakers, workshops, and training sessions, offers the *experience*. In the evenings, participants meet in small groups to *reflect* on their day and contemplate how their experiences call them to *action*. Each day, as they deepen their experience and engage in ongoing reflection on potential actions, they continually *evaluate* their learning, sustaining a cycle of transformative learning.

The social change model of leadership development (SCM) encourages students to embrace leadership as a process that can generate social change (Higher Education Research Institute, 1996). The assumptions of the SCM include viewing leadership as a process rather than a position; advocating for leadership that is socially responsible and driven by the desire to effect change on behalf of others; and promoting collaborative, inclusive, accessible, and value-driven leadership. Additionally, the model assumes community involvement and service are powerful vehicles for leadership. The SCM describes the relationship among seven key values that operate within three domains: that of the individual, the group, and the community (or society). Individually, a learner must develop consciousness of self, congruence, and commitment. As a group, learners must find collaboration, common purpose, and controversy with civility. And finally, as a community, learners must embrace citizenship, which entails understanding both individual and collective responsibilities and connections to society. Each value and domain is interactive and reciprocal; the development in any domain enhances understanding and growth in other domains, creating a continuous cycle of influence. Ultimately, once all values have been realized, the learners are then more likely to be able to effect change. In FOCI, the leader team's training calendar was developed and mapped to cultivate the seven values identified in the social change model.

In FOCI, best practices of community-engaged learning ensure participants will deepen their ability to value and participate in reciprocal relationships with community partners rather than voyeuristically engage with organizations or perform service from a charity lens. FOCI teaches participants to see themselves as members of the DC community rather than visitors inside a laboratory. It encourages participants to listen to community-voiced needs over personal pursuits; acknowledges the potential burden on a community organization of hosting participants; and underscores participants' responsibility to understand and strive for true reciprocal relationships, even if achieving them is challenging. FOCI encourages participants to reflect on how they learn and to create room for knowledge from the community to be valued as academic knowledge. Applying a racial justice lens to the program enables our participants to gain deeper insights into the systems and structures that perpetuate social injustices. The lens requires the participants to acknowledge who is most affected by the injustice and why. FOCI participants explore their own identity, biases, and prejudices as prerequisites for contributing to the creation of a more just and antiracist world.

Within these theories, pedagogies, and practices, major themes emerge, including

- building contextual understanding for students;
- reciprocity and partnership in community engagement;
- reflection and discernment; and
- iterative learning.

When integrated with the Pathways framework, FOCI's existing pedagogies and practices are complemented and enhanced rather than replaced, thereby honoring their major contributions. Ultimately, by incorporating the Pathways framework, we were able to strengthen the program's outcomes for both first-year student participants and the student leadership team (see Figure 12.1).

Existing Partnerships

When adopting the Pathways framework, we considered how it would affect our existing community partnerships. Georgetown University has established strong and enduring partnerships rooted in solidarity with community change and committed to the coeducation of our students. Over the years, we have sought to deepen our relationships with community partners, improving alignment of our regular programming with our more episodic activities (short-term or one-time service activities) such as FOCI or other short immersion programming.

In FOCI, one area of program improvement was intentionality around how we select partnership sites. While FOCI takes pride in its 40-year history with the Georgetown and DC community, new needs and issues have arisen in the community over that time. The university and our center have expanded our partners and work in the community, resulting in more potential partners than can be engaged with or learned from in just 1 week. Often, the selection of partners reflected the familiarity our student leader team had with their work and the social justice issues that felt most pressing. While informal guidelines for site selection have yielded positive results, program directors have wanted to promote greater continuity in our partnerships and deepen relationships with vital community partners. The goal is for FOCI site visits and speakers to be long-standing partners who are invited annually.

Applying the Pathways framework to existing partnerships complicated these issues but also provided a new approach to challenges in site selection. On the one hand, does utilizing pathways mean that our program should select new community partners that align with each of the pathways? An effective exploration of a pathway could involve identifying a (new) community partner that could effectively illustrate that pathway. Would it not be more beneficial to select a partner organization that can hone in on the Policy and Governance Pathway rather than mixing in Direct Service activities at the same organization? Would selecting an organization that can better serve as a coeducator within specific pathways lead to stronger understanding of the framework? Upon reflection, we decided that starting with new partners was not the best route forward for our program design.

As practitioners and educators, we recognized the important role that the Pathways framework could play in aiding our program design: By coding our partner selection for different pathways we can increase the intentionality of our choices, thereby addressing the challenges of partnership selection. Furthermore, the Pathways framework serves as a lens for program design and the building of learning experiences for our students. It is not intended to dictate how nonprofit organizations and community members should work for social justice and change. As practitioners, we uphold the value of subsidiarity—the principle that those closest to an issue should have the most involvement in determining how to address an issue. Subsidiarity is a crucial learning goal for our programming and program design. Most community-based organizations and social change individuals utilize more than one pathway in their work. As community partners and educators, it became incumbent on us to utilize pathways as a lens to view this work rather than a proscription of how this work should be conducted within the community.

Lessons Learned in the FOCI Program Implementation

To incorporate the Pathways framework into the FOCI program, we made three changes in our program design. First, as discussed previously, we modified our partner selection by incorporating the pathways to improve the intentionality of our partner choices. Second, we included the Pathways tool in our student leader training. The Pathways framework became a foundational piece of their training and program planning. We used the Pathways tool to help student leaders explore their own experiences and passions, thereby improving their capacity to serve effectively as peer mentors guiding program participants in their pathways exploration. Third, by training our student leaders in the Pathways framework, it led to improvements in our program design. Student leaders were able to choose program themes based on the Pathways framework rather than specific social justice topics, such as homelessness or education. This curriculum shift enabled more intentional selection of presession readings for participants and empowered student leaders to develop prompts for reflection sessions that aligned with the Pathways framework.

One of the challenges we confronted in integrating the Pathways framework into the program was resistance from student leaders. Some of our student leaders were past program participants, and the change felt unnecessary to them. As we described previously, student agency in implementing the program is an essential feature, so it took additional efforts to create student buy-in. Another challenge was program participants' resistance to the Pathways tool. As often with any inventory, the results did not always align with some of our students' expectations or experiences. It was common for most incoming students to have more extensive experience with direct service during their high school years and less exposure to the other pathways. For students from Catholic high schools familiar with the Two Feet framework, transitioning to the Pathways framework added complexity to the way they thought about service and community engagement. That being said, it is precisely the exposure to, and exploration of, the different pathways that makes this application so compelling and effective. Our students utilized the Pathways tool as a way to reflect on their preconceptions about themselves.

Other challenges in implementation were connected to our program intentionality and logistics. When exploring the six different pathways, we were constrained by time and the availability of our partners. For example, exploring the Policy and Governance Pathway in the nation's capital was more challenging when the programming period coincided with recess for the U.S. Congress. Existing partnerships also created some challenges, as previously discussed. A rigid implementation of the Pathways framework might risk losing past and existing partnerships. It was important to remind ourselves that the Pathways framework is a lens to enhance program intentionality rather than a tool for prescribing to our partners how their work should proceed in the community. Our partners often operate across multiple pathways to advance their goals and impact.

Potential for Applications to Other Existing Programs and New Programs

Since integrating the Pathways framework into the FOCI preorientation program 3 years ago, we have extended its application to redesigning existing programs and developing new programming, particularly as new requests or opportunities present themselves. In our existing programs, we have taken the same approach to applying the framework as we have with FOCI. It was important not to throw out what works and lose the opportunity to honor and maintain existing programming and partnerships. Applying the framework in our existing programs allowed for an internal reorganization of programming, similar to FOCI, to improve intentionality in our training and partnership selection. We have also created new opportunities for additional pathways exploration within the issue areas in our existing programs, addressing how the Two Feet framework has led to burnout or confusion for some students in the past. In several of CSJ's existing programs, roles and positions centered around specific pathways were created to offer new opportunities for engagement. For example, within CSJ's EngageDC programs—directed by both professional staff and student teams who oversee regular, weekly service commitments (Georgetown University Center for Social Justice Research, Teaching & Service, n.d.)—we introduced advocacy positions alongside our traditional direct service roles.

The Pathways framework has also informed how CSJ approaches new programming opportunities or requests and how it applies its resources. We have examined where there are areas of opportunity in our program offerings for students to explore each of the pathways. While CSJ does not seek to be the exclusive space for students to explore the pathways, we actively encourage them to connect with and participate in other opportunities across the university that also explore different pathways. Additionally, underrepresented pathways at CSJ have received additional resources to expand these opportunities.

For practitioners and educators, the Pathways framework offers significant opportunities. It can build program intentionality, provide multiple entry points for students, and facilitate the development of new partnership models for current or new community partners that align with our student learning goals. At the same time, practitioners and educators must uphold the principles and values that have guided our work. At Georgetown, the Pathways framework has offered flexibility to maintain our student learning models, animate our university's Catholic and Jesuit mission and values, and prioritize community in our partnership development.

Note

1. You can find the "Two Feet of Service" or "Two Feet of Love in Action" widely adapted by different Catholic social justice and social action committees, including on the U.S. Conference of Catholic Bishops (USCCB) website (https://www.usccb.org/beliefs-and-teachings/what-we-believe/catholic-social-teaching/two-feet-of-love-in-action). While USCCB has documentation sharing this framework in 2013, one author of this chapter was trained on this framework as early as 2004.

References

Georgetown University. (n.d.). *Mission and ministry*. https://missionandministry
    .georgetown.edu/mission/spirit-of-georgetown/
Georgetown University Center for Social Justice Research, Teaching & Service.
    (n.d.). *CSJ programs*. https://csj.georgetown.edu/csjprograms/

Higher Education Research Institute. (1996). *A social change model of leadership development guidebook* (3rd ed.). Regents of the University of California.

International Commission on the Apostolate of Jesuit Education. (1993). *Ignatian pedagogy: A practical approach*. Jesuits Global. https://www.sjweb.info/documents/education/pedagogy_en.pdf

Kolb, D. A. (2015). *Experiential learning: Experience as the source of learning and development*. Pearson Education.

U. S. Conference of Catholic Bishops. (n.d.). *Two feet of love in action* https://www.usccb.org/beliefs-and-teachings/what-we-believe/catholic-social-teaching/two-feet-of-love-in-action

Chapter 13

EXPANDING THE DEFINITION OF COMMUNITY ENGAGEMENT THROUGH THE PATHWAYS AT DRAKE UNIVERSITY

Amanda Martin

The Pathways framework has become the primary framework for how we define and talk about community engagement at Drake University. Drake first started engaging with the Pathways framework in 2019, when the director of community-engaged learning and the director of career services attended the Pathways Working Group retreat at Stanford University. We piloted the survey and framework with a small group of people that spring and took time that year to develop our own resources and web page. We officially introduced pathways to the larger Drake community in fall 2020.

The Pathways framework has provided a common language to talk about different strategies for creating change. This helps students and faculty broaden their preconceived definitions of community engagement beyond traditional concepts focused on formal volunteering and direct service.

Having a shared language helps all involved feel more connected to the work and on the same page when dialoguing about engagement.

Additionally, we encourage critical engagement with students surrounding the pathways—the good, the bad, and the ugly. History offers numerous examples when community engagement has been mishandled, "done poorly," or has perpetuated power and privilege. Through discussions of the pathways, students and faculty reflect upon and appreciate the value of different types of engagement they may not have previously considered or recognized as valuable. For instance, in some communities, mutual aid is a common way to make a difference, but it hasn't always been "recognized" when it comes to what "counts" for service hours because it doesn't involve a 501c3 organization. While the formal definition of *philanthropy* may feel out of reach for some students, knowing there are other ways to participate in philanthropy aside from donating money, such as through mutual aid, can open the door for them. The pathways demonstrate that one's engagement doesn't have to be through "formal" methods (e.g., through a registered nonprofit organization) and that diverse forms of participation allow people to see themselves represented in this work. It is a tool for students to think about their own interests and skills as well as explore how they want to get involved in changemaking as a college student and beyond. The pathways expand both what might be considered meaningful social change work as well as who is represented in each pathway.

Institution Context

Drake is a predominantly White, midsize, private university in Des Moines, Iowa. The student population is about 4,600, with approximately 3,000 undergraduates and 1,600 graduate students. Drake offers nearly 150 undergraduate majors, minors, and concentrations and 20 graduate degrees and online programs. It is home to many centers and institutes that aim to make the world a better place, including the Harkin Institute for Public Policy & Citizen Engagement, the Ron and Jane Olson Institute for Public Democracy, the Constitutional Law Center, the Principal Center for Global Citizenship, and more. Additionally, Drake has received the Carnegie Elective Classification for Community Engagement.

Drake's mission statement is "to provide an exceptional learning environment that prepares students for meaningful personal lives, professional accomplishments, and responsible global citizenship" (Drake University,

2025a, para. 1). Drake's inspiration statement is "together we transform lives and strengthen communities" (para. 2). Using the Pathways framework, students can actively participate in activities that embody these mission and inspiration statements.

Description of Pathways Usage

Staff in the Office of Community-Engaged Learning (CEL) are the primary experts in the Pathways framework at Drake. Our team consists of two professional staff—a director and assistant director—and around eight student employees. The office is housed in the Academic Excellence and Student Success Unit under the provost's office. The mission of the CEL Office is to "develop and encourage changemakers who know themselves, understand the complexities of the world they live in, and take creative action to solve problems." (Drake University, 2025b, para. 3). Pathways gives the CEL team a framework and starting point for working with students to live out this mission.

Much of the programming in the CEL Office revolves around the pathways. In the next section, I will detail how we integrate this framework in programming, courses, peer consultations, cross-campus collaborations, and partnerships with Career Services.

Programming

The CEL team visits classes and student organization meetings to deliver workshops on the broader Pathways framework and tool. The workshops typically involve an interactive case study activity, overview of the pathways, time to take the survey, and an opportunity for reflection on results. Over the past few years, pathways workshops have been offered during Welcome Weekend and to interested student organizations and classes. We intentionally reach out to organizations or classes that may have a tie to community engagement, and we also conduct mass outreach through the CEL newsletter, Drake's weekly newsletter, flyers, and word of mouth.

In the CEL Office, we structure our programming around the Pathways framework. For instance, I facilitated a 3-day January-term experience for nine students in collaboration with a local nonprofit. The staff of the nonprofit talked with students about how they utilize the six pathways in their organization—covering such areas as development, volunteer services, policy advocacy, and social entrepreneurship. This experience provided students with a fuller picture of how a local organization can leverage all these strategies to fulfill their mission.

Courses

We use the pathways as the basis for a class for a small cohort of first-year students in the Changemaker Scholars Program. This program is a 4-year experience devoted to topics of civic engagement, leadership, and entrepreneurship and incorporates academic and community-engaged learning experiences. We devote the first half of the semester to self-exploration, including values and identity exercises and discussion about why it is important to reflect on these before working in the community. The students then take the Pathways survey and receive an overview of the framework. For the rest of the semester, we devote each class period to one pathway, using a flipped classroom model whereby students read articles and watch videos to deepen their understanding of the pathway. During class sessions, we engage in field trips or host guest speakers who share real-world insights and experiences in "the field" related to that pathway. Examples include the following:

- touring the Occupational Therapy (OT) Building at Drake and visiting with OT faculty about ways they incorporate community-engaged learning and research and best practices for working with community
- touring the Harkin Institute for Public Policy & Citizen Engagement and speaking with staff members about the work they do to inform policy work and ways students can get involved in that work
- a site visit to a local nonprofit to discuss ways to engage in direct service most meaningfully in the community and how to serve with dignity

Following each of these dedicated class periods, students participate in an online discussion board where they discuss what they learned, the benefits and limitations of that pathway, their personal involvement (or lack thereof) in the pathway, and examples of other organizations that specialize in the pathway. This model has exposed students to numerous people and places in their community, helping many to clarify the paths that interest them most.

Peer Consultants

We have adopted a peer consultation program for the Pathways framework and tool. Our student staff members, known as "community engagement peers," receive training on the Pathways framework and tool prior to the start of the academic year and are equipped to lead one-on-one consulting meetings with students. Ideally, students interested in being a part of creating change and getting involved in the community complete the Pathways survey and schedule a meeting with one of the peers based on mutual interests and experience. In the meeting, they reflect on the student's survey results and ask probing questions to help connect the student to opportunities and individuals matching their interests. The peers follow up with students periodically to see if they found an opportunity or if they have any other questions.

The peer model is beneficial for several reasons. In the book *Students Helping Students,* the authors note that peers may produce positive results because they have more experience and awareness of what a student is going through and are not so far removed from the situation (Newton & Ender, 2010). Community engagement peers are typically sophomores and above, bringing valuable experiences and connections to assist their peers. They possess a deep understanding of the challenges students encounter in community engagement and can offer insights on how to navigate these challenges.

Drake alum Kirby Nelson, who served as a community engagement peer for 2 years, emphasized this point in her reflection on the experience: "I think, peer-to-peer, it is easy to understand where students are often coming from (wanting to get involved, but don't have enough time/not the right resources/not sure where to start/etc.) and empathize with those challenges." Kirby also found the one-on-one meetings to be among the most beneficial aspects of how we use the pathways at Drake: "As students shared their experience with service and their interests (kids, food insecurity, sustainability, etc.), it was simple to walk them through their Pathways results and form connections" (Kirby Nelson, personal communication, May 31, 2023).

In addition to peers being highly relatable, this model also helps the staff build capacity in the CEL Office. Oftentimes groups meet on the weekends or in the evenings, and having student peers trained to give presentations during off-business hours is helpful for the capacity of the staff.

Cross-Campus Collaboration

At Drake, we expect interested students and faculty to turn to the CEL Office for comprehensive information on the Pathways framework and various paths. A dedicated page on our website is devoted to the pathways, listing examples of activities that can be done on campus or in the local community for each path. The page also features videos of student leaders discussing their experience in specific pathways and offers ideas for addressing social issues using the six pathways. For instance, it provides suggestions on how to tackle food insecurity through the lens of each pathway.

That being said, the CEL Office doesn't feel the need to exclusively "own" the pathways; it must be a collaborative effort. As a relatively small staff, we look to other areas of campus to provide expertise and opportunities in specific paths. The CEL Office tends to take the lead on the paths of Direct Service and Community-Engaged Learning and Research, working in collaboration with others. The following sections provide examples of how we rely on other areas of campus to offer expertise and opportunities in various pathways.

Policy and Governance

Drake is widely recognized as a hub for politics, largely due to its location in the capital city of Iowa, the historic home of the first-in-the-nation caucuses. Presidential hopefuls visit our campus every few years, nationally televised town halls are held here, and the Iowa Caucus Project, Vote Smart, and the Harkin Institute for Public Policy & Citizen Engagement are all hosted at or near the university. Several academic majors at Drake are connected to politics and policy, offering a wide array of opportunities related to the Policy and Governance Pathway. While our office may not always be the experts in this area, we typically refer students to these relevant opportunities. The office does, however, employ a student who focuses specifically on voter and civic engagement.

Social Entrepreneurship and Corporate Social Responsibility

The motto of Drake University's Zimpleman College of Business (2025) is "Make Business Make a Difference" (para 1). The college's purpose statement is "to empower Drake business students to serve as a force for good, contributing to the global economy and to society" (para. 2). The college has adopted a vision of Social Entrepreneurship and Corporate Social

Responsibility. Given the experts and opportunities available, we refer students interested in this pathway to the Zimpleman College of Business. Additionally, the executive director of innovation, entrepreneurship, and human-centered design in the college comanages the Changemaker Scholars Program in partnership with the CEL Office.

Philanthropy

Philanthropic activities can be found through the work of Drake's fraternities and sororities, Student Alumni Association, and business classes. Additionally, efforts like the Little Free Food Pantries and the student-led "Help Your Shelf" provide opportunities for mutual aid, where food, hygiene, or school items are donated and accessible to all.

Community Organizing and Activism

Community Organizing and Activism opportunities and knowledge can be accessed through Drake's Office of Equity and Inclusion, the Law School, or student-led grassroots organizing efforts. Activities may take the form of rallies, petitions, or tabling events to raise awareness, among other possibilities.

Partnership With Career Services

CEL regularly partners with the university's Career Services Office. Career Services staff understand the value of the pathways when advising students about career options and ways to boost one's résumé. The offices have collaborated on a Careers in Social Change virtual panel series, inviting professionals to discuss how they leverage their careers to create meaningful change. We have themed these panels around the pathways and emphasize creating change in any career/field, including business and for-profit sectors, which have sometimes been stereotyped as incompatible with "doing good while making money."

Drake's director of career services has shared the following about their advising strategies with students:

> We in Career Services meet with students who are passionate about the need for volunteerism surrounding social change, but often, they forget there are amazing career opportunities that spur social change. The Pathways survey has been a helpful tool for students looking to identify potential paths to be civically engaged in

their communities and create social change while gaining skills for their future careers. (Chrystal Stanley, personal communication, November 10, 2023)

Challenges/Accomplishments

When implementing the Pathways framework at Drake, we celebrated a number of accomplishments, as well as continue to face a few challenges.

Accomplishments

The Pathways framework has broadened our understanding, as well as that of others, about what "constitutes" community engagement, demonstrating that creating change requires a variety of strategies. The pathways illustrate not only the various options available for people to make a difference, but also that many paths taken simultaneously by different people can have the greatest impact on the issue. For instance, while some people focus on collecting data and conducting research to uncover root causes of an issue, others engage in direct service to provide immediate relief to those in need.

Kirby reiterated this by saying,

> To me, the primary benefits of Pathways is being able to understand the different facets of service. Service isn't one-size-fits-all—it can be mended to fit people's interests, strengths, and passion areas. That was something that I was unable to understand prior to learning about Pathways. It helps group activities of service in a way that is easy to understand and easier to apply. (Kirby Nelson, personal communication, May 31, 2023)

The Pathways survey has been taken nearly 550 times by Drake students over the 3 years since its implementation. Most of those students who completed the survey also participated in an educational component, such as a workshop, that accompanies the survey completion. While some institutions use the aggregate data from the survey results to shape their programming, we do not. Instead, we use the survey tool as a personal resource and reflection tool for students. Kirby shared the importance of the survey results to her:

Since it was my first time even learning what the pathways are, these results were really crucial to my entire understanding of what service even is. Prior to that survey, I thought that service was only direct service. So, these results were extremely beneficial to me as I was first learning what service even was. I think a lot of other students go through a similar experience, especially when there is more opportunity to try out different service experiences. (Kirby Nelson, personal communication, May 31, 2023)

Challenges

It continues to be a challenge to raise awareness of the pathways within the broader Drake community. While we believe individual reflection and meetings on the pathways can be highly impactful, relatively few students have taken advantage of the one-on-one consultations—typically averaging five to 10 students per year over the past 3 years. It is unclear whether this stems from intimidation or from a lack of awareness, understanding, or caring. We have tried to incorporate the consultation meetings as a requirement for some programs, such as with Impact Explorers, aimed at first-year students. We continue to actively explore how best to market and run these meetings to encourage broader participation. Additionally, we continually seek ways to raise awareness of the pathways with faculty and explore how they might incorporate them into their classes.

Recommendations for Implementation

In the future, we would like to do more comprehensive assessment around the pathways at Drake. Particularly, we would like to understand how students' engagement with the Pathways framework impacts them. Are they more connected to opportunities, and what specific impacts have these connections had? Has it helped students view themselves as an agent of change in new ways? Has it helped them clarify their career interests?

We would also like to secure buy-in from other parts of campus on ways to utilize and promote the pathways. For example, Drake is in the process of implementing a blended advising model, which supports students' academic paths by offering access to both professional advisors and faculty mentors. It would be beneficial to train advisors on the pathways and help them become aware of the resources available. Ideally, we'd like to incorporate the pathways into even more classes, allowing more students the opportunity for deeper engagement with them. When paired with a course and faculty advising, the potential for impact on students is substantial. Our next step involves identifying courses we think are aligned with the pathways and collaborating with faculty to offer class presentations.

Additionally, we'd like to assist our community partners in envisioning how they can collaborate with the university through the Pathways framework. One way to enhance their understanding of pathways and highlight opportunities is to create marketing materials showcasing examples of each pathway. This initiative could expand their awareness of potential collaboration possibilities.

Conclusion

The Pathways framework has broadened our definition of community engagement at Drake and given us structure for discussing it with the campus community. It empowers individuals to find "their fit." It underscores the importance of diverse pathways in creating positive social change, while also emphasizing that individuals do not need to do *everything* in order to create that change. They can do what interests them and what is within their skillset, while others may choose to pursue work in other pathways. Kirby summarizes this idea by saying, "I can't remember the last time I was genuinely this passionate about something. Pathways has opened so many new doors to finding the things I love at Drake University" (Kirby Nelson, personal communication, May 31, 2023).

The Pathways framework and tool are not static. A benefit of being a part of the international Pathways Working Group is that it allows us to engage in ongoing dialogue and assessment, continuously evolving the framework and tool. This dynamic approach is vitally important in community engagement work, and the Pathways Working Group serves as a strong example of this adaptability.

References

Drake University. (2025a). *Mission & values.* https://www.drake.edu/about/mission/

Drake University. (2025b). *Learning & service.* https://www.drake.edu/community/learningservice/

Drake University Zimpleman College of Business. (2025). https://www.drake.edu/zimpleman/

Newton, F. B., & Ender, S. C. (2010). *Students helping students: A guide for peer educators on college campuses.* Jossey-Bass.

Chapter 14

PUBLIC SERVICE, PERSONAL GROWTH

Cultivating Civic Mindsets in a
Living-Learning Community

Kemi A. Oyewole and Luke Terra

The founders of Stanford University envisioned an education that would prepare students for lives of active and engaged citizenship. Writing to the trustees in 1902, Jane Stanford reminded them, "While the instruction offered must be such as will qualify the students for personal success and direct usefulness in life, they should understand that it is offered in the hope and trust that they will become thereby of greater service to the public" (Stanford University, n.d., para. 5). We see this commitment reaffirmed in Stanford's 2019 Long-Range Vision, which includes "Preparing Citizens and Leaders" as one of four institutional priorities. The Haas Center for Public Service has served as a hub of public service and civic engagement efforts at Stanford since its founding in 1985. Since 2009, it has also sponsored a living-learning community for students interested in exploring public service in a residential setting. The Public Service and Civic Engagement Theme House ("Public Service House") was designed to "foster healthy civic identities that enable students to become ethical and effective agents of positive social change at Stanford

University and beyond" (Schnaubelt et al., 2021, p. 1). The theme program draws from four frameworks—including the Pathways of Public Service and Civic Engagement—to broaden students' understanding of different approaches to public service. In this chapter, we outline the ways we use public service frameworks and a differentiated track structure to engage a diverse cross-section of students in a four-class, residential environment.

Living-Learning Communities

A living-learning community (LLC) is characterized by students sharing academic and residential experiences around a theme (Inkelas et al., 2007). These communities first emerged in the 1920s as a tool for using an interdisciplinary approach to foster civic mindsets (Smith, 2001). By the 1960s, the explosion in university student populations transformed LLCs into a tool for maintaining interpersonal connections. Though LLCs vary in their level of coordination, they are associated with an enhanced sense of belonging, conception of leadership ability, appreciation of diversity, and willingness to dialogue on sociocultural issues (Inkelas et al., 2006; Spanierman et al., 2013). Especially promising is the positive connection between LLCs and outcomes for first-generation students (Inkelas et al., 2007).

Drawing from an analysis of over 600 LLCs, Inkelas et al. (2018) developed a best-practices model for LLCs that emphasizes four key components: infrastructure, academic environment, cocurricular environment, and intentional integration. The infrastructure of effective LLCs includes clear goals and objectives, the intentional selection of student and professional staff, strong connections to academic affairs and residential life, and adequate resources. The academic environment encompasses credit-bearing courses, advising, and an academically and socially supportive climate. Meanwhile, the cocurricular environment includes theme-related activities designed to build community and connections (Felton et al., 2023). Intentional integration focuses attention on how these components interact in mutually supportive ways to create a coherent and robust residential and academic experience. The Public Service House was designed with each of these elements in mind.

Developmental Frameworks

Effective LLCs articulate clear learning goals and provide a robust academic and cocurricular program to support students in achieving them.

Core Commitments and Building Blocks of a Healthy Civic Identity	Principles of Ethical and Effective Service
Core Commitments • Commitment to the values, practices, and institutions of liberal democracy • Focused commitment(s) to an issue(s) • Commitment to integrity • Communitarian mindset Building Blocks • Capacity to engage constructively across difference • Democratic knowledge, habits, and skills • Knowledge of social change frameworks and tools • Deep content knowledge • Resilient mind, body, and spirit	• Humility • Respect and Inclusion • Reciprocity • Preparation • Safety and Well-being • Accountability • Evaluation • Learning and Reflection
	Pathways of Public Service and Civic Engagement
Cultural Humility Practices • Practice critical self-reflection • Recognize the dynamics of power and privilege • Build inclusive and accountable structures	• Community-Engaged Learning and Research • Community Organizing and Activism • Direct Service • Philanthropy • Policy and Governance • Social Entrepreneurship and Corporate Social Responsibility

Figure 14.1. Public service frameworks in a living-learning community.

The learning goals of the Public Service House draw from four frameworks developed or adapted by the Haas Center for Public Service (Figure 14.1).

The Core Commitments and Building Blocks of a Healthy Civic Identity are based on a working paper written by Thomas Schnaubelt (2022) during his tenure as executive director of the Haas Center. Recognizing the difficulty of defining a civic identity, Schnaubelt developed a set of core commitments and building blocks to guide Haas Center staff. We integrate many of these in our programming in the Public Service House, especially in building students' capacity to engage constructively across difference, focusing their commitment to an issue, and developing their knowledge of social change frameworks and tools.

The Cultural Humility Practices, adapted from the pioneering work of Melanie Tervalon and Jann Murray-Garcia (1998), originated as a critique of cultural competence training in medical education. We have found that their emphasis on critical self-reflection, understanding positionality and power, and fostering equitable structures is equally relevant in preparing students for various public service experiences. In the Public Service House, this cultural humility approach informs how we prepare students to be cognizant of their identities and power as they engage in public service.

Stanford's Principles of Ethical and Effective Service were first developed in 2002 through a series of conversations with students, staff, faculty, and community partners. They have been revised several times over the years, most recently in 2019. As we tell our students, these principles are not an exhaustive list but are intended to inspire questions and reflection. In the Public Service House, these principles anchor our opening retreat and serve as a touchstone throughout the year as students engage in service activities.

The Haas Center's pathways have had the most direct impact on the overall structure of the LLC program. The Pathways framework was initially designed as an advising tool to help students broaden their understanding of the multiple ways to approach public service, and specifically to expand their perspective beyond direct service and government service. One of our primary goals in the Public Service House is to help students connect their academic and public service interests. Many students arrive at Stanford with a clear commitment to a particular issue, such as housing, environmental justice, or educational equity, among others. It is part of our program's mission to introduce students to the many tools available for addressing these societal challenges. The Pathways framework provides the curricular structure for the house's academic program, allowing us to spotlight cross-cutting approaches to social change.

Public Service Theme House History

Stanford introduced a public service theme in 2009, partly in response to a lack of residential programming for sophomores. With a focus on sophomores, the theme program was anchored around a yearlong service commitment that students made during their year in residence, along with a set of programs designed to introduce students to public service frameworks and provide opportunities for deeper engagement and reflection. In 2021, Stanford reorganized its undergraduate housing, standardizing all theme houses to accommodate students at any stage of their undergraduate career, resulting in four-class residences. The Public Service House would be weighted heavily toward first-year students, with 44 of 79 residents being in their first year. Incoming first-year students would rank academic theme houses among their housing options, while sophomores, juniors, and seniors would apply directly through a housing preassignment process. From 2021–2024, the student population of the Public Service House has been broadly representative of the demographic makeup of the undergraduate student body, with a slightly higher percentage of female-identifying students, students of color, and first-generation and low-income students than the university's overall student population.

The 2021 reorganization of undergraduate housing also brought about a change to the location of the Public Service House, along with new leadership—namely, the authors of this chapter. In our first year as a four-class house (2021–2022), we kept the program structure largely unchanged from its previous iteration. Residents were required to complete a yearlong service commitment with an organization of their choice. They also participated in an opening kickoff event to introduce them to the Principles and Pathways frameworks, participated in two mandatory community conversations each quarter, explored each pathway through attendance at events in 5-week segments, took part in a 1-day service experience in San Francisco, and came together for an end-of-year reflection event.

However, we quickly learned that this program structure—ideal for a community of sophomores—presented several challenges in engaging students at different stages of their collegiate experience. First, many students were concerned about the amount of time the public service theme required. The 2-day kickoff, six community conversations, six pathways explorations, public service commitment, off-site field trip, and closing reflection were daunting, especially for first-year students adjusting to campus life. Furthermore, it felt inaccessible to create a program with so many requirements while students juggled other demands, including athletics, employment, and family. Secondly, most first-year students felt unprepared to make a yearlong commitment without first having some exposure to local service organizations. As staff, we also felt uncomfortable ushering students toward service commitments they were not equipped to fulfill. Lastly, our sophomore, junior, and senior students voiced a different set of needs. They sought to go beyond understanding the service landscape to sharpening their leadership skills.

New Model for a New House

Responding to this feedback, we made two key changes to the program for the 2022–2023 academic year: introducing a differentiated track structure and launching a credit-bearing course entitled Pathways of Public Service (i.e., Pathways course).

Differentiated Track Structure

We developed program tracks to tailor the theme-based program to meet students' needs in a four-class environment. Residents could choose one of four options depending on their interests and commitment:

- *Explore*: Students seeking a flexible introduction to public service committed to attending two theme events per quarter. Theme events included Pathways class sessions, service events, guest speakers, community partner visits, and other service-oriented programs.
- *Engage*: Students new to public service and/or Stanford could deepen their engagement with service by participating in two direct service events per year and enrolling in at least one quarter of the Pathways course.
- *Sustain*: Students who were ready for ongoing service made a year-long commitment to an issue or organization and enrolled in the Pathways course for two quarters. They were not required to identify their commitment in advance; instead, we supported them in identifying one at the start of the year.
- *Lead*: Students in this track committed to a leadership role on or off campus and enrolled in the Pathways course for two quarters. These students led through student service organizations, student staff positions at the Haas Center, community service work-study with local community organizations, and service activities within the house community.

In the new model, the only mandatory house events were a shortened kickoff and year-end reflection event. Beyond that, the minimum requirement of just two theme events per quarter was designed to ensure that any student—regardless of other commitments—could participate in the theme program.

Pathways of Public Service Course

First-year residents who found it challenging to prioritize house programs suggested we use course credit to honor the time students devoted to the

LLC. Following the example of other Stanford theme houses, we designed a one-unit survey course. In line with our principles of inclusivity and accountability, we convened student focus groups to define our course objectives:

- *Broadening conceptions of public service and civic engagement (PSCE)*: Students will consider ways PSCE can be part of their lives regardless of their vocation.
- *Serving as a Stanford student in the Bay Area*: Students will grapple with ways their affiliation with Stanford shapes their service in the region and intersects with other identities they hold.
- *Holding respectful dialogue in a community of service*: Similarly well-intentioned public servants have a range of life experiences and values that lead them to different positions on complicated topics. Students will expand their ability to engage in respectful dialogue across a range of perspectives.

The Pathways course met weekly for 10 weeks, with each session featuring a pathway or discussion of ethical tensions and dilemmas that arise in service work (Appendix C in the Online Companion includes class topics and objectives). Class sessions were a mix of guest speakers, panels, and direct instruction followed by small-group conversations. The course also allowed us to host intimate dialogues with public service leaders already on campus. We used readings to provide necessary context and exit tickets to assess students' ability to apply course content to their own contexts. A typical exit ticket would ask for a short, written response that prompted reflection on the class discussion or presentation. We discovered that with a brief 50-word response, we could get a pulse from the class on their learnings and lingering questions from the session.

Responding to feedback from our sophomore through senior residents, we offered a two-unit option for students interested in joining a leadership cohort that met biweekly to focus on specific leadership skills. Drawing on the work of Marshall Ganz, we define public service leadership as "accepting responsibility to enable others to achieve shared purpose under conditions of uncertainty" (Ganz & Lin, 2011, para. 2). This perspective underscores that leadership in public service is *relational rather than positional*. It focuses student attention on the importance of cultivating the relationships and shared commitment with others that are necessary to effectively organize and sustain public service efforts. Students in the cohort were trained to provide coaching to their peers on leadership challenges, work in teams to organize events for the campus, and conduct interviews with leaders in fields of interest.

We encouraged students to take the Pathways course in the fall quarter to establish relationships and further shared understandings of the Pathways framework. In our first quarter teaching the course, 46 students enrolled in the course, with 21 also enrolling in the leadership cohort (out of 79 residents). In alignment with our commitment to community engagement and accessibility, we opened our class to the broader community and welcomed students living outside the house to register.

Student Response

Implementing these changes significantly improved students' experience and engagement in the theme program. At the end of winter 2023, 63 residents completed a survey that found

- 95% had a broader understanding of the Pathways of Public Service and Civic Engagement,
- 90% felt deeper awareness of the ways their service is shaped by their positionality and Stanford affiliation, and
- 87% were better equipped to have respectful dialogue with others holding different perspectives.[1]

We inductively coded the 30 open responses that suggested improvements to the program and found that students desired more

- exposure to guests with diverse backgrounds: individuals working in STEM, business, lobbying, and local government as well as speakers with LGBTQ+, first-generation, and low-income identities ($n = 12$);
- opportunities for direct service, especially off campus ($n = 11$);
- events during different times of the day and week to support students with recurring conflicts with the Pathways course ($n = 9$);
- opportunities for student leadership ($n = 6$); and
- partnering with campus organizations to better publicize events ($n = 6$).

We saw this feedback as an opportunity to expand student leadership. We mobilized residents on our lead track to organize additional student-led events for the house in spring 2023. Beyond this change, student feedback will continue to guide us in further strengthening our program in the years ahead.

Recommendations

Our central learnings from reenvisioning the Public Service House were the need to provide a differentiated program to meet a range of student needs and the advantage of consolidating the academic program into a credit-bearing course that leveraged the Pathways framework effectively. The benefit of a tailored experience and credit-bearing coursework is consistent with scholarship on effective LLCs. This approach also prioritizes accessibility, ensuring that all students can be a part of the theme program. Public service should not be a domain of the privileged, exclusive to those who can easily volunteer their time, free from competing work, family, and other commitments. A principled approach to public service leadership provides multiple entry points to the Pathways framework, offering diverse perspectives on issues and approaches to social change. This ensures that all students can access and integrate public service and civic engagement into their college experience.

We encouraged students to explore pathways beyond those that are most common on university campuses, such as direct service and activism. Additionally, early in the academic year, we held a Pathways class session to highlight some of the ethical tensions of participating in one-time service events. Still, residents expressed a strong desire to transition from intellectualizing service to more "hands-on" involvement, preferably without making long-term commitments. This reality prompts us to consider ways to offer meaningful service experiences that do not exploit or extract from community partners while also engaging students with less familiar pathways like social entrepreneurship.

Finally, our best-received content suggests that students crave opportunities to grapple with critical perspectives and ethical practices in the digital age. Though our location in the Silicon Valley amplifies this need, the implications of technological advances, the contraction of stable middle-class employment, and growing income inequality can be seen across the globe. Similarly, students welcomed opportunities to deepen their understanding of surrounding communities, especially about minoritized people displaced by our regional economy. The pervasiveness of the town–gown divide suggests the need for other institutions of higher education to center their local context in Pathway initiatives.

Conclusion

Our first 2 years leading the Public Service House have been an adventure in iterating the program to prepare students to serve. Though we have found success in our current model, many questions remain. How do we balance building developmental trajectories in the residence with directing students to external resources? How do we celebrate students deepening their expertise in one pathway while also expanding their proficiency across all pathways? Where are the opportunities to leverage a residential space to interrupt a culture that prioritizes personal achievement by fostering dedication to public service? We look forward to contending with these quandaries as we navigate meeting the ever-changing needs of our thriving community.

Note

1. Indicated by responding "agree" or "strongly agree" on a 5-point Likert scale.

References

Felton, P., Lambert, L. M., Artze-Vega, I., & Miranda Tapia, O. R. (2023). *Connections are everything: A college student's guide to relationship-rich education*. Johns Hopkins University Press.

Ganz, M., & Lin, E. S. (2011). Learning to lead: A pedagogy of practice. In S. Snook, N. Nohria, & R. Khurana (Eds.), *Handbook for teaching leadership: Knowing, doing, and being* (pp. 353–366). SAGE.

Inkelas, K. K., Daver, Z. E., Vogt, K. E., & Leonard, J. B. (2007). Living–learning programs and first-generation college students' academic and social transition to college. *Research in Higher Education*, 48(4), 403–434. https://doi.org/10.1007/s11162-006-9031-6

Inkelas, K. K., Jessup-Anger, J. E., Benjamin, M., & Wawrzynski, M. R. (2018). *Living-learning communities that work: A research-based model for design, delivery, and assessment*. Stylus.

Inkelas, K. K., Vogt, K. E., Longerbeam, D., Owen, J., & Johnson, D. (2006). Measuring outcomes of living-learning programs: Examining college environments and student learning and development. *The Journal of General Education*, 55(1), 40–76.

Schnaubelt, T. (2022). *The building blocks and core commitments of a healthy civic identity* [Working paper]. Stanford University Haas Center for Public Service.

https://docs.google.com/document/d/1NCHS-IIurSjAlV8zOZxAbwr7Aop
8vNMC/

Schnaubelt, T., Schnaubelt, M. E., & Stipek, D. (2021). *Public service and civic engagement theme house application* [Unpublished internal document]. Stanford University.

Smith, B. L. (2001). The challenge of learning communities as a growing national movement. *Peer Review, 3*(4), 2–4.

Spanierman, L. B., Soble, J. R., Mayfield, J. B., Neville, H. A., Aber, M., Khuri, L., & De La Rosa, B. (2013). Living–learning communities and students' sense of community and belonging. *Journal of Student Affairs Research and Practice, 50*(3), 308–325. https://doi.org/10.1515/jsarp-2013-0022

Stanford University (n.d.). Becoming of greater service. https://facts.stanford.edu/service/

Tervalon, M., & Murray-Garcia, J. (1998). Cultural humility versus cultural competence: A critical distinction in defining physician training outcomes in multicultural education. *Journal of Health Care for the Poor and Underserved, 9*(2), 117-125.

Chapter 15

DEEPENING THE CONNECTION

Reimagining Service

Vernette Doty and Andrea Tafolla

I n the shared spaces of the Community Engagement Center at the
University of California, Merced, conversations occur regularly that
grapple with questions and concerns surrounding tensions within our
communities and nation—challenges such as racial and gender inequity,
food insecurity, lack of access to clean water, growing numbers of unshel-
tered individuals, and more, contributing to heightened political polarization. While these issues are not new, they present significant hurdles that
our nation continues to grapple with. For many of our students, these challenges may be new, requiring them to learn how to engage in discussions
and understand how these issues manifest within local organizations. At
UC Merced, we have implemented the Pathways tool and framework to
equip students with skills to identify potential solutions, language to navigate difficult dialogues, and confidence to demonstrate resilience in the
face of adversity.

Institutional Context: Location, Community, and Campus Population

In 1995, the University of California System identified Merced, California, as the location for the 10th University of California campus. Placed with the intention to serve California's Central Valley, UC Merced opened its doors to the first class of students in 2005. On land originally inhabited by the Penutian-speaking Northern Valley Yokuts Indians, in the heart of the Central Valley, Merced became a city in 1889 (County of Merced, 2020). In contrast to the faster-growing, sprawling cities of Los Angeles, San Francisco, and Sacramento, Merced has retained its agricultural focus, sustained by generations of families and entire communities who migrated here to tend dairies and farm crops.

While the Central Valley produces roughly one quarter of the nation's food, as of June 2023, childhood food insecurity rates in Merced County stood at 19.6% compared to the California state average of 13.5%. Numerous communities in the Central Valley lack reliable access to clean drinking water due to deteriorating water systems and ongoing struggles between agricultural interests and low-income communities. Compounded by the region's desert environment and fueled by drought conditions, this issue remains a critical challenge (Feeding America, 2023). Serving as an incubator for many of the most pressing needs and wicked problems facing global societies today, the Central Valley has potential for becoming a valuable reciprocal partner with a research university like UC Merced. At the same time, UC Merced acknowledges the mutual benefits of such partnerships, as research addressing the region's needs has implications and applications of global significance.

Enter a population of bright, high-performing, problem-solving students, the majority of whom (70%) are the first in their family to go to college. UC Merced boasts the most diverse student population in the UC System, comprising 52.3% Hispanic, 20.4% Asian, 9.3% White, and 5.1% Black students. UC Merced students reflect the communities and challenges mirrored in the Central Valley (Center for Institutional Effectiveness, 2023). Of the university's approximately 9,000 students, 58% are Pell recipients, 8% are DACA or AB540 eligible, over 70% report participating in service with the community (Center for Institutional Effectiveness, 2019), and many arrive seeking ways to make positive change in the community. Enter students who bring with them a desire to serve.

Introduction to the Pathways

The mission and vision of the Community Engagement Center (CEC) at UC Merced prioritize the development of reciprocal partnerships, student learning, and capacity building aimed at fostering positive social change. The following student learning outcomes inform all CEC programming and assessment:

- *civic responsibility*: capacity to express an understanding of issues within the community and the responsibility to participate in democratic processes to work toward positive changes
- *consciousness of self*: ability to identify individual values and interests, to gain the confidence to act consistently with values, and to respect and appreciate the perspectives, values, and life situations of others
- *academic success*: ability to apply academic concepts to community issues and concepts of community issues to academic learning, alongside the development of professional skills

Since their inception in 2006 and 2011, respectively, the CEC and our partner center, the Margo F. Souza Student Leadership Center, have employed the social change model (SCM) of leadership development (Higher Education Research Institute, 1996). This framework serves as an introduction to help students identify their values and develop skills to collaborate in partnerships aimed at social change. While the SCM effectively motivates students to make a difference and facilitates service through teamwork, further efforts are required to help students envision multiple methods for creating effective change within communities. Many UC Merced students, some of whom have been recipients of community outreach programs as children, are limited not in their passion but in their understanding of how to engage with community beyond direct service interventions. At the same time that we began to look for ways to broaden and deepen students' engagement opportunities and experiences, conversations about the Pathways to Public Service and Civic Engagement tool and Working Group began to emerge as a survey tool and catalyst for community engagement opportunities.

Once UC Merced joined the Pathways Working Group and began to explore the examples provided by the Pathways framework and tool, it sparked conversation on our campus about potential ways our unique student population could engage with our local community. Additionally, conversations about the impact of community engagement on our diverse student population as individuals within the diverse community of Merced emerged institutionally. These conversations stimulated further dialogue about the pathways and the need to address frameworks of oppression, microaggressions, biases, the knowledge of the community, respect, inclusion, and acceptance. As we began to use the Pathways tool, and students began to take the survey and receive their results, the comments and questions generated helped us develop language for defining and discussing the pathways with our students. In addition, students' comments and questions opened up ideas for new applications for pathways.

Implementing Pathways: Leadership and Service Living–Learning Community

To foster dialogue on community engagement, social impact, and preparing students for ethical and effective community involvement, we initially introduced the Pathways tool and framework within our Leadership and Service Living–Learning Community (LLC). The LLC provides a year-long experience where first-year students live together in a residence hall and share academic courses and cocurricular learning and events. Weekly lessons and small-group exchanges in the residence hall helped students think through their pathways and discuss hypothetical situations. However, for first-year students at UC Merced, the actual contact with community was minimal, for a variety of reasons, the primary reason being lack of available transportation. The absence of real-life, hands-on opportunities for application led students to perceive the pathways as more theoretical than practical. As we have continued to introduce each cohort of our first-year Leadership and Service LLC to the pathways, we have worked to be more intentional by simultaneously connecting them with a community service project, even at the most introductory level. We have found that using pathways provides a framework that supports students in reimagining their concept of service. It helps them explore the real-life implications and impact from their unique pathway perspective, encouraging them to think critically about community issues and personal challenges. As one LLC student stated,

> When I learned of the multiple ways people can serve, it opened my eyes to many possibilities. If I wanted to serve the community around me, I didn't just have to do direct service, I could actually

spur on change legislatively or rally the community to get more people engaged [using] multiple forms of service.

Additionally, introducing our LLC students to the Pathways survey and framework in their first year at the university gives them the opportunity to apply their learning and experiences. This allows them to reflect on how they can integrate these insights into their classes, leadership roles, and extracurricular activities throughout their time at UC Merced and beyond.

Only two LLC cohorts have completed 4 years at the institution. Of those approximately 40 students, 60% graduated in 4 years. Close to 80% participated in campus clubs and organizations, employing the Direct Service Pathway via club-related community service. Also employing the Direct Service Pathway in addition to the Community Organizing and Activism Pathway, two students from the 2019–2020 LLC class began a new club with a focus on mentoring and tutoring undocumented high school students to prepare them for college application. The club also applied for and received funding from the Merced Union High School district to expand participation and impact.

CollegeCorps

In 2022, the Pathways tool became part of our CollegeCorps preservice program training. CollegeCorps is an "AmeriCorps-style" California statewide grant initiative designed to achieve the following three goals:

- create a generation of civic-minded leaders with the ability to bridge divides and solve problems
- help low-income students graduate on time and with less debt
- address societal challenges and help build more equitable communities across California (Office of the Governor, 2023)

Our UC Merced CollegeCorps program places students at local community partner host sites whose work addresses one of three focus areas: education, climate action, or food insecurity. Student participants in the program complete 450 hours of service over 11 months at their site, while maintaining their degree progress. During the CollegeCorps service year, similar to the AmeriCorps model, students, or "fellows," as they are called, receive a monthly "service" stipend to help cover their living expenses.

Adding pathways to the CollegeCorps training agenda provided new opportunities for discussion about community needs, how social patterns and structures may combine to create inequity, and how to apply a social justice lens to potential solutions. It opened a space for students to examine their service placements not only in terms of their preferred pathway but also the range and variety of positive and/or negative potential impacts on their host site and the population(s) they serve. The Pathways framework opened the door to a new level of dialogue about ethics, equity, civic responsibility, and multiple perceptions of social impact.

Public Service and Leadership Certificate

Despite being an "early adopter" of the Pathways framework, our campuswide vision for the pathways has been slow to develop. Beginning with application at a programmatic level, we have just launched our Public Service and Leadership Certificate, which is open to all students. Students apply to participate and must complete the following requirements during their time at UC Merced:

- a Pathways survey and workshop/consultation
- 80 hours of pathways-identified and -recorded service
- at least one course with a service-learning/community-based learning component
- a capstone project

Upon completion of all requirements, students receive a certificate and graduation cord that acknowledges their commitment to community engagement and their significant contribution to social impact.

One Public Service and Leadership Certificate student recipient, in response to a question about how the Pathways had informed their engagement, replied,

> My involvement in the community has been strongly shaped and guided by identifying my Pathways, which include direct service and community-engaged learning & research. Through these paths, I have developed a deeper appreciation of the distinctive needs and obstacles that our community faces. My participation in community-engaged learning and research allowed me to value the interactions between academic institutions and the

community at large. Through direct service, I have been able to establish relationships with locals, interact on a personal level, as well as offer practical support where it is most relevant

CollegeCorps and LLC students, through their program activities, nearly meet all Public Service and Leadership Certificate requirements. We anticipate the interest and participation in the Public Service and Leadership Certificate will continue to grow and students from all disciplines and majors will participate. The newest campus partnership is embedding the Public Service and Leadership Certificate within the engineering programs, from first-year experience course to capstone. This partnership will provide students with the opportunity to apply pathways throughout their learning at UC Merced, and to open conversations with community partners around social impact and projects that do no harm. We envision opening campus-wide dialogues surrounding social impact that introduce the diverse pathways available to students to contribute to their communities, now and as college graduates. We also look forward to gathering data that inform both campus and community and that support a growing network of social impact locally, statewide, nationally, and globally.

Lessons Learned, Next Steps

Every time we have applied the Pathways framework and tool, we have seen positive results. Our CollegeCorps Fellows use their pathways knowledge to identify ways in which other pathways could contribute to the mission of their community host site. One fellow organized a community food drive (Philanthropy) to support the small community in which the kids they tutor (Direct Service) live. Another fellow began attending city council meetings to learn more about how policy change (Policy and Governance) might impact their site. As we open expanded opportunities for students, we highlight the community relationships that foster synergy and drive positive social impact. Relationship development also illuminates areas of our community where systems of oppression, discrimination, and bias continue. Introducing students to pathways provides a gateway to broader conversations about diversity, respect, ethics, and acceptance. Ultimately, they are conversations about relationship building. Not only do we need to continue to learn how to engage in these conversations safely and respectfully, but we need to imbue students with the skills, insight, and empathy to be participants and leaders of these conversations within their peer groups, course-related workgroups, campus organizations, and their families. Perhaps other living–learning communities will begin to use the Pathways tool, or we might see campus service clubs adopt the pathways. Do our first-year LLC members continue to use their pathways knowledge? Do our CollegeCorps Fellows, our LLC students, and our PSLC participants employ the pathways knowledge in their club leadership and participation? To their course dialogues? To their student employment? How do we measure this potential ongoing application and/or the impact? Expansion and assessment are the direction our next steps will take.

Community Partners

As we continue to expand our use of the Pathways framework, an additional direction that we are beginning to pursue is to provide training and education for our community partners. As a result of hosting our initial introduction of the Pathways tool to community partners, one site, the senior center, immediately inquired to identify students for whom advocacy and organizing is their dominant service pathway. They are losing their building to high-speed rail and are seeking support from the city for new space. They hope to engage students to organize broad support and to speak out on their behalf.

We hope to gain insight as to whether our partners see the Pathways framework as supporting their work. How might they use the pathways to define their needs or desires? Are some pathways more valuable to certain partners due to their capacity, knowledge, or access? How comfortable are partners in participating in difficult conversations that may emerge? Are there trends and/or community challenges the pathways bring to light? These and many other questions emerge as we consider pathways dialogue with our community partners.

For other campuses considering the use of pathways, the tool is ever evolving to remain relevant to an ever-changing student population. The capacity for student growth and engagement is boundless, and the potential for contributing to positive social change is only limited by vision and capacity. Start small, plan for growth, and be sure to have trained staff (professional or student) to support whatever programming or outreach you plan. Think outside the box to engage academic and cocurricular applications and assess and reassess both engagement and outcomes frequently.

Conclusion

The future of the pathways at UC Merced is to remain responsive to creative opportunities for application and growth. As we introduce our partners to the Pathways framework and tool, and the capacity they provide for bold and honest conversations, it is exciting to imagine what new doors may open. As we continue to introduce new classes of students from more disciplines and majors, improve our efforts to assess, reimagine and implement new applications and programs, and engage in honest and challenging conversations, the potential for positive social impact is boundless, and the opportunities for our remarkable students are limitless. The tensions that exist in our communities and our nation won't disappear overnight, nor are the Pathways tool and framework a "magic bullet," but as we employ them to help our students reimagine how they engage in and with community, we will begin to see deep change occur.

References

Center for Institutional Effectiveness. (2023). *All student statistics*. https://cie.uc merced.edu/analytics-hub/student-statistics

Center for Institutional Effectiveness. (2019). *Graduating Senior Survey*. https:// visualizedata.ucop.edu/t/UCMerced/views/GSSLongitudinalTableauDash board/GraduatingSeniorSurveyStory?%3Aembed=y&%3AisGuestRedirect FromVizportal=y

County of Merced. (2020, November). *Cultural resources*. https://www.countyof merced.com/DocumentCenter/View/26171/44---Cultural-Resources#:~: text=The%20Yokut%20Indians%20originally%20inhabited,in%20the%20 San%20Joaquin%20Valley

Feeding America. (2023). *Central Valley map*. https://map.feedingamerica.org/ county/2021/child/california

Higher Education Research Institute. (1996). *Social change model for leadership development*. Astin. A.W., Astin, H.S.

Office of the Governor. (2023). *California volunteers*. https://www.california volunteers.ca.gov/californiansforall-college-corps/

Part Three

THEORETICAL, EMPIRICAL, AND CRITICAL REFLECTIONS

Chapter 16

PATHWAYS DATA

An Overview

Annabel Wong

The Pathways of Public Service and Civic Engagement survey tool has not only enhanced student advising but has also enabled the collection and analysis of aggregated data from participating organizations and institutions since the 2015–2016 academic year. Although the data are limited and conclusions may not be representative, trends have emerged that may help shape future academic and programmatic inquiry. This chapter will provide an overview of the Pathways data collection, discuss emerging trends, and explore their implications.

Pathways Working Group member institutions and organizations receive an updated electronic version of the survey tool at the beginning of each academic year. Additionally, they are provided access to the Pathways data on the Qualtrics survey platform, enabling representatives to view responses from their respective institutions. Each summer, responses from participating institutions are aggregated, providing implicit and explicit perspectives on the pathways, as well as issues or concerns relevant to different geographical areas. While the nonrandom sample and ambiguities in data collection limit the conclusiveness and representativeness of the data, some sample-specific trends have emerged.

The survey tool and its results have been useful at individual, cohort, intrainstitutional, and interinstitutional levels, informing advising,

Table 16.1. Pathways of Public Service and Civic Engagement and Their Abbreviations Used in This Chapter

Full Pathway Name	Abbreviation
Direct Service	DS
Community-Engaged Learning and Research	CELR
Community Organizing and Activism	COA
Philanthropy	Phil
Policy and Governance	PG
Social Entrepreneurship and Corporate Social Responsibility	SECSR

programming, and deeper understandings of the student body of each campus. The questions and data available can also inform the development of future iterations of the survey tool to meet the evolving needs of students, staff, and administrators. Table 16.1 describes abbreviations for each Pathway that will be used throughout the chapter.

Data Collection and Limitations

At the end of the academic year, responses from participating institutions are aggregated with comparable populations, specifically university and college students (henceforth referred to interchangeably as "respondents"). The collected observations are retained only if they are complete, meaning all questions related to four different dimensions—interest, experience, personal impact, and general social impact—are answered for every pathway. Responses to other questions may be incomplete or missing. In addition to these dimensions, the survey tool collects quantitative and qualitative data from additional multiple-choice questions, a pick-and-rank question, and a variety of short-answer questions.

Complete responses have contributed to a dataset of more than 14,000 respondents at nearly 90 partner institutions and coalitions, collected between the 2015–2016 and 2021–2022 academic years. The institutions involved have varied over time; some join for a single year, others have consistently used the Pathways tool for many years, and still others participate intermittently. Each year's data provide a snapshot of trends for that period, and with multiple years of data, it is possible to identify broader trends.

Sources of Data

The 2022–2023 survey tool, complete with examples for each data source or question, is provided in Appendix D (Online Companion). The survey tool has been updated over the years, most notably with the additions of Part A and Part C in 2019–2020. The first question on the survey presents a list of general public service activities and asks respondents to "pick and rank ONLY the activities that [they] want to try or engage in" (Part A of the survey). While the list includes two activities representing each of the six pathways, totaling 12 activities, the pathways are not mentioned on this page. This approach solicits respondents' preferences based on their perceptions of the activities themselves, which can contrast or reinforce results that explicitly include the named pathways.

In Part B, the survey asks respondents to identify what they consider to be the most important issues or concerns by geographic area (i.e., campus, local region/community, and the world at large). This section aims to capture respondents' perspectives in their own words.

In Part C, respondents are asked to select the topic that most closely aligns with their service experiences or interests, including options such as Diversity, Equity, and Inclusion; Education and Youth Development; Environmental Sustainability; Health; Human Services; and General. The addition of Part C to the 2019–2020 survey generated the topic-specific examples listed in Part D.

After reviewing the definitions and examples of the six pathways, respondents indicate their experience, interest, personal impact, and perceived general impact on social issues for each pathway in Part D of the survey. Finally, they select the two pathways they are most likely to explore after college as part of their career or personal pursuits, indicate whether they have participated in a workshop about public service pathways (Part E), and optionally provide demographic information (Part F).

Limitations

The sample is nonrandom and includes institutions that use the survey tool in a variety of settings, such as with all first-year students, cohorts of highly engaged students living in a service-minded housing community, or those within student leadership courses. Results are derived from responses from institutions willing to use the tool with their students, facilitated by faculty, administrators, civic engagement staff, and other affiliated individuals. While some institutions gather data broadly (e.g., from all incoming students during a first-year orientation), allowing extrapolation to other similar students, the aggregated data cannot be considered representative of the college population nor support analysis for establishing causation.

The survey tool does not collect personal identifying information, thus precluding the longitudinal tracking of individual responses. Some campuses do use the tool in pre- and postactivity situations, allowing for comparisons of aggregate responses or enabling individual respondents to track their own results. As a result, the dataset may thus include multiple responses from the same individuals over time.

Ambiguity may also affect the data collected from the survey tool, as the responses are self-reported. In Part D, the survey does not standardize the definitions for the levels of experience, interest, personal impact, or general impact, which are categorized as "none," "very little," "some," and "a lot."

The short-answer questions in Part B of the survey require students to articulate responses in their own words rather than offering a drop-down menu with predefined examples of issues or concerns. A review of feedback received from students at the end of the survey indicates that incoming first-year or transfer students, especially at the campus level, often express inexperience and a lack of familiarity with identifying their top issues or concerns. This inexperience may result in respondents providing answers with less information or consideration than desired.

Some respondents have also expressed confusion and frustration about certain demographic questions (gender, race, and ethnicity, etc.) in Part F. These issues may potentially influence responses or response rates, despite these demographic questions being the last set shown in the survey before the results appear. These questions are critical for advising, programming, and inquiry purposes, but some respondents may perceive them as irrelevant or intrusive.

Additionally, because the pathways overlap, some activities may be categorized under multiple pathways. For example, collecting and distributing donations and supplies for wildfire survivors could be categorized under both Direct Service and Philanthropy activities. Similarly, organizing a town hall discussion to generate ideas to increase low-income housing availability could be seen as both Community Organizing and

Activism as well as Community-Engaged Learning and Research. The indistinct boundaries between pathways may lead to confusion for respondents.

Data Overview

This section provides an overview of the aggregated data collected between the 2015–2016 to 2021–2022 academic years. Part A and Part C have data available between 2019–2020 and 2021–2022, when they were added to the survey. While demographic data is collected optionally in Part F of the survey tool, it is incomplete and may not be wholly accurate, so it will not be incorporated in this analysis.[1] However, the demographic data illuminate patterns of engagement in public service through institutional channels, identify which populations are missing or underrepresented, and shed light on how existing structures, narratives, and opportunities may encourage or deter participation. The myriad ways that respondents wish to participate in social change is a valuable area of ongoing and future examination, discussion, investment, and action.

Multiple sources of data allow some degree of corroboration for articulating trends and substantiating hypotheses. For instance, respondents' choice of example activities in Part A and their selected pathways for future exploration in Part E may overlap or contrast with their reported experience, interest, personal impact, and general impact in Part D. Similarly, respondents' identified issues or concerns in Part B may intersect or diverge with the topic they prioritized in Part C to determine the survey tool's examples.

Example Activities

The example activities question of Part A (see Table 16.2) was introduced in 2019–2020, when it was piloted with a subset of all respondents. While the number of years of collected data is limited, clear trends have emerged (see Figure 16.1).

The option "Volunteer your time to help on a local project you care about" is consistently selected by 80% of respondents, and over 40% of those respondents rank it first among their choices. "Gather supplies to help a population you care about," which is most typically ranked second when selected, and "Donate to a charity drive that benefits a population

Table 16.2. Example Activities and Associated Pathways

Pathway	Example Activity
CELR	Survey neighborhood residents regarding the effects of an issue you care about.
CELR	Review books or articles on best practices to create a policy paper for an organization.
COA	Organize your peers through social media to participate in an event to support an issue you care about.
COA	Write an editorial or blog post about an issue you care about.
DS	Gather supplies to help a population you care about.
DS	Volunteer your time to help on a local project you care about.
Phil	Donate to a charity drive that benefits a population you care about.
Phil	Participate in a walkathon or fundraising event for an issue you care about and ask friends or local companies to sponsor you.
PG	Serve on a student government association or council.
PG	Attend or organize a debate, forum, or town hall.
SECSR	Sell items and donate a portion of your profits to support a cause you care about.
SECSR	Work with a tech company to design a mobile app that helps a population you care about.

you care about," which is most commonly ranked third, have similarly maintained consistent results and relative positions across 3 years of data.

Data highlight: The top two most-selected activities are associated with Direct Service, and the third activity is associated with Philanthropy.

The option "Sell items and donate a portion of your profits to support a cause you care about" (SECSR) was selected less frequently over time, despite remaining among the most selected overall. Conversely, one Community Organizing and Activism activity ("Organize your peers through social media to participate in an event to support an issue you care about") and one Community-Engaged Learning and Research activity ("Review books or articles on best practices to create a policy paper for an organization") were selected slightly more frequently over time. The option

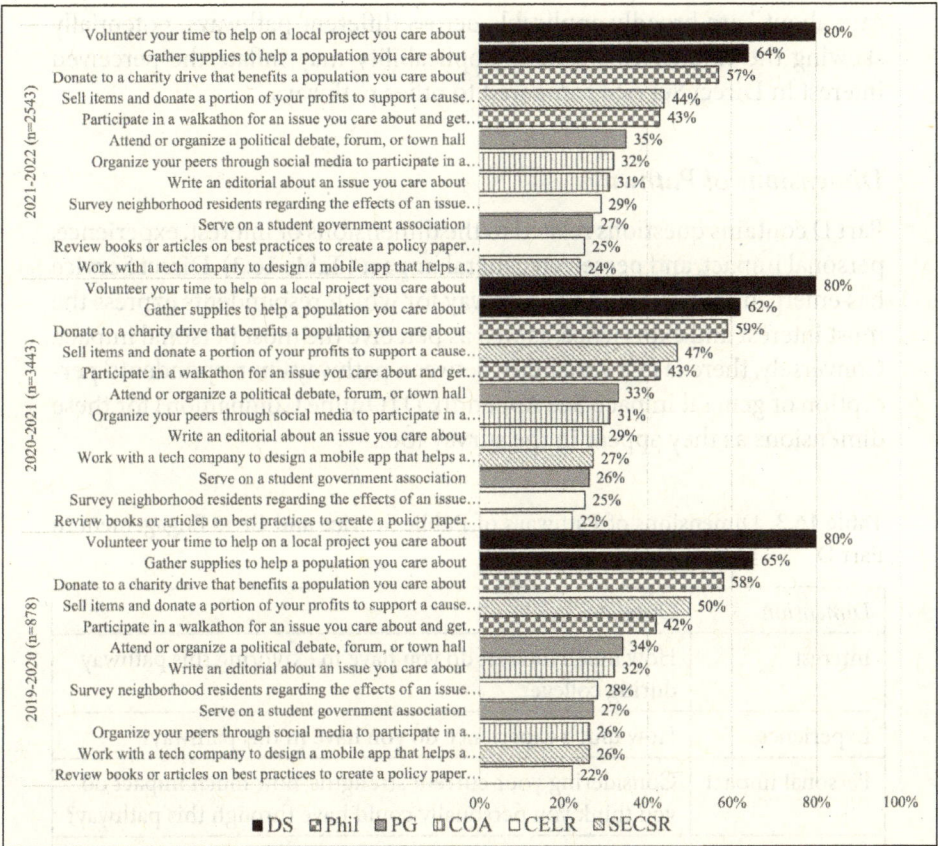

Figure 16.1. Example activities, by year (from 2019–2020 to 2021–2022).

on reviewing books or articles, however, was the least frequently selected until 2021–2022, when it was surpassed by "Work with a tech company to design a mobile app that helps a population you care about" (Social Entrepreneurship and Corporate Social Responsibility).

Data highlight: Policy and Governance activities ("Attend or organize a debate, forum, or town hall" and "Serve on a student government association or council") were favored by relatively few respondents (between one fifth and over one third of respondents).

While the pathways are not mentioned in Part A, respondents familiar with the framework may infer the associated pathway for activities. Some activities, like "Volunteer your time to help on a local project you care about," are broadly applicable across different pathways, potentially skewing the results. This general applicability may inflate the perceived interest in Direct Service compared to other pathways.

Dimensions of Pathways

Part D contains questions related to the dimensions of interest, experience, personal impact, and perceived general impact (Table 16.3). Direct Service has emerged every year as the pathway for which respondents express the most interest and experience, as well as perceive the most personal impact. Conversely, there is less variability between pathways in respondents' perception of general impact. See Appendix D (Online Companion) for these dimensions as they appear in the survey tool.

Table 16.3. Dimensions of Pathways of Public Service and Civic Engagement in Part D

Dimension	Question
Interest	How much interest do you have in exploring this pathway during college?
Experience	How much experience do you have in this pathway?
Personal impact	Considering your current strengths, how much impact do you think you personally could have through this pathway?
General impact	In general, how much impact do you think this pathway has on social issues?

Interest

Over 80% of respondents consistently select "a lot" or "some" for their interest in Direct Service. During 2015–2016, respondents expressed greater interest in Philanthropy compared to other pathways, but the relative interest in COA and CELR quickly caught up in subsequent years (Figure 16.2, Online Companion).

CELR has become the second most "interesting" pathway for respondents since 2019–2020. Interest in PG has consistently been the lowest among the pathways, with between 47% and 55% of respondents expressing "a lot" or "some" interest in PG each year. Interest in COA and PG follow a similar trajectory in the available period (2015–2016 to 2021–2022,

Figure 16.3, Online Companion). While impossible to ascribe causation, one use of the Pathways tool and aggregated data may be to observe trends and consider possible correlated events, such as humanitarian disasters, technological breakthroughs, or in the case of COA and PG, major election campaigns and contentious political circumstances. These events may highlight opportunities or motivations for public engagement.

Data highlight: Students consistently express the most interest in Direct Service. Interest in CELR and COA have increased relative to other pathways, while interest in Philanthropy has declined in the same period.

Experience

Between 65% and 80% of respondents select "a lot" or "some" for their experience in Direct Service. After Direct Service, early respondents (until 2018–2019) expressed greater relative experience in Philanthropy than other pathways (Figure 16.4, Online Companion). In 2019–2020, 50% of respondents selected "some" or "a lot" of experience in Philanthropy, while 41% selected "some" or "a lot" of experience for COA, the next pathway with greatest relative experience. One year later, in 2020–2021, the gap between Philanthropy and COA decreased to approximately 3%, as 38% of respondents selected "some" or "a lot" of experience in Philanthropy, and 35% selected "some" or "a lot" of experience in COA (Figure 16.5, Online Companion). Experience in CELR trailed closely behind, and by 2021–2022, respondents expressed virtually the same relative experience in Philanthropy, COA, and CELR. Experience in SECSR is consistently the lowest, though reported experience in PG was comparably low in 2015–2016, 2020–2021, and 2021–2022. Like with reported interest, experience in COA and PG follow a similar trajectory in the given period.

Data highlight: Students express the least experience in SECSR and PG, and later cohorts of students expressed less relative experience in Philanthropy than earlier cohorts.

Personal Impact

Respondents consider themselves relatively impactful in Direct Service, with 85% or more selecting "a lot" or "some" each year (Figure 16.6). Like interest, respondents in 2015–2016 express greater personal impact in

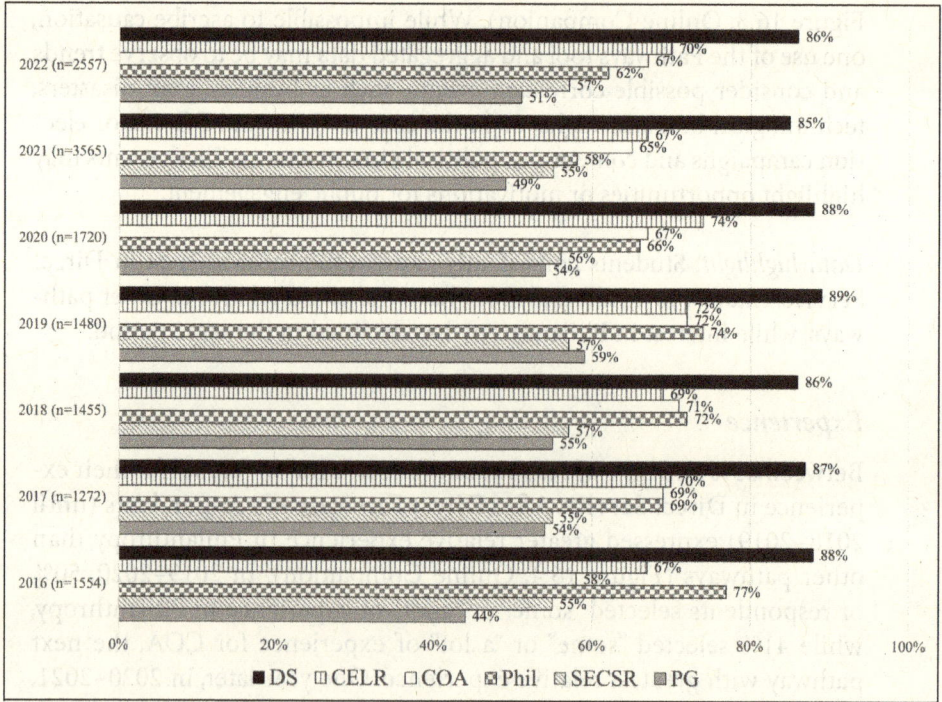

Figure 16.6. Aggregate personal impact by pathways, from 2015–2016 to 2021–2022.

Note: Pictured is the percentage of "a lot" and "some" responses for each pathway.

Philanthropy compared to other pathways, but it is overtaken by COA and CELR beginning in 2019–2020.

Like interest and experience, personal impact in COA and PG follows a similar trajectory in the given period. The portion of respondents who selected "a lot" or "some" personal impact increased by approximately 10% for COA and PG between 2015–2016 and 2016–2017, which was not seen in the dimensions of interest or experience. Respondents expressed an increase in the impact they believed they could have through COA and PG in that period, and they have not since reverted to the lower number observed in 2015–2016, though levels have declined from a peak in 2018–2019 (Figure 16.7, Online Companion).

Data highlight: Despite the early increase, PG remains the pathway for which respondents express the least relative personal impact nearly every year.

General Impact

While Direct Service remains the top pathway relative to others in perceived general impact—over 90% of respondents consistently select "a lot" or "some" for Direct Service—there is much less variability between pathways in students' responses compared to the other dimensions (Figure 16.8).

In 2015–2016, respondents selected "a lot" or "some" least frequently for PG, but that increased in subsequent years to match the other pathways, save for Direct Service. Starting in 2016–2017, respondents selected "a lot" or "some" least frequently for SECSR, except in 2018–2019, but all pathways seem to be considered comparably impactful on social issues.

Perceived general impact of PG stands out when isolating "a lot" responses (Figure 16.9). As before, respondents selected "a lot" least frequently for PG in 2015–2016, but that increased in subsequent years to levels comparable with Direct Service. Direct Service and Policy and

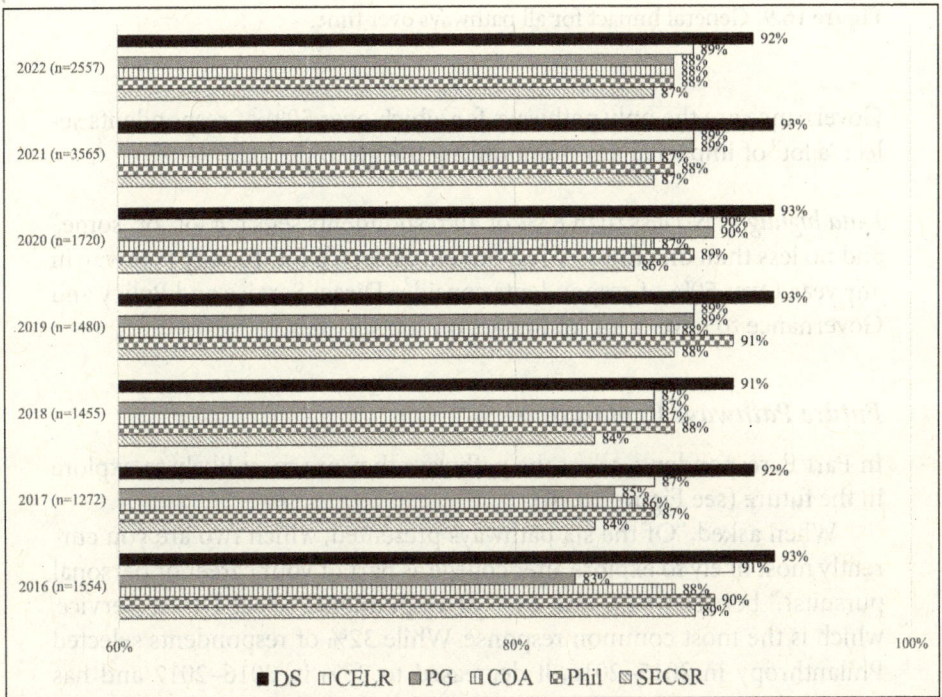

Figure 16.8. Aggregate general impact by pathways, from 2015–2016 to 2021–2022.

Note: Pictured is the percentage of "a lot" and "some" responses for each pathway.

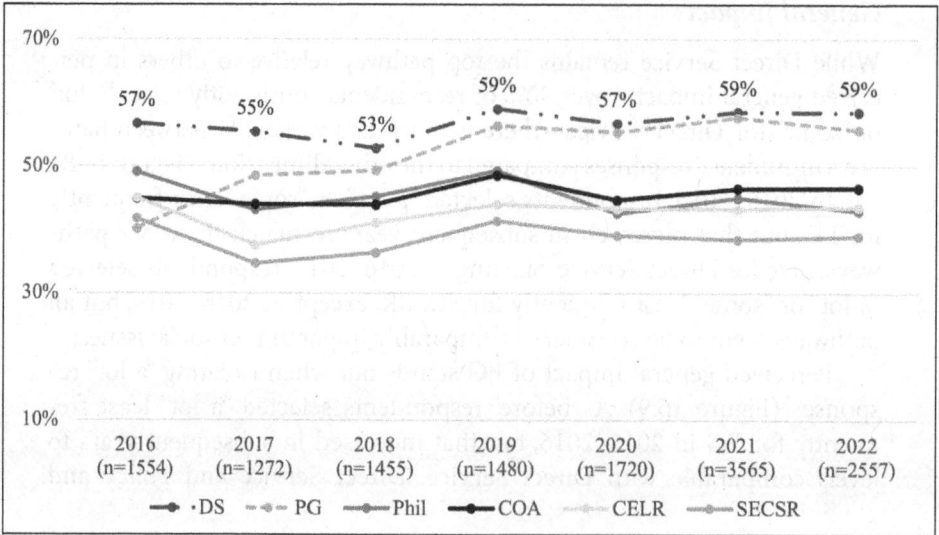

Figure 16.9. General impact for all pathways over time.

Governance are the only pathways for which over 50% of respondents se-lect "a lot" of impact at any point during the given period.

Data highlight: No less than 83% of all respondents select "a lot" or "some," and no less than one third of respondents select "a lot" for any pathway in any year. Over 50% of respondents consider Direct Service and Policy and Governance to have "a lot" of impact on social issues.

Future Pathways Exploration

In Part E, respondents select the pathways they are most likely to explore in the future (see Figure 16.10).

When asked, "Of the six pathways presented, which two are you cur-rently most likely to explore after college as part of your career or personal pursuits?," between 51% and 61% of respondents select Direct Service, which is the most common response. While 32% of respondents selected Philanthropy in 2015–2016, it decreased to 23% in 2016–2017 and has remained at approximately 21% since 2019–2020. In contrast, while 20% of respondents selected COA in 2015–2016, it increased to 35% and 36% in the following 3 years and has remained above 30% since. After Direct Service, COA and CELR are the most frequently selected pathways, with one third or more respondents selecting CELR every year.

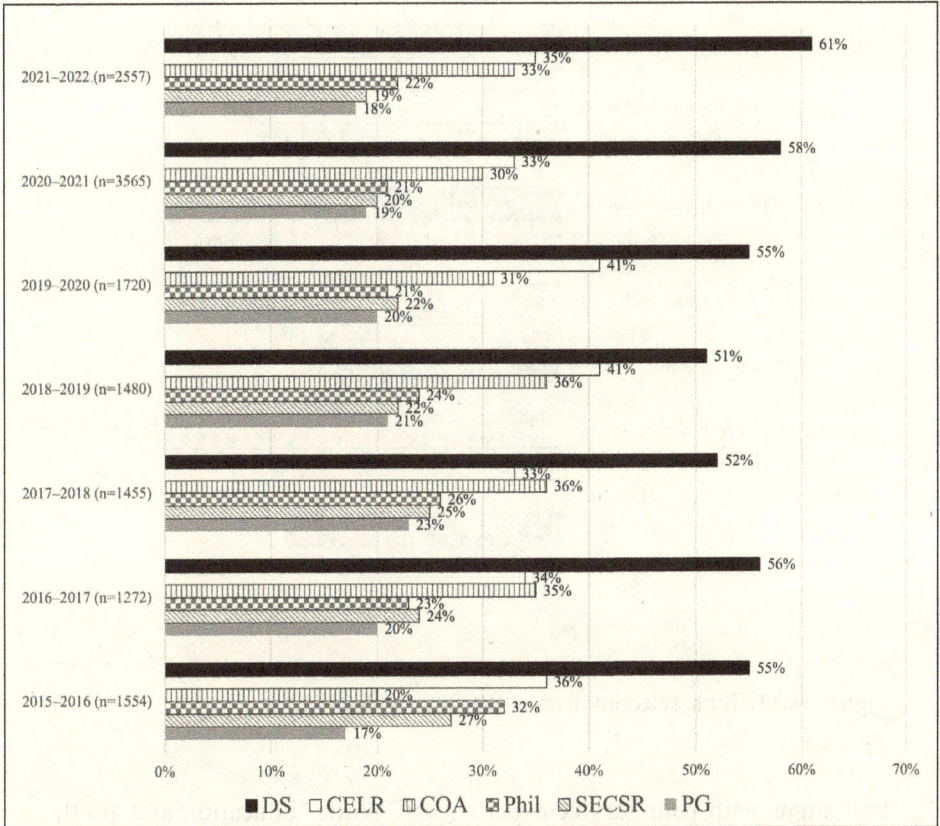

Figure 16.10. Selection of future pathways for exploration, from 2015–2016 to 2021–2022.

Note: Respondents can select multiple answers.

Like COA, respondent likelihood of exploring PG increased from 17% to 20% and then to 23% between 2015–2016 and 2017–2018 but declined in subsequent periods. The likelihood of exploring SECSR has declined steadily over the given period.

Topic Selection

As in the Example Activities question, the ability to choose a topic for subsequent examples (Part C of the survey tool in Appendix D, Online Companion) was introduced in 2019–2020 (see Figure 16.11). Respondents select from six options in response to "Among these, which topic

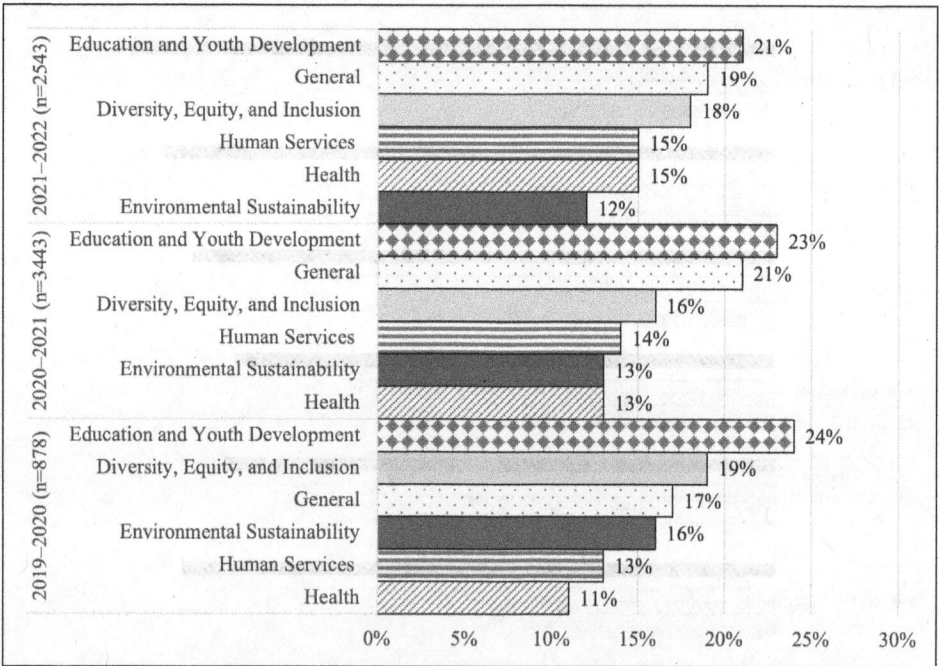

Figure 16.11. Topic selection from 2019–2020 to 2021–2022.

best aligns with your service experiences?" While "Education and Youth Development" is the most frequently selected topic, no more than one quarter of respondents selected any given topic. Though "Diversity, Equity, and Inclusion" was second in 2019–2020, "General," which refers to a broad range of examples, from community gardens to municipal politics, overtook it. "Health" was the least selected topic in 2019–2020, but "Environmental Sustainability" replaced it in 2020–2021 and 2021–2022.

Issues of Importance

Since 2016–2017, respondents have provided their opinions on the top three social issues or concerns on their own campus, in the local region/community, and in the world at large (Part B of the survey tool in Appendix D, Online Companion). Analysis focuses on the single top concern for each of the three geographical areas. Every year, this qualitative data is reviewed and sorted into themes. Themes are ranked according to frequency, and counts are divided by total respondents to the entire survey for a percentage of respondents (Appendix E, Online Companion). Multiple themes are possible per response.

At the campus level (Figure 16.12, Online Companion), issues of diversity (e.g., acceptance, inclusion, representation, etc.) have been identified among top concerns most frequently, and related ideas are also prominent (e.g., race and racism, discrimination, equity). Issues related to well-being, such as finances, mental health, sexual violence, safety/security, social interactions, and alcohol use, made up much of the rest of the top 10 campus concerns over time. Other recurring concerns include campus environment (infrastructure and local environment), academics, sustainability, engagement/involvement, food, and academics. The COVID-19 pandemic appeared frequently in the relevant years (2020–2021 and 2021–2022).

In the local region/community category (Figure 16.13, Online Companion), there was less consistency. Top concerns rotated to inequality (especially economic), poverty, and housing/homelessness. Also appearing in the top 10 regional/community concerns were diversity, racism, and discrimination; environment and sustainability; substance/drug use; economy and unemployment; safety and crime; education; mental health; and COVID-19 and public health.

For the world at large (Figure 16.14, Online Companion), respondent concerns were dominated by climate and environmental sustainability, which comprised the most frequently identified theme for 4 of the 6 years of available data. Only poverty was more prominent in 2016–2017, and COVID-19 and inequality were more prominent in 2020–2021. Poverty, economic inequality, and food/hunger, as well as discrimination, diversity, racism, and inequality more broadly were also frequently identified. War and conflict issues and politics/political climate were unique to issues identified in the world at large. Health, violence, terrorism, and justice also appeared frequently.

Discussion

In questions related to the Pathways framework, respondents show a clear preference for Direct Service. This preference is evident when respondents are asked about their interest, experience, personal impact, and general impact regarding Direct Service (Part D of the survey), as well as when they select activities they want to try or engage in (Part A). However, as noted, the example "Volunteer your time to help on a local project you care about" is widely applicable across public service and civic engagement activities, and therefore across different pathways, and may skew results.

While explicit interest in Philanthropy has fallen relative to COA and CELR over time, more than 50% of respondents selected "Donate to a charity drive," and more than 40% selected "Participate in a walkathon." These activities, as well as "Volunteer your time" and "Gather supplies to help," could be more familiar activities to respondents as they may be encouraged or required in religious and workplace contexts.

After Direct Service, respondents express most interest in CELR as a pathway and select CELR and COA most frequently for future exploration. In contrast, they select CELR activities ("Survey neighborhood residents" and especially "Review books or articles") relatively less frequently than other activities. Respondents may be primarily interested in aspects of CELR outside of reviewing books or may not perceive reviewing books to be among CELR activities. Activities associated with COA ("Organize your peers through social media" and "Write an editorial or blog post about an issue") are more frequently selected than CELR ones. In contrast, respondents tend to express comparable or in some cases more explicit interest and personal impact in CELR, though they express comparable or more experience in COA.

"Sell items and donate" is selected by 40% to 50% of respondents, and far more frequently than the other SECSR activity, "Work with a tech company," but respondents express relatively low interest and experience in SECSR compared to other pathways. Respondents express the lowest relative interest and personal impact in PG, yet PG activities ("Serve on a student government association" and especially "Attend or organize a debate") were selected more than CELR activities. Respondents may understand the pathways differently based on their experience, available definitions, and examples. It is also possible that creators of the survey tool have miscategorized the example activities into the associated pathway.

Respondents seem to consider all the pathways comparably impactful on social issues; in particular, DS and PG are most frequently identified as having "a lot" of impact. This impression of PG as having "a lot" of impact contrasts with reported levels of relatively low interest, experience, and personal impact among respondents. Respondents may think of PG as being influential on social issues but do not necessarily see themselves as able or interested to effect social change through involvement in PG.

Responses to the short-answer questions (Part B of the survey) regarding significant social issues or concerns varied widely, but diversity and inclusion emerged as a prominent concern at the campus level, poverty and homelessness at the local region/community level, and climate and environment at the world level. In the topic selection section (Part C of the survey), "Education and Youth Development" is most frequently chosen (between 21% and 24% of the time). Respondents are asked to pick the topic that best aligns with their experiences, so responses may reflect their interest and available opportunities more than their issues or concerns in Part B. It is nonetheless interesting to note that education is rarely represented among those issues or concerns. "Diversity, Equity, and Inclusion," "Human Services" (which covers "topics related to helping people navigate through crisis or chronic situations, toward self-sufficiency and improved quality of life"), and "Environmental Sustainability" were less infrequently selected (18%, 15%, and 12%, respectively, in 2021–2022).

Implications and Further Questions

Survey tool results that align perfectly with what respondents or administrators anticipate can leave limited room for exploration. The existence of areas of contrast and reinforcement, whether from differing understandings or creator errors, surface many questions that can lead to rich discussion in advising and classroom settings, This has always been a core intention of the survey tool and framework. Topics for discussion might include the following:

- The pathways are an attempt to categorize different types of civic and community engagement activities. What are alternative taxonomies or ways to categorize activities?
- What activities have been most available to you? What have you embraced or avoided, and why? What opportunities would you like more access to?
- Who do you think is effective at public service and civic engagement? What do they do well? How could they be more effective?

Respondents have received their survey results in various formats over time, initially with a spiderweb graphic or radar chart for each of the four dimensions (Appendix F, Online Companion), and now with a simpler bar chart for each pathway. These individualized results offer a reflection of respondents' dispositions. With the 2019–2020 additions of example activities and topics for pathway-specific examples to contrast or reinforce results from other sections, respondents may be prompted to reexamine their perceptions. These results can serve as an advising aid for course planning, career counseling, leadership development, and other areas.

Advisors can also use group survey results to create a cohesive cohort experience and inform programming decisions, such as for the selection of speakers, discussion topics, and service opportunities. Aggregated results, whether across cohorts or institutionally, provide valuable insight into the student body and facilitate comparisons between programs, classes, and demographic groups. Detailed case studies on the use of the framework and tool are provided elsewhere in this volume.

Aside from applying insights, many questions can be explored using the available data, despite their incomplete and inconsistent demographic aspects. It is possible to trace connections between responses from different parts of the survey tool. For example, for respondents who select "Diversity, Equity, and Inclusion" in Part C, one may ask: What are their main pathways of interest, experience, personal impact, and general impact? Or, what issues or concerns do respondents who express "a lot" of personal impact in Philanthropy name? What opportunities or experiences might be tailored to these profiles?

With multiple years of data confirming that respondents express the most interest, experience, and personal impact in Direct Service, it may be valuable to explore other aspects of affinity or engagement with the pathways. For example, how confident are respondents about being able to identify and pursue opportunities relevant to specific pathways, such as Philanthropy or Policy and Governance? More broadly, research questions for qualitative study might explore why there is a persistently low level of interest in exploring PG while the perception of PG's impact on social change has been relatively high. What are the relationships between interest and general impact, or experience and personal impact? How do students conceive of their self-efficacy in social change?

The form and content of the survey tool has remained largely the same since 2015–2016, notwithstanding the additions in 2019–2020. Use of the survey tool increased during the years of the COVID-19 pandemic, reflecting the heightened need for online tools that support students' journeys in civic engagement and provide staff guidance. With recent technological advances, there is an opportunity to creatively design new tools that apply the Pathways framework. These tools could incorporate simulations and multimedia resources, artificial intelligence–assisted guidance, or real-time synthesis of responses. Seven years of accumulated data from the original and updated versions of the survey tool should inform future iterations that continue to challenge and educate users, whether they be students, staff, faculty, or administrators.

Conclusion

While data from the Pathways survey tool may paint a somewhat limited picture of trends over time, they nevertheless prompt deeper exploration into the pathways by highlighting what is absent. With reliable demographic data, for example, it would be possible to explore the preferences and profiles of specific groups (e.g., respondents who identify as Black/African American, first-generation college students, health sciences majors, rural background students, etc.) or the identifiers of those with certain preferences (e.g., those who express "a lot" of interest in PG or how those who select "review books or articles on best practices to create a policy paper for an organization" identify). It is currently not possible to ensure that the optional demographic questions are accurately completed, nor is generating profiles necessarily the goal. Demographic data that are available suggest that current respondents largely identify as women, White, and non-first-generation and are frequently first-year college students. There is ample opportunity to expand the use of the Pathways framework across a broader range of institutions and a more diverse audience. By doing so, we can make the framework and tool more inclusive by incorporating the diverse narratives and approaches through which students and other users engage in their communities and effect social change.

Stepping beyond data from the Pathways survey tool, integrating them with those of other sources, such as UCLA's CIRP Freshman Survey, National Survey of Student Engagement, Beginning College Survey of Student Engagement, or College Senior Survey, could yield valuable insights into social change education. By combining data from similar cohorts, we could develop a more robust and reliable understanding of student engagement.

Seeking to further community engagement in our times calls for deeper inquiry into how individuals interact with each other across differences and engage with democracy. What preconceptions and tensions do students hold about community engagement? What means of data collection might allow research into these questions? Existing data from the Pathways survey tool provide a foundational starting point and catalyst for future investigations. These could benefit from creative narrative approaches, diverse engagement methodologies, and rigorous critical analysis.

Note

1. Stanford University staff and consultants presented some demographic data results and analysis for a Campus Compact webinar on October 8, 2020, which can be viewed at https://compact.org/resources/pathways-of-public-service-and-civic-engagement.

Chapter 17

WHERE REFUSAL MEETS THE PATHWAYS

A Relational Praxis in, but Not of, the University

Agustin "Tino" Diaz, Brenna Lambert, and Priscilla Villaseñor-Navarro

(Content warning: This book chapter contains material that discusses suicide and the story of a child taking their life)

I n November 2021, in Utah, a tragedy unfolded. A young Black girl who was autistic took her own life amid reports of intense bullying related to her disability and race. Her name was Izzy Tichenor. The impact shook local community members in the Davis School District. Prior to that, a Department of Justice report was released revealing a lengthy and disturbing pattern of racist and ableist incidents throughout the school district. Many of these issues were not addressed or were poorly handled (Elizabeth, 2021). At Utah Valley University (UVU), the impact of Izzy's suicide was also felt among student leaders and educators. The three of us (a program director [Tino] and two student leaders [Bre and Priscilla]) from the UVU Center for Social Impact (CSI) were compelled to take action because of our proximity to local, racially minoritized communities.

CSI at UVU is a unique space within the campus. The CSI Office had undergone a transformation of mission and practice over the 2 prior years that allowed it to become a more forward-thinking, progressive, and action-oriented space that valorized social justice themes and motivated its students to engage in local issues. CSI did this by redesigning their programs through the Pathways framework (Haas Center for Public Service, 2023). The center typically has an outline of programming and events that are laid out at the beginning of the year, similar to student life centers in other universities. However, given our feeling that what happened to Izzy needed to be immediately addressed, we chose to depart from the center's timeline of programming and events, disinvesting from the idea that we had to identify a measurable return on investment for the event, and instead engaging in extra work to highlight the issue within our community.

It's important to note that our writing in this chapter operates from a decolonial and abolitionist perspective, viewing the university as a site of both interpersonal and systemic violence due to its colonial heritage and corporatist agendas (Stein, 2021). Building on this critique, we add that normative university discourses frequently resist politically charged events and programming that challenge the complicity of educational institutions in societal violence (Gaston-Gayles et al., 2005). Despite the CSI being a space for students aligned with justice-oriented thinking and principles, we still felt ourselves having to push against the dominant discourse of university programming, which typically adheres to specific departmental strategies and metrics. What we were doing was a response to a need as well as an issue that the three of us felt personally tied to, and we have come to frame our response as an act of refusal within the university.

Our chapter begins by examining a study that highlights the emerging neoliberal agenda in higher education student affairs. We then delve into the concept of refusal as a guiding framework that motivated our response to Izzy's suicide, prompting us to develop an event that diverged from CSI's preplanned programming. Finally, we share a transcribed dialogue among the three of us, reflecting on our efforts at refusal and how we leveraged the Pathways framework to create relational praxis across the university.

Literature Review

In the following section, we offer a literature review that lays the foundation for our conceptual approach of refusal within the context of the university. First, we provide a critique of the university as a colonial and corporate institution that perpetuates historical and contemporary forms of harm rooted in colonial and capitalist logics. These logics include assimilation, epistemic exclusion, the commercialization of student bodies, and the prioritization of metrics over relationships, among others. Afterward, we provide the theoretical background of refusal as a framework, tracing the history of the concept and drawing mainly from Black radical traditions and Indigenous political thought. Together, these sections provide the necessary foundation for understanding the dimensions of our conversation and analysis.

Institutional Settings—A Colonial and Corporate Critique

In discussions among the authors leading up to this piece, we noted time and again that while the university can be a place where communities form organically, fostering healthy relationality is not inherently prioritized in the design of the university (Stein, 2021). Gaston-Gayles et al. (2005) point out that educators and practitioners in student affairs did not truly become student advocates, change agents, and resistive actors till the 1960s and 70s (Wolf-Wendel et al., 2004). Scholars of higher education also point out that the historical legacy of the university is one rooted in the violence of assimilation, the centering of Eurocentric knowledge and hierarchy as universal truths, and the application of Western modes of being, such as individualism, as the only valued experience (Harney & Moten, 2013; Stein, 2021). Indeed, today's university is the embodiment of the sociohistorical forces that have perpetuated the genocide of Indigenous communities across the Americas, the transatlantic slave trade, scientific racism, and more (Naepi et al., 2017; Wilder, 2013).

While this scholarly critique highlights the colonial origins of the university, it also integrates critical scholarship on the corporatist agenda, or neoliberalism, within the university context. A study published in 2021 offers insight into the contradictions present in the ongoing corporatization of the university, particularly within student affairs (Cairo & Cabal, 2021). Cairo and Cabal interviewed numerous educators and practitioners within a university's student affairs division, as well as conducting focus groups and soliciting letters with additional feedback from these educators and practitioners. The results demonstrated that the messaging of student success and care clashed with the institution's metrics-driven strategies, putting overwhelming pressure on employees. For example, viewing students as data or numbers often meant that they were treated without specialized care or humane treatment. Metric-driven strategies also meant that students couldn't be viewed with their full humanity, which often meant treating them like mass consumers versus people with unique histories and contexts embarking on a journey of learning. Ultimately, the study suggested that the corporatization of student affairs has significant negative consequences, such as the treatment of students as consumers and numbers. The tensions among university staff are not only present within the institution but also affect their personal lives and ability to support students. This strain also negatively influences how they build relationships and community with students.

Refusal as a Framework

Refusal, as a political and ontological ethos, originates from Indigenous scholars and activists (Coulthard, 2014; Simpson, 2007, 2014), Black feminists (Ferreirra da Silva, 2018), fugitivity philosophers (Moten & Harney, 2004; Wynter, 2006), and cultural anthropologists (McGranahan, 2016). While refusal as praxis is informed by numerous traditions, we mainly draw from Black radical and Indigenous political thought. The concept of refusal serves as a means to deny the state or other institutions access to and authority over the body, mind, and spirit. This act fundamentally alters relationships with societal institutions while also opening up space for radical futures and new forms of relationality. For example, Kelley (2016) highlights the actions of student activists on campus while also challenging them to question why they seek belonging in an institution that would fail to love them as they are. Instead, the act of refusal to an institution can be the intellectual and material pursuit of alternative ways of existing *within* but not being *of* the university (Harney & Moten, 2013). Harney and Moten (2013) similarly advocate for rejecting the university's professionalization to engage in an "undercommons" that values study, struggle, and relationality. Thus, instead of severing relations with an institution as an act of refusal, they propose a creative mode of being, whereby refusing or ignoring that which is, one can have the space and freedom to *be* something and somewhere else.

Inspired by Black radical and Indigenous politics and praxis, Grande (2018) outlines three core principles of refusal in the context of the university: First, commit to a collectivity that refuses individualized praxis; second, commit to a reflexivity that is answerable to the community you are a part of and that you intend to serve; lastly, commit to mutuality, which transcends capitalist relationships and relies not on exploitation but instead emphasizes solidarity and familial relationships, particularly in relation to land. Indeed, Grande's (2018) work in writing "Refusing the University" is an invitation for racially minoritized educators and students to (re)relate to one another, and in doing so, honor the theoretical origins of such work.

Refusing Institutionalization Through Pathway Praxis—Usage, Challenges, and Recommendations

In this section, we offer a conversation between the three of us in which we discuss and reflect on an event organized by one of the authors to honor Izzy. The event was a vigil for which we worked closely with the Black Lives Matter chapter of Utah, several Black community organizers and leaders, and the UVU African Diaspora Initiative. We had speakers, artists playing music and sharing spoken word poetry, and we heard directly from Izzy's family. One of the Latine organizers of the event asked that we honor Izzy with an *ofrenda*, or an offering that is often reminiscent of the Northern Mexican tradition of the Day of Dead, so at the end of the vigil, we displayed our *ofrenda* to Izzy and the community was invited to light candles and place them at her *ofrenda*. We not only sought to bring community members and organizers into the university space to bring attention but made this event a very emotional and personal part of who we were as well.

To fully grasp the context of the event, we recorded this dialogue on Zoom, transcribed it, and dedicated time to taking notes and reflections to ensure inclusive consideration. In presenting the dialogue, we emphasize our efforts as praxis, so it is important to connect how we mean the term. Brazilian educator and philosopher Paulo Freire (1996) defines *praxis* as a mode of reflection and action that challenges systems in need of change. This suggests that the notion of critique, and acting on that critique, is not only a mode of critical thinking; it is an act of engaging the world around us for better conditions. However, not all forms of resistance or critical engagement (i.e., praxis) look the same. Zembylas (2021) notes that refusal in higher education can manifest as affective disinvestment, when not everything done at the university is accepted as absolute truth or practice. Similarly, our conversation in the next section reflects our capacity to refuse the colonial and neoliberal agenda pervasive in university programming, framing the pathways as avenues for relational praxis in this context.

A Conversation on Refusal, Izzy's Event, and the University

Tino: It's good to see everyone again! Let's talk about Izzy's event and how what we did was a type of refusal of the university and the way it offers events and programs. I'd love to start by sharing what motivated me to create the event. To be honest, your pathways, along with Bre's identity as a Black woman, made sense to me. COA [Community Organizing & Activism] and CELR [Community-Engaged Learning and Research] are community-facing pathways that I believe present a visible tension to higher ed because real community-based organizing/activism and engaged learning and research represent the means by which we reimagine the university and dismantle its systems. Building on this idea of systems, and after reflecting on this event, I realized I had to challenge my own internal thinking on programs at UVU. I had to tell myself, "Why can't we do this?" or "Why not?"

Bre: I get emotional when I think about Izzy's event. I remember wanting to become a fellow to be able to experience what we felt that night. The programming that was already established was well intended, but I never felt the sense of community or doing something till that night was done. I felt like we did something that meant something in our community. Working on podcasts and research competitions as part of my pathway meant something, but what I did with y'all was a spiritual experience, I felt it so deeply within myself and that meant something and changed me.

Priscilla: Love being in this space with everyone. Personally, this really has been one of the few things done at UVU that hold space for community. I think a lot of places on campus claim to hold space for faculty, staff, and students but they don't actually do that. This event was the only time where I felt there was real community building in a spiritual sense. We were souls coming together for a common cause and feeling. It's what we need in Utah County, because in SLC [Salt Lake City] there is that, but we don't have that here. This also put my COA pathway into practice, like I got to witness what real community building is and do it.

Tino: Let's talk about how the other pathways play into what we did, because while COA and CELR were critical in starting this, we didn't apply them in isolation with the others.

Bre: Right, for example, the first ones that come to mind for me are Direct Service and Policy and Governance. For example, as soon as we began to share the event with our local community and student offices, we had so many organizations that often weren't involved want to help. The Party for Socialism and Liberation came to help us pass hand warmers out, and our local BSU [Black Student Union] offered music and spoken word. That felt like Direct Service to me.

Priscilla: Agreed, and Policy and Governance were at play because we were literally participating in helping drive a political process. You remember when BLM leadership told us this would be a good event to help remind the public of the case, as lawyers were compiling info for the investigation at the school district? The news stopped by, and I think we were able to help in that process!

Tino: What about Philanthropy and SECSR [Social Entrepreneurship and Corporate Social Responsibility]? I'm having a hard time seeing how those fit into what we did.

Bre: The African Diaspora [a UVU initiative] helped us promote the fundraising that was already happening with our BLM chapter, and I remember us spreading that info around online prior and after the event.

Tino: I forgot about that!

Priscilla: SECSR is hard. I feel like the university is its own business in some way, and we were able to utilize it to offer the space we needed for our event. But in another way, we were able to work with local Black- and POC-owned businesses to spread the word. I think that's part of ethical practices in business. Saying and taking a stance on an issue and not remaining silent. Honestly, just allowing people to feel what we were doing through some of these channels helped us a lot.

Tino: Y'all are so right. This event came out of a desire to be in relationship with community, but now I'm realizing the emotional element, and I never thought about that. I did not expect y'all to mention feeling and spirituality. I'll add my voice to yours as well. Izzy's event felt very different from a lot of the work I did in my years of higher ed. Not sure if I ever told you guys, but that event was the thing that made me realize I could leave. That night I went up to the center [Center for Social Impact] to help pack things away from the event, and I ended up finding some corner and crying out of joy. Like we did something. We really did something.

Bre: It was so needed. It was a responsive event. We were transitioning back from COVID, BLM, and trauma after trauma, and as a Black woman and being able to be with Izzy's family was powerful! It was a sorrowful event, and I love that it was allowed. And then having it be in a place that's so focused on "education" felt so resistive. In some way, having the event in a place where what we felt that isn't happening or allowed, made it spiritual.

Priscilla: Yes! It granted us a moment to feel what Izzy's family felt and where we're at, in this county, in this city. Proximity of these issues isn't around or isn't felt, particularly Blackness and neurodivergence, and yet these communities exist here. Holding that grief with Izzy's family isn't something that Western academia appreciates or acknowledges as something conducive to education or learning. Western academia isn't centered on community and focuses on the individual, and it definitely doesn't value vulnerability. We were holding the event on the grounds of an institution that doesn't do that or doesn't allow for it.

Tino: This makes me think that to refuse the university, one has to *feel*, and be okay with feeling, and I don't think we're allowed to feel in some ways. I love the center. At the same time, things felt very rote and traditional. Priscilla's Clothesline project felt very contextual, which was great, but the emotional charge of the event needed to be addressed, and it was work for us, it wasn't easy, and as I reflect on what's being said now, I'm thinking that feeling and emotion is a refusal of institutionalization.

Bre: A big motivator for us was our emotions, and if that wasn't allowed, it wouldn't have happened. This event was loud. We made it to the news, we had tons of community members show up and support, and we did it without the planning and processes that we'd take on during our normal programs and events. We had to be loud because there were restrictions. Our center is devoted to making impact, organization, and so on, but our emotional response was our impact. It took some bravery on my part to be part of this, because I was nervous of how it would be received, and we didn't do any of the typical program things like record how many people attended and track metrics. It's almost as if we were refusing to be told what impact should look like.

Tino: It's almost as if emotion was positioned within the pathways to carve out a new form of impact? I'm not sure if I'm doing it justice, but I felt like we were humanizing the pathways, possibly? Maybe leading to new visions of what impact could look and feel like? Pushing against Western academic interpretations of the pathways and the Pathway framework?

Priscilla: I can see that, but honestly, I am so frustrated with academia and the university's data-driven strategies. It is so discouraging to have programs and events to help motivate people to think, reflect, and feel, but you're just asked about how many people showed up or how many flyers did you pass out? Like does any of that humanize the process? Why are we so caught up in numbers and stats? Being in the current position I've been in [UVU presidential intern for equity, inclusion, and diversity] and around the higher admin, a lot of them don't care about emotions amongst students, faculty, and staff, and that's disappointing. They just care about the numbers because that is what our systems rely on.

Bre: I think you can humanize the pathways, but the numbers aspect can't be at the center of it. The university is the same way, because you can't be an effective administrator if you're getting halted by emotions. Especially in the United States, and as a therapist at the university, I'm seeing this more in college students, especially those from degrees and majors that stress numbers, products, and data-driven programming, where stifling that emotion cuts off connections to living and community. It is so sad that a place like the university, that has so much wealth to create those kinds of environments, falls so short of that. In the end, social and emotional well-being are not a priority, and when these thoughts come out, they have to be validated with metrics. But why can't we do things on a whim and respond to things when we need to?

Tino: Honestly, I wasn't expecting y'all to say this, but I'm not surprised either. Studying what I have of the university placed such a focus of the place and program rather than the impact of people.

Tino: And you work in DEI? And you would think that's where the focus is to transform the university, but there's even a dehumanizing effect there as well.

Priscilla: 100%. It's very discouraging, and it's hard. I had this event that I did, not long ago. My emotions were very much part of building that event and thinking through it. But that was all lost in the process of our EDI (equity, diversity, and inclusion) office. People were excited initially about having powerful conversations amongst faculty, staff, and students because legislators were beginning their attack on our work in 2022, and I wanted to have these events so people can come as their full selves and be vulnerable. But as time went on, everything was lost, because it became about RSVPs and expansion rhetoric, and eventually I was like, why does that matter? I was emotionally charged, and like Izzy's event, I wanted to respond, and it just kind of fell apart because it had to be institutionalized.

Bre: Planning it through your office probably didn't leave you enough autonomy to enact what we did. Despite being a part of the university, people in the center worked hard to dismantle power dynamics in a way that we could do what we did. I felt like everyone was my peer and [it was] so healing for me because our relationships were so well stressed, which makes me ask, How do you perform refusal when those power dynamics can't be ignored?

Priscilla: Personally, I love at the center how Cassie and Tino introduced that and made that part of our work. I saw y'all as my advisors and mentors, but I could talk to y'all about anything. I could truly be my full self with each of you. Western academia and institutionalization does the opposite; it shuns and shames students and doesn't allow students and staff to have emotional and horizontal relations. Honestly, it feels like that's why my event didn't pan out, because my relationships with staff were very vertical. I'm your boss and you are my subordinate, and that was hard for me. I couldn't stand up for myself.

Tino: The center really did a great job in centering relationality in our process and ethics. Personally, I saw it play out with the pathways as well. We were encouraged to look at them as a piece to a whole and interweave them in a lot of our programs and events. I do think using them as organically as we did at Izzy's event feels different though. It was as if we didn't have to force any of them into the event. Each one kind of fell into place as we built everything. But is that because relationships were at the core of what we did?

Bre: From the beginning, we set our ethics as priority. Cassie was able to offer that systematic approach when she recommended space for relationships, personal discussions, and even discomfort in our program conversations with our diversity of opinions, and we weren't going to judge each other. At times those convos kept going on for so long! I wonder if this type of approach allowed us to think and act critically, which in my mind, informs the way we approach each pathway as well, viewing them as connected pieces to create change.

Priscilla: So involving emotion humanizes our work [the pathways], which is only possible when relationships are centered. That's why things like EDI within the university don't work. The kinds of spaces like the ones we're talking about would not be possible, because the approach is data-driven first. There should be a critical glance at how we're viewing EID work in the first place, which sucks because conservative circles are also attacking it, but we question that kind of work with the intent to humanize it. We need to dialogue about these things and about how we all see it and then discuss what the impact of those views are with students. It's frustrating when those higher up use a top-down approach. Cassie and you [Tino] were like, we want everyone to have good relationships with us and each other, because all of this takes time.

Tino: So how do we do this within the university?

Bre: Well, why would we want to institutionalize what we've done?

Conclusion—Relational Praxis as a Mode for All Six Pathways

We decided to end our section with Bre's statement asking why does everything have to be institutionalized because it demonstrates the tension of radical praxis within an institution, emphasizing that our work doesn't need to be binary, such as inside or outside of systems. Instead, we engage the gray, the middle, the borderlands, the messiness of doing this kind of work within institutions. As change agents committed to collectivity, we navigate beyond the romantic educational mirage that higher ed often projects (Stein, 2021). Embracing our messiness in the work as refusal means that, despite being within the university and part of an institutional center, we can still deliver on work that challenges the systems we operate in. This is what it means to be within the university, but not of it, or existing within places of institutional violence, but not living or enacting those logics.

How, then, does our work constitute refusal? As mentioned previously, Grande frames refusal at the university as an extension of Black and

Indigenous politics and praxis that refuses individuality, inspires reflexivity with community, and works toward mutuality outside of institutions and with land. While land was not specifically engaged in our work, Izzy's event allowed us to connect with local Black organizations and community members in a way that made it more than just about our center or the university. This inspired further reflections from all of us on the impact of relationality within and outside of campus, because everything surrounding Izzy's event became about deepening connections with our own communities—and not in a profit-driven or exploitive fashion. It became about feeling the trauma of Izzy taking her own life and feeling like we were all woven into her story—to make sure it never happened again.

As mentioned previously, emotion plays a role in refusing academia's coldness to a life lost outside of the institution. Zembylas sees refusal enacted as pedagogy when we help students affectively disinvest from the university. Izzy's event wasn't built with a metrics-first approach. It wasn't about institutional PR or a headline. Instead, we centered the event around Izzy's life and invited Black poets, musicians, and political activists to share their words. We created an altar honoring Izzy's life, and members of several communities responded with their participation, lighting candles at the altar. Refusal in this case meant not waiting for the university to create spaces for us, but for people to make and claim them for themselves. We need to realize that emotions and feelings are okay, and even necessary, in spaces of learning. We need to be vulnerable. We need to have hard conversations. We need to build trusting relationships, and we need to be willing to engage difficult moments in our communities. This doesn't mean abandoning existing frameworks and methodologies of our offices or centers. As Rodríguez (2019) encourages, we should think beyond the boundaries of classroom, or in this case, beyond our centers and programs—and reroute our investments toward community and collectivity in ways that humanize the methods we are utilizing, such as the pathways. In the case of the event for Izzy, we did so by creating what we came to feel was an interconnected and relational form of praxis.

We did not apply a singular pathway to this effort, nor did we predetermine how this aligned with our values, mission, or structural purposes. We saw a need, and we engaged it with all the tools at our disposal such that the multiplicity of pathways could be adapted to the context. In this way, we saw each pathway in our framing of the event as a tool for community engagement, woven into our praxis. This led to refusal, which in turn opened pathways of relationship building and deeper engagement with our community. Viewing the pathways as an interconnected form of praxis also puts into context how oppression operates in our society. It doesn't happen in a vacuum or a universal context but confronts our humanity in multiple ways. In viewing the pathways as an interconnected and relational praxis, we experience our engagement as intersectional, pluralistic, and context-driven. We are who we are, where we need to be, and on January 27th, we organized a vigil for Izzy Tichenor in collaboration with Black-led organizations from both on and off campus. Our intentions were to show solidarity with Izzy's family, remind local institutions and community members of what had happened, and be in better relationship with those organizations leading the fight against systemic racism in Utah, where Izzy took her life. We'd like to thank Izzy's family, UT BLM, and all our friends in CSI and our local community.

———

It's October 29, 2023, almost 2 years after Izzy's vigil on campus. We all just received a personal invitation to join her family and other community members at a celebration event of Izzy's life. With the support of BLM Utah and other organizers, Izzy's mom was able to push for stronger accountability in schools and policies that better protect students like Izzy. News coverage of our vigil served as a powerful reminder to the local community of Izzy's story as the case made its way to court. We were proud to do something that helped Izzy's cause and equally proud to refuse the university.

References

Cairo, D. K., & Cabal, V. (2021). *Corporatization of student affairs*. Springer.

Coulthard, G. S. (2014). *Red skin, White masks: Rejecting the colonial politics of recognition*. University of Minnesota Press.

Elizabeth, J. (2021, November 12). *10-year-old Utah Black and autistic student dies by suicide weeks after scathing DOJ report on school district*. CNN. https://www.cnn.com/2021/11/12/us/isabella-izzy-tichenor-utah-bullying-claims-suicide/index.html

Ferreira da Silva, D. (2018). Hacking the subject: Black feminism and refusal beyond the limits of critique. *PhiloSOPHIA, 8*(1), 19–41. https://doi.org/10.1353/phi.2018.0001

Freire, P. (1996). *Pedagogy of the oppressed* (Revised ed.). Continuum.

Gaston-Gayles, J. L., Wolf-Wendel, L. E., Tuttle, K. N., Twombly, S. B., & Ward, K. (2005). From disciplinarian to change agent: How the civil rights era changed the roles of student affairs professionals. *NASPA Journal, 42*(3), 263–282. https://doi.org/10.2202/1949-6605.1508

Grande, S. (2018). Refusing the university. In E. Tuck & K. W. Yang (Eds.), *Toward what justice?* (pp. 47–65). Routledge.

Harney, S., & Moten, F. (2013). *The undercommons: Fugitive planning and Black study.* Minor Compositions.

Kelley, R. D. (2016). Black study, Black struggle. *The Boston Review.* http://boston-review.net/forum/robin-d-g-kelley-black-study-black-struggle

McGranahan, C. (2016). Theorizing refusal: An introduction. *Cultural Anthropology, 31*(3), 319–325.

Naepi, S., Stein, S., Ahenakew, C., & Andreotti, V. D. O. (2017). A cartography of higher education: Attempts at inclusion and insights from Pasifika scholarship in Aotearoa New Zealand. In C. Reid & J. Major (Eds.), *Global teaching: Southern perspectives on teachers working with diversity* (pp. 81–99). Palgrave MacMillan. https://doi.org/10.1057/978-1-137-52526-0_5

Rodríguez, Y. (2019). Pedagogies of refusal. *The Radical Teacher, 115,* 5–12. https://doi.org/10.5195/rt.2019.672

Simpson, A. (2007). On ethnographic refusal: Indigeneity, "voice" and colonial citizenship. *Junctures: The Journal for Thematic Dialogue, 9,* 67–80.

Simpson, A. (2014). *Mohawk interruptus: Political life across the borders of settler states.* Duke University Press.

Stanford Haas Center. (2023, July 3). Pathways of Public Service and Civic Engagement. https://haas.stanford.edu/about/our-approach/pathways-public-service-and-civic-engagement

Stein, S. (2021). What can decolonial and abolitionist critiques teach the field of higher education? *The Review of Higher Education, 44*(3), 387–414. https://doi.org/10.1353/rhe.2021.0000

Wilder, C. S. (2013). *Ebony and ivy: Race, slavery, and the troubled history of America's universities.* Bloomsbury.

Wolf-Wendel, L. E., Twombly, S. B., Tuttle, K. N., Ward, K., & Gaston-Gayles, J. L. (2004). *Reflecting back, looking forward: Civil rights and student affairs.* NASPA.

Wynter, S. (2006). On how we mistook the map for the territory, and reimprisoned ourselves in our unbearable wrongness of being, of desêtre: Black studies toward the human project. In L. R. Gordon & J. A. Gordon (Eds.), *A companion to African-American studies* (pp. 107–118). Wiley.

Zembylas, M. (2021). Refusal as affective and pedagogical practice in higher education decolonization: A modest proposal. *Teaching in Higher Education, 26*(7–8), 953–968. https://doi.org/10.1080/13562517.2021.1900816

Chapter 18

EXPANDING ACCESS AND REFRAMING PERSPECTIVES

Exploring Community Engagement Professionals' Use of the Pathways Framework

Renee Sedlacek Lee

T here is no shortage of complex problems to be solved in this world, and I firmly believe that institutions of higher education play a critical role in preparing the future leaders needed to tackle them. However, most institutions have not found a way to lean into the prevailing social, economic, political, and environmental issues facing communities and successfully develop a cohesive approach to teaching students about social change (McBride & Mlyn, 2020). In the book *Connecting Civic Engagement and Social Innovation Toward Higher Education's Democratic Promise*, Amanda Moore McBride and Eric Mlyn (2020) argue for "a reinvigoration of purpose and even a new organizing framework for higher education's approach to social change" (p. 164). One framework gaining popularity among community engagement professionals is the Pathways of Public Service and Civic Engagement.

Recognizing the need for a more cohesive approach to teaching students about social change is what initially drew me to the Pathways framework. At the time, I was serving as the director of community-engaged learning for Drake University, and we were beginning to explore how we might integrate a broader emphasis on social innovation and changemaking into the student experience. My attendance at the Ashoka U Exchange in 2019 provided me with valuable insights, revealing striking parallels between the new-to-me world of social innovation and the more familiar field of service-learning and community engagement. This experience at the exchange sparked my interest in understanding how institutions of higher education operationalize and engage students in these distinct but seemingly similar movements. Although the original creators of the Pathways framework probably never intended it to be used as a strategic planning tool (Schnaubelt & SchwartzCoffey, 2016), it quickly became the guiding framework around which we organized our community engagement efforts at Drake.

During this period of exploration, I was already enrolled in a doctoral program. As my understanding of the Pathways framework grew, it also sparked an academic curiosity about social innovation and changemaking. This curiosity paired with the practical application of pathways in our work at Drake naturally led me to explore how these emerging concepts could inform my dissertation research. And although my doctoral studies were not initially intended to advance our initiatives at Drake, as I delved deeper into the topic, it became clear that my findings were also contributing valuable insights to my colleagues and the broader community engagement efforts at Drake. This dual benefit reinforced the importance of my research and further motivated me to explore how the Pathways framework could meet the pressing need for a cohesive approach to teaching students about social change.

So when it came time to select a dissertation topic, I thought, "Here's this framework that we have found very useful in bringing these two movements together in practice; therefore, I wonder what value other community engagement professionals have found in using it? Could pathways be an answer to Mcbride and Mlyn's call for a new organizing framework?" The shift from practitioner to scholar, initially undertaken for academic purposes only, became a pivotal factor in advancing my understanding of the pathways, informing our practice at Drake, and as any starry-eyed doctoral student can hope for, making a tiny contribution to the broader conversation of an emerging field.

Setting the Context

While service-learning and social entrepreneurship programs share the common goal of equipping students with the skills to solve social problems, they often operate independently on college campuses (Butin, 2010; Enos, 2015; McBride & Mlyn, 2015, 2016, 2020; Schnaubelt & SchwartzCoffey, 2016). The absence of a shared framework across the broader fields of civic engagement and social innovation makes it difficult to unify language and practice, compare programs across institutions, and understand their impact on students, communities, and campus organizations (Kim & Krampetz, 2016; Schnaubelt & SchwartzCoffey, 2016; Stanford Haas Center for Public Service, n.d.). Furthermore, Kim and Krampetz (2016) argue that departmental divisions and the lack of shared language often result in redundant staffing structures that hinder collaboration among faculty and staff and confuse students seeking clear paths.

Developing a holistic civic engagement and social innovation model requires universities to rethink their organizational frameworks. It also requires an institutional strategic leader dedicated to the cause (Mathias & Banks, 2015). Uniquely qualified for this role are community engagement professionals (CEPs), higher education practitioners whose formal administrative responsibilities are to support student community engagement programming and service-learning (Dostilio, 2017a, 2017b; Dostilio & McReynolds, 2015; Dostilio & Perry, 2017; McReynolds & Shields, 2015). With a campus-wide perspective, CEPs have the capacity to identify initiatives across the institution that target related social issues or have similar civic goals (Dostilio & McReynolds, 2015). While there is an expanding body of research on CEPs, there is limited information available about the frameworks they are using to involve students in civic engagement and social innovation. Research exploring how institutions of higher education are implementing the Pathways framework and how CEPs' perceptions of using the framework to educate students for social impact lays the foundation for establishing a shared framework across the fields of civic engagement and social innovation.

Research Purpose and Background

My doctoral dissertation aimed to explore how the Pathways of Public Service and Civic Engagement framework supports CEPs in their efforts to educate students for social impact and engaged citizenship. The study followed a basic qualitative design, with the Pathways framework serving as the conceptual framework. Participants were recruited through their affiliation with the Pathways Working Group, and data were collected through semistructured interviews. A total of 12 participants, representing six private 4-year institutions, four public 4-year institutions, and two community colleges, participated in the study. Institution size varied from 1,300 to 40,000 full-time students. On average, participants had 5 years of experience with the pathways. All but two participants were using both the framework and the survey tool; two participants indicated they were utilizing only the framework. The participant sample was predominantly White and female, with four identifying as male and only one participant identifying as a person of color.

Relevant Insights

Interviews with the CEPs in this study confirm that the Pathways framework is a valuable tool for several reasons. The findings indicate it is a critical tool for expanding the types of engagement that are traditionally offered on campuses as well as diversifying participation in community engagement initiatives. Each participant articulated how the pathways had helped them organize the work of social impact and emphasized the value of belonging to a network of people from different colleges and universities using the same tool. The following insights offer salient themes distilled from the study.

How the Pathways Show Up

As evidenced by the case studies in this book, CEPs are using diverse approaches to engage students in the various pathways. While deeper analysis of the pathways-specific activities shared by each participant was beyond the scope of my study, some relevant insights emerged from the interviews to help characterize each pathway. Example activities and characteristics shared by study participants are presented in Table 18.1. For example, the Community-Engaged Learning and Research Pathway appears to be the most heavily resourced and where the most intentional integration of reflection occurs. Direct Service was frequently identified by participants as the pathway that students are most familiar with and the one they regard as the "most accessible." Participants noted the Policy and Governance Pathway is typically leveraged to help students

Table 18.1. Pathway-Specific Activities and Characteristics as Described by Participants

Value	Example Activities	Key Characteristics
Community-Engaged Learning and Research		
"Deepens understanding of social issues"	• course designation • grants • faculty fellows • awards • student scholarships • certificate program	• experiential learning • discipline agnostic • reflection often required
Direct Service		
"Exposure to community issues"	• days of service • alternative breaks • volunteering • service awards • employee VTO • opportunities database • paid student coordinators	• episodic and sporadic • issue-based • decentralized • reflection not monitored or required • most accessible entry point
Policy and Governance		
"Understanding the role of government"	• voter education and registration • hosting officials and candidate debates • internships • student government	• decentralized, but often led by the Political Science Department • heavily focused on voter engagement
Community Organizing and Activism		
"Opportunity to have agency in an issue"	• dialogue trainings • awareness programming • awards • online activist resource guide	• heavily focused on identity-based factors • often led by DEI or multicultural office or student culture groups • CEPs feel tension with supporting it • grassroots and reactionary
Philanthropy		
"Mobilizing others to give money or goods"	• giving campaigns and fundraising • donation drives • experiential philanthropy courses	• least developed • organic, often not coordinated • most often initiated by student clubs or driven by Institutional Advancement Office • concerns with students' lack of financial resources
Social Entrepreneurship and Corporate Social Responsibility		
"Business as a force for good"	• pitch competitions • courses • centers for entrepreneurship	• siloed to business schools • appeals to business-minded students

understand the various roles of government in social change; however, example activities cited by participants were primarily limited to voter registration and education. Participants frequently mentioned examples of student engagement with Community Organizing and Activism that were reactionary to point-in-time issues of injustice. Only one participant was proactively working on resources to support students in effective Community Organizing and Activism. On several campuses, the Philanthropy Pathway was focused primarily on institutional fundraising, while some institutions integrated philanthropy activities into coursework or cocurricular programming. The pathway that was the least understood by the CEPs in the study was Social Entrepreneurship and Corporate Social Responsibility, often articulated as the pathway for engaging business students.

Organizing and Explaining the Work of a CEP

Similar to the practitioner examples included in this book, CEPs in my study shared that they utilize the pathways as a guiding framework in a variety of ways: as an institutional planning tool, a departmental organizing framework, a basis for course design, and a blueprint for cocurricular program design, among other uses. For example, when asked what they would like others to know about the Pathways framework, one participant highlighted its use to help "faculty integrate into their class different ways of thinking about community impact. . . . You could integrate it into your career services, into your student programs, your leadership programs, or housing programs. . . . There's so much flexibility." Another CEP described the Pathways framework as the field's "next practice" due to its forward-thinking nature and practical elements that guide students in engaging with social change. Participants frequently mentioned using the pathways to help students understand how to "make a difference," "make an impact," or "create social change," further emphasizing the focus on social transformation. However, for most campuses, the office in which CEPs operate does not directly facilitate programming across all the pathways. As campus size and operations scale, the engagement opportunities of each pathway are even more siloed.

Inevitably, the pathways play a pivotal role in efforts to coordinate social impact efforts across a campus. Moreover, they are instrumental in pushing CEPs, understanding of community engagement beyond traditional concepts of service-learning. As one participant explained,

We decided as a college to shift away from the term service-learning . . . and I don't think I could have gotten to that place, and have been comfortable with that, if I hadn't been introduced to the [framework] and really pushed to think beyond the orthodoxy of service-learning.

Another participant shared how the pathways help her explain her work to others. "My parents cannot articulate what I do," she said, "but when I told them about the pathways, they were like, oh, okay, that makes sense." These insights highlight that CEPs are broadening their scope of practice and the Pathways framework is providing them with a vocabulary and visual aid to do so.

Access and Inclusion

The Pathways framework is highly praised for its simplicity and accessibility, especially when compared to other models like the Social Change Wheel 2.0 (Iowa & Minnesota Campus Compact, 2024). "The language [of the framework] is overall student-friendly," commented one participant. Another shared, "The framework has really helped us talk about our work in a context that feels really accessible for students." Several participants mentioned how their students often come from a direct service mindset and that the framework helps them recognize that there are other ways to create change in their community. For example, a participant described how students initially view their campus community engagement requirement as merely performing tasks like "petting cats or painting fences." However, after being introduced to the pathways as a visual, their understanding expands. She said, "You show them [the pathways diagram] or refer back to the [survey] tool that they took, and they say, 'Oh, I didn't realize it could take all these forms, and oh, hey, I'm already on Student Government [so] I'm already doing this policy and governance thing and I didn't really think of it that way [before].'" And for CEPs working with community college, commuter, or part-time students the framework has proven particularly helpful in overcoming barriers commonly associated with participation in direct service activities, such as time constraints and transportation issues. As one participant explained, "I don't want students to think that [direct service] is the only way they can make change in their community . . . some [students] already know that they're doing the other pathways, and I think it's important to give equal value to those."

Consequently, as the Pathways framework helps CEPs expand the types of engagement traditionally offered on their campuses, it is also expanding who is involved. Many CEPs in the study shared specific examples of how including the Social Entrepreneurship and Corporate Social Responsibility Pathway helps them appeal to business majors and students with "different motivations" than those who are typically drawn to the Direct Service Pathway. "I think it can grab the attention of students in a different way than some of the other pathways," commented one participant. "It's helpful," she continued, in demonstrating that "even business has a role in social change."

The framework also helps faculty recognize how their teaching and research can contribute to positive social impact in ways that may not always occur under narrow definitions of *service-learning*. A CEP described her strategy of utilizing the framework with faculty to initiate discussions about diverse methods of incorporating a community experience into their courses, illustrating with specific examples from different pathways. She shared how the Pathways framework helps faculty "close the loop" between their disciplinary expertise and the various pathways by demonstrating how their work can benefit a community or be utilized by citizens or organizations. "Using the framework, and talking in that language, has helped a lot of faculty understand that their research is actually publicly engaged scholarship," she explained. "It's changing the way they think about what they're doing!"

A Network of Resources and Support

CEPs in this study affirmed that the Pathways Working Group, with its diverse perspectives from institutions of various types and sizes, is invaluable for brainstorming and adapting the framework to suit specific institutional contexts. The Working Group also offers CEPs a crucial network of support, especially those who often feel siloed in their work. One participant mentioned, "When you are a solo person doing this work, being able to chat with people who do similar work is huge . . . the fact that there is a working group that I can be a part of has been really nice." Another participant shared that the Working Group is what has motivated them to stay involved. "The opportunity to get on the [quarterly] calls, and [share] what you are struggling with [and hear other's ideas] . . . that kind of is where the magic happens."

Several CEPs in this study also expressed how belonging to a collective effort validates their work. A participant shared how "the fact that there is a working group, there are people focused on these pathways, it's not just us, it's not just some crazy idea," helped them gain buy-in from their administration. Another participant described how motivating it has been to participate in the Working Group, commenting, "I feel like we're contributing to something [bigger than ourselves], to a movement, a shift in the way higher ed does this." And for others, the sense of accountability to peers in the network presents the opportunity to rethink their work. For example, one participant commented, "If I'm pushing this broader international network to consider, 'Have you thought about this?', the question then is, Have I thought about this in my own work?"

Recommendations and Implications

The findings of this study suggest a fundamental shift is taking place in how CEPs perceive their work, how students conceptualize service, and how faculty integrate community engagement into their teaching and research. Moreover, while many findings align with existing research, some warrant further exploration. I offer the following implications for practitioners and recommendations for future research.

Find Ways to Intentionally Integrate Reflection

The CEPs I interviewed frequently shared stories about the conversations, dialogue, and advising prompted by the Pathways framework. For example, one participant explained, "I have always found the conversations around the framework more informative than the tool itself." Another participant shared, "I just haven't found anything that has facilitated those conversations in the same way. . . . It has sparked some of the most meaningful and rich conversations around how change happens with students that I've ever had." Comments like these affirm that engaging students in reflection on the pathways is when the learning happens.

However, when considering how various pathways show up across a campus, it is clear that the quality of reflection can vary considerably across pathways. For example, reflection was a prominent feature within examples of the Community-Engaged Learning and Research Pathway, but rather sparse or absent altogether in the other pathways. While this observation is not surprising given many CEPs' theoretical grounding in service-learning, it presents an opportunity for CEPs to strategize on how to strengthen students' learning across the pathways. As research indicates, reflection is a critical component to high-impact student learning experiences (Ash & Clayton, 2009; Kuh, 2008). Therefore, a recommendation for all Pathways practitioners is to find a way to intentionally integrate reflection into experiences across all the pathways. However, this could prove challenging since most CEPs don't "own" all programming across the pathways. Therefore, leaning into the pathways as a shared campus framework can serve to unify the language and goals of diverse, and often decentralized, units across campus.

Contextualize the Pathways to the Local Campus

While we all can acknowledge the intersectionality between different pathways, the organizational structures within our institutions often create silos in our programming. For example, multiple participants reflected on how being positioned within student affairs can limit their ability to support students across all the pathways. Likewise, factors like campus culture, institution type (private or public 4-year, community college, or trade school), structure of the academic calendar (semester, quarter, trimester), student demographics, and the broader community context are important to consider when determining how to use the pathways at your institution. My study affirms that the Pathways framework does not constitute a typology but a guiding framework that can be molded and adapted to fit specific campus needs. I liken it to the analogy of shoes. While we all wear shoes and understand them as universally essential, the specific shoes we wear depend on a variety of factors, including our personal style, the activity at hand, our budget, the size of our feet, and the shopping options available to us. Similarly, to effectively contextualize the pathways may require modifying the name to fit the campus culture, creating a resource that lists local nonprofit groups for each pathway, or redesigning the pathways graphic and other support materials to fit your institution's brand and style.

Develop an Awareness of Your Implicit Biases

Although the study did not analyze data with sociopolitical positionality in mind and this chapter is not intended to offer an in-depth exploration of sociopolitical influences on CEPs' understanding of the various pathways, it is important to acknowledge, nevertheless. Several participants' comments hinted at implicit biases that seemed to influence which pathways hold prominence on their campus and might affect their approach to student engagement. To create a new organizing framework for higher education's approach to social change, it is imperative for Pathways practitioners to be mindful of their implicit biases.

A CEP's personal experience (or lack thereof) in a particular pathway should not serve as a justification for how they guide (or fail to guide) students. For example, one participant commented on how social entrepreneurship wasn't their "area of expertise" and in essence excused themselves from needing to care about it as a legitimate strategy for social change. In a contrasting case, another participant expressed how the pathways gave them freedom to engage students in organizing and activism, an activity that they were personally interested in but that otherwise would have been condemned on their campus. While it's human nature to rely on our personal experience while advising students, our bias toward or against specific pathways shouldn't be used to indoctrinate students to our way of thinking or dismiss a student's specific interest and engagement. Otherwise, we run the risk of missing opportunities to broaden the scope of who and what is included in the realm of social impact.

Conclusion

The CEP participants in this study affirmed that the Pathways framework is expanding their thinking beyond the confines of traditional service-learning, pushing their students to engage beyond direct service, and bringing more students into social impact approaches that they might not have otherwise seen themselves fitting into. While the Pathways framework was originally intended for student advising, it is now catalyzing a shift in mindset and practice. This transformation is evident by changes to titles and language, underscoring the profound influence of the Pathways framework on reshaping the landscape of community engagement in higher education.

I began this chapter invoking McBride and Mlyn's call for a new organizing framework for higher education's approach to social change. While the findings of this study support the idea that a universal typology should not be the goal, they affirm that the Pathways framework is playing a pivotal role in unifying and advancing the field of social impact education. The world faces a multitude of complex challenges, and their solutions are far from simple. Addressing these problems requires the engagement of diverse problem-solvers globally, equipped with the disposition, skills, and knowledge to drive meaningful change. To create a more equitable and inclusive world, institutions of higher education must teach students how to approach these issues from multiple perspectives. By focusing on various pathways to social impact, they can integrate social innovation and civic engagement and provide a guiding framework for how to do so.

References

Ash, S. L., & Clayton, P. H. (2009, Fall). Generating, deepening, and documenting learning: The power of critical reflection in applied learning. *Journal of Applied Learning in Higher Education, 1*, 25–48.

Butin, D. W. (2010). *Service-learning in theory and practice: The future of community engagement in higher education.* Palgrave Macmillan.

Dostilio, L. D. (Ed.). (2017a). *The community engagement professional in higher education: A competency model for an emerging field.* Campus Compact.

Dostilio, L. D. (2017b). The professionalization of community engagement. In C. Dolgon, T. D. Mitchell, & T. K. Eatman (Eds.), *The Cambridge handbook of service learning and community engagement* (pp. 370–384). Cambridge University Press.

Dostilio, L. D., & McReynolds, M. (2015). Community engagement professionals in the circle of service-learning and the greater civic enterprise. *Michigan Journal of Community Service Learning, 22*(1), 113–116.

Dostilio, L. D., & Perry, L. G. (2017). An explanation of community engagement professionals as professionals and leaders. In L. D. Dostilio (Ed.), *The community engagement professional in higher education: A competency model for an emerging field* (pp. 1–26). Campus Compact.

Enos, S. (2015). *Service-learning and social entrepreneurship in higher education: A pedagogy of social change.* Palgrave Macmillan.

Iowa & Minnesota Campus Compact. (2024). *Social Change Wheel.* https://iamn campuscompact.org/resources/social-change-wheel/

Kim, M., & Krampetz, E. (2016). The rise of the sophisticated changemaker. *Diversity & Democracy, 19*(3), 8–10. https://dgmg81phhvh63.cloudfront.net/content/user-photos/Publications/Archives/Diversity-Democracy/DD_19-3_SU16.pdf

Kuh, G. (2008). *High-impact educational practices: What they are, who has access to them, and why they matter.* American Association of Colleges and Universities.

Mathias, N., & Banks, B. (2015). Institutional strategic leader. In. M. McReynolds & E. Shields (Eds.), *Diving deep in community engagement: A model for professional development.* Iowa Campus Compact.

McBride, A., & Mlyn, E. (2015, February 2). Innovation alone won't fix social problems. *The Chronicle of Higher Education.* http://www.chronicle.com/article/Innovation-Alone-Won-t-Fix/151551

McBride, A., & Mlyn, E. (2016). Social innovation and civic engagement: Toward a shared future? *Diversity & Democracy, 19*(3), 4–7. https://dgmg81phhvh63.cloudfront.net/content/user-photos/Publications/Archives/Diversity-Democracy/DD_19-3_SU16.pdf

McBride, A. M., & Mlyn, E. (Eds.). (2020). *Connecting civic engagement and social innovation: Toward higher education's democratic promise.* Stylus.

McReynolds, M., & Shields, E. (2015). *Diving deep in community engagement: A model for professional development.* Iowa Campus Compact.

Schnaubelt, T., & SchwartzCoffey, C. (2016). Public service and civic engagement: Multiple pathways to social change. *Diversity & Democracy, 19*(3), 24–25. https://dgmg81phhvh63.cloudfront.net/content/user-photos/Publications/Archives/Diversity-Democracy/DD_19-3_SU16.pdf

Stanford Haas Center for Public Service. (n.d.). *Pathways conceptual foundations and evidence.* https://haas.stanford.edu/about/our-approach/pathways-public-service-and-civic-engagement/pathways-public-service-and-civic

Chapter 19

CHALLENGES, POSSIBILITIES, AND CONSCIOUS RESPONSIBILITY

Directions for the Field

Aaliyah Baker

C urrent approaches to developing student civic identity through civic engagement risk exacerbating or endorsing systems of oppression unless there is a simultaneous commitment to addressing structural and systemic oppression in society. There is an opportunity to strengthen the Pathways of Public Service and Civic Engagement framework if societal oppression is addressed as a central focus of its integration.

There has never been a more opportune time to reimagine civic engagement through an emphasis on both individual and collective agency. To achieve this, developing a critical consciousness of structural and systemic issues (influenced by Freirean pedagogy) will occur alongside understanding pathways of service. This is our starting point. Political engagement is connected to the development of civic identity in students;

however, becoming engaged members of society is only one part of civic identity. Higher education should seek additional strategies that call on students to challenge the inherent perpetuation of historical injustice and connect civic learning directly to social action. If the goal of civic identity is to invite the development of a theory of mind around human agency, it is essential to reflect on the philosophy of service through the lens of socially constructed isms stemming from sociological categories of difference, such as racism, sexism, and ableism. This process begins with critically examining and challenging the inherent power structures embedded in the concept of service.

Freire's (2005) idea of *conscientização* refers to "learning to perceive social, political, and economic contradictions and to take action against the oppressive elements of reality" (p. 35). Expanding on this concept, I aim to support the commitment to foster intentional focus on social issues such as race as an ideological construct that perpetuates injustice to inform a process for understanding the problem of internalized oppression even when we articulate our democratic imperative. In this chapter, I explore possibilities for examining individual and group identity in relation to civic identity in a racialized society. I then offer suggestions for integrating theoretical and interpretive frameworks of critical consciousness in ways that invite a deeper analysis of race and racism and center strategies to develop a stronger lens for racial justice. The suggestions are informed by my scholarship and teaching and are deeply embedded in both the formal and informal work of a community engaged practitioner-scholar. To strengthen our commitment to community-engaged learning and research, I offer a critique of civic identity frameworks and suggest ways to align current critical literature with emerging goals in the field. I pursue deeper questions and thought experiments, using the Pathways framework to explore specific examples of what it would look like in practice to shift toward critical consciousness in civic identity as a vision for change. Without taking into account a collective commitment to solving the social crisis of racism, civic identity development efforts risk becoming part of the problem.

Civic identity and critical theory are complementary approaches to social change (Suzina & Tufte, 2020). Developing critical consciousness can transform institutional and individual practices, disrupting ingrained habits of mind that perpetuate social isms and systemic injustice. Emphasizing critical consciousness in civic identity is crucial, as it lies at the heart of understanding how both individual and collective civic identities relate to social change. This chapter articulates the need for more carefully constructed models of public service and civic engagement initiatives to transform institutional and individual practices during troubled times.

Civic identity, as defined by Hart et al. (2011), is "a set of beliefs and emotions about oneself as a participant in civic life" (p. 773). A heightened awareness of social issues, coupled with a commitment to fostering critical consciousness, is essential for nurturing a moral compass in community engagement work. This is an important topic of conversation among practitioners and scholars alike. However, postsecondary education often seems less committed to addressing the ethical and intellectual injustices faced by communities of color and more focused on protecting power and privilege associated with wealth, gender, and race. This is evident in the continued marginalization of Black and Indigenous people of color who are frequently treated as second-class citizens perceived to have been granted special permission to be present on college campuses and universities rather than being treated as individuals whose presence has been fully represented and included all along (Ladson-Billings & Tate, 1995). Substantial literature, data, and current events indicate that our social systems have not only perpetuated inequity but, in many cases, have exacerbated disparities for people of color. The onset of a global health, racial, and economic pandemic in 2020, followed by recent landmark court decisions overturning affirmative action in college admissions, has intensified our commitment to this dialogue. If we are not increasing our ability to recognize where and when systems of oppression are creating unnecessary barriers, then we have failed to learn from the lessons of the past. Similarly, without applying a lens of equity and justice to our work on civic identity development, we fail to practice the common good.

This chapter is a call for institutions of higher education to consider the responsibility and commitment to addressing social injustice as a fundamental purpose of their mission. The questions, key points, and examples raised in this chapter urge community engagement professionals in higher education to continue to challenge the exclusionary, marginal, and mediocre attempts to equitize social systems. Critical consciousness is often lacking in the work of service-learning (including "critical service learning") and civic or community engagement. This chapter elucidates the essential link between civic identity and the development of critical consciousness, framing it as crucial for pursuing paths to public service, engagement, and social justice.

Theoretical Framework

Critical theory provides an analytical and philosophical framework that underscores the need for critical consciousness in learning. It focuses on empowering critical thought and deconstructing ideological roadblocks that hinder change. Increasing one's awareness of personal agency improves responsiveness to social issues, particularly given the insights gained from practitioners in the field and from reviewing literature and research by critical thought leaders, both past and present, on issues of injustice. However, the practices, behaviors, attitudes, and habits of mind aligned with structural and systemic issues have created injustices and negative outcomes for students. This has led to an inability to recognize their own agency in disrupting injustice, their participation in hegemonic structures, and/or their complacency with oppression. As individuals become more aware of their role in society, they must also understand historical contexts to guide future decisions aimed at slowly undoing oppression, and recognize that perception of both reality and experiences are forms of possession (Freire, 2005). By critically reflecting on and analyzing our experiences, we can develop a consciousness that helps us unlearn past mistakes and, consequently, change future habits and behavior. Community-based practitioner scholars at institutions of higher education can offer unique opportunities for students to develop their critical and reflective lenses. These practitioners bridge the gap between theory and practice, driving the application of theoretical concepts in real-world scenarios.

Critical consciousness can and should be a critical component of the day-to-day business of higher education, not just as an academic concept but also in practice. It should inform institutional, organizational, and structural justice in areas of hiring, compensation and budgets, purchasing, partnerships, as well as in other social, political, and economic practices within the institution. New directions in the field of higher education community engagement can arise from the willingness to explore existing injustices within our social systems and how each pathway interacts with, influences, and is influenced by these systems. Current social systems and structures that are rooted in oppression ingrained in our society and part of our day-to-day practices preclude the ability to have robust critical consciousness that can effect change. Using critical consciousness both as a tool and lens for consciously unpacking institutional inequities would allow the field to operationalize the goals of social justice both in theory and in practice.

Critical Consciousness in Practice

As a new faculty member at a small liberal arts college in the Midwest, I integrated the Pathways survey tool into a doctoral seminar on service theory within an educational leadership program that I was teaching. The use of the survey was intended to support students' reflection on the philosophies of service, particularly in relation to socially constructed isms stemming from sociological categories of difference (i.e., race, sex, ability). The goal was to engage in a deeper discussion around how the Pathways framework can support the development of civic identity by serving as a point for critical reflection and understanding of agency and power and encourage a critique of service from a social justice lens. The seminar contextualized four major components of service (parameters, application, integration, and transformation) as course outcomes on transformational leadership. Moving forward, these four components can also be mapped and incorporated with the shared knowledge, skills, and attributes identified across the Pathways Practitioner Profiles. For example, critical consciousness is essential in understanding the historical and contemporary context of social issues, lived experiences of the community, and, especially, power structures and relational dynamics between stakeholders, environments, and organizations.

While the tool served as a conversation starter to critically analyze and assess service theory and civic engagement, I was interested in exploring the awareness of the development of a critical civic identity. The conversations in the doctoral seminar centered on critical reflection by prompting the following questions:

- What is your definition of *service*?
- Which pathway does your service philosophy most align with and why?
- What role does experience play in the definitions of *service* based on the survey?
- Does the survey offer a complete picture of service—why or why not?
- How can we invite a more critical approach to service for social justice?

It is necessary to remain critical of the embedded assumptions about power and privilege that can endorse and exacerbate systems of oppression. The Pathways framework invites opportunity for profound exploration around socially responsible service. To invite the opportunity to develop critical consciousness as a civic identity, the pathways invite an opportunity to explore ideas that serve to empower critical thought and deconstruct ideological roadblocks that hinder change. Current societal issues signal the importance of engaging in critical reflection through questions that seek to challenge the inherent power structures within the concept of service. This invites a more robust development of theory of mind around human agency, beginning with the construction of self-assessment of opportunities to serve and the awareness of the level of advocacy necessary for change.

In our current society, human beings have found ways to impose a dominant ideology of citizenship, norms, and values upon civilians. This then alienates some and effectively perpetuates inequality.

> Western Civilization is historically oppressive. Domestically, its history is one of oppressing women, slaves, and serfs. Internationally, its history is one of colonialism and imperialism. It is no accident that the works in the Western tradition are by white males, because the tradition is dominated by a caste consisting of white males. In this tradition, white males are the group in power. (Searle, 1996, p. 96)

Searle (1996) and Mills (1997) have framed this idea effectively. As students prepare for their work and roles in society, they must be ready to engage critically by challenging ideology that has served to stratify people into layers according to socially constructed interpretations of value to society. Critical consciousness encounters mechanisms of alienation, separation, and ostracization when students have learned to break down barriers of hegemony rooted in racism, cultural dominance, and/or colonialism. Critical consciousness brings with it a realization of the dangers and disadvantages of thinking of people in castes, such as living in a racially unjust society. A huge concern is that the majority of people have become complacent with castes that stratify and oppress based on sociological and socially constructed categories of difference, and consequently we have, as a society, developed mindless practices that are endemic to inequity. A renewed awareness of community engagement work in higher education will reestablish a commitment to a philosophy of service rooted in social justice.

Even in spaces that appear to be progressive, we neglect to examine how knowledge can be subjective due to the diversity of experiences from person to person, and thus the institution of higher education will continue to cast out the work of justice without a critical and intentional focus on social issues as the vehicle that drives praxis. Freire has argued that the educational system has been the enemy of the people because it serves as a way to perpetuate oppressive ideals. Since the educational institution functions as an "instrument to bring about conformity" (Freire, 2005, p. 34) rather than liberating young men and women for the creation of a new world, it causes the people to become oppressed and to "internalize the image of the oppressor and adopt his guidelines and fear freedom" (p. 47), thus becoming controlled or governed not by outside forces but by oneself (Foucault, 1991). The development of critical consciousness for racial justice in students' civic identities, for example, starts with an analysis of race, class, and ability ideologies that have led to racial injustice in order to understand the path to justice, which would promote critical self-reflection that would immediately change outcomes. As students develop their critical consciousness, the pathways offer a framework through which students can expand their analysis to include how social change may be enacted to reduce or eradicate racial injustice. Since we live in a racialized society, race needs to be further theorized and contextualized to provide structure to serve as analytic learning for understanding inequity. The interconnectedness of race, politics, and law represents an important underlying analytical framework for formal educational settings. Education is not separate from race, politics, and law. Therefore, education must be critically analyzed, explored, and juxtaposed with the development of civic identity.

Critical Consciousness of Systemic Issues in the Development of Civic Identity

The development of civic identity is essential to leading individuals to live out humanistic values on the firm basis and commitment to a social justice–related mission. In 2023, the *Michigan Journal of Community Service Learning* published a Special Volume on Civic Identity, in which each paper engaged with the civic identity core commitments and building blocks:

- capacity to engage constructively across difference
- democratic knowledge, habits, and skills
- knowledge of social change frameworks and strategies

- deep content knowledge
- resilient mind, body, and spirit (Schnaubelt et al., 2023)

Centering on isms, like racism, as a forging issue in higher education should be a collective commitment of embracing the courage to disrupt racial injustice and support the improvement of empowered civic identities.

Pathway to Civic Engagement for Justice and Social Change: A More Robust Civic Identity

Research on civic identity suggests that its cultivation is developmental (Johnson, 2017). Johnson argues that "educators should anchor their work in explicit theoretical models that help students interpret their experiences and promote growth" (p. 54). However, much of the research on civic identity focuses on individual growth and transformation as opposed to a collective process for social change. It is important for educators/practitioner-scholars to scaffold these elemental concepts in order to move students toward collective action and liberation. Instructional approaches such as critical reflection, storytelling, and counterstorytelling are effective ways to deconstruct notions of the "other." These can also illuminate how idealized notions of identity badges translate to unequal power distribution. There is power and agency in the collection of stories, and this must be driven by the counterstories of wealth, power, and privilege that make up the complete picture of civic and democratic participation. Without a collective process for understanding civic identity, we run the risk of elevating privileged perspectives of civic engagement and smothering the stories of civic identity that help to expose inequality.

The Politics of Racial Difference and Political Engagement in Civic Identity: A Critical Theory of Social Impact

An age-old question persists: Would service be necessary in the presence of social justice? Experience molds one's epistemology of knowledge. Moreover, our experiences provide clarity and obfuscate our epistemics. In many cases, students of color come to us with diverse knowledge and experiences that are necessary to lead social change. It is widely understood in social change work that those who are most impacted by the issues have a necessary perspective of how issues impacting them should be addressed. We should build on that experiential knowledge for our students. Understanding a theory of service as social justice is necessary for students to feel empowered to change systems. Otherwise, the knowledge of the experiences they've had do little to invite multiple perspectives and critique the epistemological frameworks they hold as truths. The knowledge of a collective experience is the only way to demystify the epistemological frameworks that shape one's own experiential knowledge. Critical theory empowers individuals to step outside of their own reality and to embrace, if even for a brief moment, the reality of someone else's experience and, to add, suspend judgment on that experience. We witness epistemic agency that speaks to mobilizing movements seeking to end oppression and injustice when students have opportunities to employ a critical theory of service. Service, in the sense of leadership for social justice, is indeed unnecessary in a society that lacks injustice. Cultural evolutions have enhanced our ability to imagine justice. The ability to imagine this also leads to impact and change. We begin to act in accordance with our collective vision. We begin to experience education around a critical theory of service. Human beings do not need to suffer collectively in order

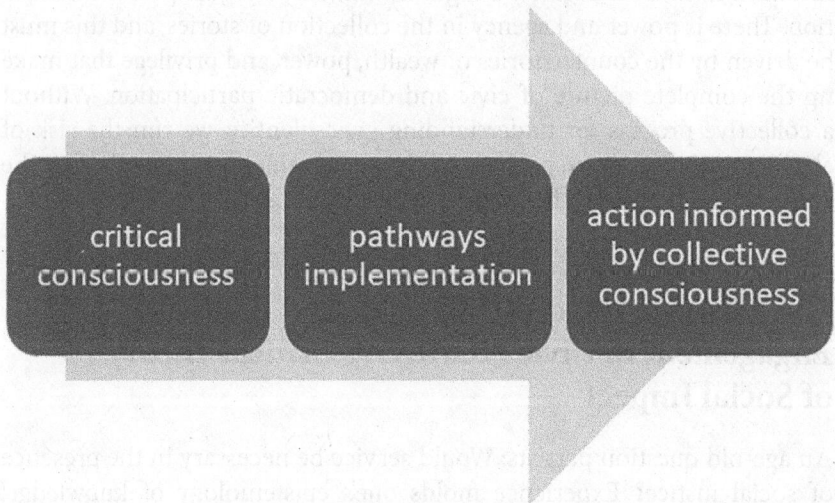

Figure 19.1. A visual teaching model for developing a theory of service for social justice.

to be inspired to change. As shown in Figure 19.1, we can teach students how to theorize a collective vision around a philosophy of service for social justice.

Teaching in higher education during a global pandemic was no easy feat. Furthermore, teaching through the exploration of issues of racism, classism, sexism, xenophobia, gender differences, heteronormativity—to name a few—during a global and social crisis when social disparities were confounded by civil unrest and civic divide brought with it an unimaginable journey toward shared responsibility. The social-emotional and cognitive experiences that usually come to pass in the learning through pedagogies that have withstood the test of time are increasingly challenged by shifts in cultural, political, and technological alterations. As institutions were impacted by the COVID-19 health pandemic, we were forced to adapt to rapid changes with speed, humility, gratitude, and patience. Social distancing changed the landscape of learning that occurred during the COVID-19 pandemic in 2020 for all of us, particularly for our most vulnerable communities. The impact on what constituted mental and emotional health—as well as physical, cognitive, and social domains of existence—could not be taken for granted. Higher education witnessed systemic disparities emphasized in social and higher education affairs during the 2020 pandemic (Chronicle of Higher Education and Fidelity Investments, 2020). Higher education also demonstrated its capacity and potential as a public good, through the distribution and coordination of student aid. We learned from the pandemic that service was in even more demand, and our current social constructs and constraints around justice are unavoidable.

Conclusion

An interdisciplinary nature of social science places civic identity within multiple coordinated concepts found in several disciplines: history, geography, psychology, economics, sociology, government/political science, anthropology, humanities, law, archaeology, and citizenship. Civic visioning will occur within a framework for social justice and as a process that centers a commitment to addressing social issues. Strengthening moral solidarity should be at the core of civic engagement. Therefore, civic identity is increasingly important in considering the project toward resolving the legacies of isms such as racism in the United States. Careful and selective attempts to solve the problems we face will lead to greater concerted effort. Key challenges facing institutions of higher education live in the legacy of racism, which means that current initiatives and innovations in higher education must focus on antiracism if we are to nurture civic identity to enrich our democracy that is currently threatened by racial divide.

In order for us to commit to critically engaged community work, we must continue to forge a commitment to understanding civic identity as doing away with hegemonic social issues. When we allow opportunities to deconstruct dangerous and divisive attitudes, either/or thinking, individualism/separatism, and competition, we can embrace a more just image of a kind of civic identity that is inviting and inclusive for all (Okun, 2021). Community-based scholars and professors of professional practice can therefore utilize the Pathways of Social Impact with an emphasis on social justice, which has the ability to empower and unite rather than perpetuate the destruction of individuals, communities, and society. Practitioners can generate environments that embrace a realistic alternative to the one we live in that will be necessary for developing hope, intellect, courage, and innovation that bring us steps closer to justice. We have an opportunity to create shared language around a commitment to civic identity for social justice that begins with a critical analysis of social issues. To start, we must

- trace our social, intellectual, and philosophical roots to a radical concept of love (as described in various ways by authors such as bell hooks, Cornel West, Satish Kumar);
- bridge the distance between cultures and do away with the practice of racializing human beings that are separated by distinctions of unearned and socially constructed ideals of power and privilege;
- renew our connections between self and others in this global ecology, particularly a rejuvenation between Indigenous and marginalized communities and knowledges;
- design onramps that build connections across disciplines;
- listen empathetically and lean in to the experiences of people living across multiple realities that stem from structural and institutional economic divides—a critical education beginning with awareness of oppression; and
- universalize our systems to leverage goods and services rooted in collectivism and human capital to equitize inequality.

Oppressive isms such as the burden of racism continue to harm personal, physical, professional, and psychological domains for us all. Transformative resistance helps to create visioning and action for the work of undoing and exposing the deeply rooted and inherent destruction that comes with social injustice. Every issue can be linked back to systemic and structural injustice—food insecurity, homelessness, racism, sexism, heterosexism, xenophobia, religious oppression, adolescent suicide, low income, college access, inadequate housing, job security, human trafficking/slavery. The systemic and structural injustices have resulted in widespread oppression. Transformational resistance has been used as a lens on student agency to counter systemic oppression (Talavera & Solórzano, 2012). There is an opportunity to create shared language around a commitment to understanding civic identity as doing away with social issues. The pathways equip higher education to assess a willingness/readiness to equitize systems through critical consciousness and transformational resistance in civic identity learning and community engagement.

References

Chronicle of Higher Education and Fidelity Investments. (2020). *"On the verge of burnout": Covid-19's impact on faculty well-being and career plans* [Research brief]. https://connect.chronicle.com/rs/931-EKA-218/images/Covid%26 FacultyCareerPaths_Fidelity_ResearchBrief_v3%20%281%29.pdf

Foucault, M. (1991). Governmentality. In G. Burchell, C. Gordon, & P. Miller (Eds.), *The Foucault effects: Studies in governmentality* (pp. 87–104). The University of Chicago Press.

Freire, P. (2005). *Pedagogy of the oppressed.* Continuum.

Hart, D., Richardson, C., & Wilkenfeld, B. (2011). Civic identity. In S. J. Schwartz, K. Luyckx, & V. L. Vignoles (Eds.), *Handbook of identity theory and research* (pp. 771–787). Springer Science + Business Media.

Johnson, M. (2017). Understanding college students' civic identity development: A grounded theory. *Journal of Higher Education Outreach and Engagement, 21*(3), 31–59.

Ladson-Billings, G., & Tate, W. F. (1995). Toward a critical race theory of education. *Teachers College Record, 97*(1), 47–68.

Mills, C. W. (1997). *The racial contract.* Cornell University Press.

Okun, T. (2021). *White supremacy culture: Still here.* https://www.whitesupremacy culture.info/

Schnaubelt, T. J., Bass, S., Terra, L., & Lobo, K. (2023). Introduction to the special volume on civic identity. *Michigan Journal of Community Service Learning, 29*(2). https://doi.org/10.3998/mjcsl.5136

Searle, J. (1996). The case for a traditional liberal education. *The Journal of Blacks in Higher Education, 13*(2), 91–98.

Suzina, A. C., & Tufte, T. (2020). Freire's vision of development and social change: Past experiences, present challenges, and perspectives for the future. *International Communication Gazette, 82*(5), 411–424. https://doi.org/10.1177/1748048520943692

Talavera, V., & Solórzano, D. (2012). Resistance theory. In J. Banks (Ed.), *Encyclopedia of diversity in education* (Vol. 4, pp. 1856–1858). SAGE.

AFTERWORD

Moving Forward

Sean P. Crossland, Thomas Schnaubelt, and Annabel Wong

The Pathways framework has existed for nearly a decade at the time of this writing. The Pathways were a necessary innovation for articulating shared language in an adolescent field and for addressing concerns about overly simplistic, binary thinking related to social change. Its distinctive collaborative and evolving approach has not slowed since its inception. The authors' contributions in this book speaks to the pathways' continued potential to reimagine and reshape higher education's alignment with the public good.

There are many remarkable examples within the Working Group that are not represented in this book and good reason to believe not all the work being done with the pathways is represented in the Working Group. We hope this book will serve as a catalyst for future projects, collaborations, and a broader body of cocreative work centered on the pathways as a means for reimagining higher education's role in transforming democracy. This work situates the pathways as an opportunity to address the urgent need to stabilize democracy in the United States. In light of the dynamic, ongoing challenges to democratic processes and institutions, democratic renewal demands continued innovation, knowledge sharing, and commitment to democratic values.

In the closing section, we present considerations for advancing the public purpose of higher education through intentional engagement with the Pathways framework. These considerations are organized into three categories: individual, institutional, and field building. However, as with much of this book, these categories are fluid and interconnected.

Individual

Considering the individual when engaging with the Pathways framework offers rich potential for growth. In this section, individual primarily addresses the work of students and practitioners and can extend to community partners committed to transformative work.

Reflection

Reflection has been a pillar of community engagement work for several decades. We emphasize reflection as a "whole-body process of transforming experience into meaning to shape the future" (Cavagnaro, 2023, p. 3). It offers an opportunity for students, faculty, and practitioners to deepen the meaning-making process of experiential learning and content exploration with the Pathways framework.

In the introduction, Sean shared his initial interest in pathways as driven by a desire to engage more deeply with the Community Organizing and Activism Pathway. At the same time, his teaching approach was resistant to meaningful engagement with Philanthropy and Social Entrepreneurship and Corporate Social Responsibility Pathways due to his own ideological stances toward capitalism and neoliberal agendas. Through critical and intentional reflection, Sean has grown to appreciate and value the Pathways framework as a whole, recognizing each pathway's unique potential for social impact. Although he still views capitalism as a barrier to human and ecological sustainability, he acknowledges that the challenges moving forward demand equal attention to harm reduction and envisioning a future when human rights are more equitably realized globally. Many of us who have used the pathways have found them to be a valuable framework for examining biases, assumptions, and predispositions, not just with our students but ourselves. Sometimes our instincts are affirmed upon reflection; other times we are called to radically rethink our perspective on the ethical implications of any particular approach to social change. Reflection nearly always allows for new insights and questions to emerge.

Historical Analysis

Historical analysis of efforts to utilize the pathways as a lens at local, regional, national, and global levels will deepen our understanding and ways of thinking about the public purpose of higher education and the dynamics of social change. Individuals' histories are conveyed through their relationships while community histories emerge from the interplay of relationships and shared information. Understanding how different neighborhoods and regions interact with and are impacted by the pathways is an essential foundation for advancing transformative work within any pathway.

Questions about when history should be viewed as a contested space can be approached through various forms of narrative analysis. Additionally, community histories must be safeguarded against the risk of being coopted. In *The Dawn of Everything: A New History of Humanity*, Graeber and Wengrow (2021) emphasize the fundamental imperative to question any narrative that implies a single, inevitable path of social evolution, or assumes that our path to the current state of the world was predetermined. Future work should focus on compiling people's histories within and across pathways as they relate to social impact so that we might continue to illuminate the ways in which struggles for dignity and quality of life have made meaningful contributions to the public good.

Democracy as Hidden Curriculum

The Working Group has striven to craft descriptive language in the Pathways tool and share resources while avoiding the pitfalls of partisan or ideological alignment. Certainly, we see this work as value-oriented and requiring the same intentionality as all effective community and civic engagement strategies. There is an inherent tension between the goal of making educational theory or practice inclusive of any worldview a student might bring and the recognition that an apolitical educational experience becomes impossible once it is situated within the lived realities of educators and students.

Meaningful engagement with the pathways requires continual questioning and exploration of our own political and ideological perspectives, especially as they relate to social change and the public purpose of higher education. Partisan polarity coupled with hyperindividualism is wreaking havoc on the civic sphere. As practitioners, it is essential that we examine our own dogmatic stances and remain dedicated to fostering adaptive, compassionate learning environments. At the same time, the community engagement field is teeming with a sense of urgency to slow the erosion of democracy within our institutions and communities.

Interpretations of hidden curriculum range from the unintended consequences of a learning experience (a change in student perspective outside the learning outcomes) to the sociocultural factors influencing a learning experience (departmental dynamics, influence on faculty state of mind). Democracy as the hidden curriculum as it relates to the pathways highlights opportunity to infuse democratic values, principles, and action into our work. While democracy as the hidden curriculum has a place in the institutional and field-building themes in the following list, it appears in the individual theme as this stance starts with individual behavioral and mindset shifts.

Democracy as the hidden curriculum of pathways work asks questions:

- How might we infuse the notions of civic friendship and compromise (Manville & Ober, 2023) when using the Pathways framework and crafting engaged learning experiences?
- Can we strive to preserve and uplift marginalized epistemologies, especially the lived experiences of those who have been systematically excluded from the democratic enterprise of the United States, while simultaneously advancing an overt agenda of democratization?
- What advances can be made in reconciling higher education's exploitative history with the recognition of its unique position to operate at the intersection of diversity and civic engagement (Sturm et al., 2011)?

Institutional

Considering the institution when engaging with the pathways framework offers opportunity to explore programs, processes and approaches. This section offers consideration for areas with rich potential for further development, acknowledging there are many additional ways not discussed the Pathways framework might work to rethink institutional efforts.

Programming

The Pathways framework continues to develop and gain momentum. Part Two of this book provides examples of curricular and cocurricular programming, showcasing a range of institutional support at a variety of institutions. While institutional adoption and support can have the benefit of providing more resources, greater student access, and enhanced inter-disciplinary collaboration, smaller programs offer unique opportunities for students and can circumvent the pressures of institutionalization. Pro-gramming of all types and sizes can offer meaningful contributions to the efforts of the Working Group and our understanding of the impactful use of the Pathways framework and tool.

Emphasizing creativity and centering creative self-belief (Karwowski et al., 2019) in Pathways programming provide students with opportunities to expand their creative confidence, creative self-awareness, and creative self-image through the lens of social change. Social-emotional imagina-tion is the "ability to conceive of multiple possible cognitive and affective perspectives and courses of action and to skillfully reflect about each of these and their ties to one's own value and understanding of the world" (Gotlieb et al., 2019, p. 710). Perspective-taking, identity construction, constructive internal reflection, and cultural awareness are all elements of social-emotional imagination. The broaden-and-build theory of positive emotions (Fredrickson, 2001) posits that positive emotions (which can be intentionally cultivated through positive psychology practices) should be viewed as both an ends and a means for enhanced well-being and psycho-logical growth. The broaden-and-build theory posits that some positive emotions can "broaden people's momentary thought-action repertoires and build their enduring personal resources, ranging from physical and intellectual resources to social and psychological resources" (p. 219). This theory can help practitioners navigate emotionally charged conversations and support students in making meaning of their often strong emotions about issues affecting them and their communities. By integrating cre-ativity and positive psychology into Pathways programming there is rich potential to create meaningful student learning experiences that focus on cocreating ideas and action for social change that are unconfined by the current state of the issue or world.

Local Contextualization

Local contextualization of the pathways can mean several things. There is ample opportunity for institutions to leverage the Pathways framework to advance community partnership development and larger community engagement strategies. Striving for reciprocity with community partners and practicing relational care with all stakeholders is essential. These ef-forts should be balanced with a strong focus on prioritizing the student learning experience. The framework can also be used to examine how community organizations are approaching their work. For example, Utah, which boasts the highest volunteer rates in the country, might show a preference for the Direct Service Pathway, whereas the San Francisco Bay Area, with its long history of social activism, might emphasize Community Organizing and Activism.

As practitioners work to reimagine higher education's role in transforming democracy, hyperlocal approaches may offer nuanced insights into specific communities, neighborhoods, and groups that are both affected by and have an impact on higher education. Community engagement efforts within higher education institutions are notorious for abstracting *community* to mean "anything outside the institution." Institutions can clarify their roles in supporting the meaningful social impact work occurring within communities by applying the pathways as a lens in the analysis. Recognizing the nuanced ways in which different communities and organizations engage with one or more pathway can also improve the likelihood of connecting students with transformative experiences that align with their personal goals.

Careers and Work

The creation of the Pathways Practitioner Profiles was largely motivated by the need to more clearly articulate the potential use of the Pathways framework as a model for student career development. The profiles are designed to provide additional support for advising students on academic and professional decisions using the pathways. They aim to guide students to make more informed decisions based on their interest in social impact. Expanding the use of the pathways in internships, service-learning placements, and more expansive capstone experiences will create practical ways for students to intentionally develop the knowledge, skills, and attributes to be effective practitioners in roles within and across the pathways.

There is an urgent need to define and better map the onramps for which students can start, pivot into, and advance within social impact careers. Too often, students receive career guidance constrained by disciplinary perspectives, stakeholder access, or financial motivations. Infusing the pathways into these conversations opens possibilities to inform their thinking and align their career choices with the issues they find most pressing. Alongside the daily work of supporting students in their academic and career growth, there is a need to articulate the economic potential for such shifts in economic terms, taking into account the lived realities of students and the communities from which they enter higher education. Historically, higher education has contributed to perpetuating stratification, elitism, and hierarchies of human worth. How might we shift the conversation of the value of higher education toward a framework that balances individual social mobility with the collective good?

Field Building

As was described in the introduction, there is a broad assemblage of nomenclature for the field of higher education community engagement. At times, these nuances are important to differentiate, clarify and complicate. The following considerations invite readers to contemplate how the pathways framework might contribute to field-building efforts within specific distinctions and especially within the broader field.

Resource Building

One priority area for growth is the development of more shareable learning resources. The Working Group currently maintains a shared drive containing advising resources, sample syllabi, activities, presentations, and more. As practitioners continue to experiment with new applications of the framework and tool, there is significant potential to expand these shared resources and learn from each other's efforts.

Collaborative Research

The lack of robust, comparable, and replicable research across institutions was a major impetus for the creation of the pathways. This challenge remains prevalent today, hindering progress within the field. The Pathways framework and tool offer significant potential to move the field forward through shared language and opportunities for multisite research. Chapter 16 ("Pathways Data") offers some insights and explorations with the existing data around the pathways, and hopefully stimulates further thought on how researchers might use the pathways in inquiries focused on higher education's role in sustaining and transforming democracy. Collaborative inquiries using the pathways should be a central feature of this exploration.

Another promising area for growth is to align Pathways research with existing studies on civic identity (Hart et al., 2011). There are many significant questions about how civic identity develops and the role it plays in democratic participation. The building blocks and core commitments, discussed in the Chapter 19, are a feature of Pathways curriculum that offer potential to expand our understanding of civic identity and how it can be intentionally cultivated.

Interaction and Integration

The pathways were informed by a range of different models and frameworks and now have the potential to inform and inspire the creation and application of new frameworks and models. In Part Two, authors illustrate how they use the pathways in conversation with other models and theories. There is nearly limitless possibility in the continued exploration of how the pathways can complement additional approaches. For example, overlaying the pathways with the United Nations Sustainable Development Goals could provide students with new perspectives on how to contribute to these goals within their local communities and academic studies.

The conclusion of *The Cambridge Handbook of Service Learning and Community Engagement* outlines five theories, practices, and principles that can ground future community engagement work: feminist pragmatism, anticolonialism and antiracism (versus inclusion and diversity), class and economic power, the practice of freedom through arts and humanities, and the recognition of "a legacy of suffering and struggle, without falling victim to fatalism or cynicism" (Dolgon et al., 2017, p. 531). Each of these five concepts offers opportunities to enhance our analysis of Pathways praxis. Feminist pragmatism might ask how gender influences and is influenced by each pathway. Anticolonialism and antiracism offers the opportunity to rethink where Western ideologies and whiteness appear and/or dominate within a pathway and with our notions of social change as a whole. Pathways work has yet to venture into asking where Indigeneity fits into our understanding of leadership for social change. Class and economic power influence students' perceptions of where they fit (or do not fit) within each pathway as well as a pathway's potential impact. The Pathways framework offers opportunities to reconsider what "humanities careers" look like. Art as a form of social change is well established and warrants more consideration within each pathway and not just Community Organizing and Activism. Where the pathways fit within the practice of freedom as a whole may warrant another volume. Many students, especially those most impacted by social issues, enter college disillusioned by what they have experienced and seen inflicted on and in their communities. Other students begin with the best intentions and become overwhelmed as their understanding of the complexity of social problems increases. As educators of social change practitioners, we too can fall victim to the velocity with which wicked problems become intractable. Urgent optimism (McGonigal, 2022) is not submissive naivety but rather an active stance that embraces psychological flexibility, realistic hope, and future power.

Closing

There is little doubt that higher education is in the midst of substantial shifts. Studies indicate that the public perception of higher education is at an all-time low, in line with all-time low confidence in U.S. institutions (Fry et al., 2024; Jones, 2022, 2024; Pew Research Center, 2024). In 2024, numerous state legislatures introduced measures directly challenging diversity, equity, and inclusion efforts, while many states are preparing for significantly reduced enrollment based on declining college-going populations. At best, this represents a challenging period for both higher education and democracy in the United States; at worst, it marks the beginning of a worsening trend from which they may never fully realize their potential.

One reason for this crisis in confidence in higher education may lie in our collective failure to acknowledge a fundamental polarity in the purpose of the university: that of advocacy and critical inquiry. As Yuval Levin (2024) states, the university's fundamental purpose is the "pursuit of knowledge of the truth . . . and to form adult human beings and citizens in its light" (para. 11). For others, academic institutions are flawed as evidenced by the fact that they often reproduce social hierarchies and inequalities; hence, the purpose of the university must be to challenge the status quo and foster critical consciousness. This is the implication in Audre Lorde's (1983) statement, often quoted by those who advance community engagement: "The master's tools will never dismantle the master's house." (p. 94)

Amna Khalid and John Tomasi explore the tension between advocacy (civic engagement) and inquiry (the search for truth) in the Heterodox Academy podcast *The Role of Universities in the Age of Campus Activism*. Khalid asserts the institution has a dual purpose that includes both critical inquiry and training for citizenship, to which Tomasi suggests an even more expansive view. He says universities are about "learning to be a person . . . not only to seek the truth, not only to be citizens . . . but to be a less stunted being, to be a more expansive being, beings who understand the possibilities for our own situatedness" (Tomasi & Khalid, 2024, 13:54). Indeed, these ideas are codified in most college and university mission or vision statements.

Commitment to individually and collectively wrestle with the inquiry–advocacy polarity is central to our being able to effectively discharge the mission of higher education.

In a society infected with toxic levels of affective polarization, we suggest that universities can and must name this polarity, accept that it is an enduring tension, and open ourselves to the idea that universities can both preserve and transform society. Moreover, we must model the capacity to wrestle with this tension in front of students.

In "The Heart of a Teacher: Identity and Integrity in Teaching," Parker Palmer (1997) suggests:

> We need to open a new frontier in our exploration of good teaching: the inner landscape of a teacher's life. To chart that landscape fully, three important paths must be taken—intellectual, emotional, and spiritual—and none can be ignored. Reduce teaching to intellect and it becomes a cold abstraction; reduce it to emotions and it becomes narcissistic; reduce it to the spiritual and it loses its anchor to the world. Intellect, emotion, and spirit depend on each other for wholeness. They are interwoven in the human self and in education at its best, and we need to interweave them in our pedagogical discourse as well. (pp. 15–16)

How does this relate to the pathways? One of the more common questions we get when introducing the framework to educators is "Which pathway should we encourage for students?" The only right answer is "None of them and all of them." Our role is to expose students to frameworks that help them surface complexity and clarify their own values, whether it is in the levers they pull to create social change or the issues they choose to be passionate about. When we present different levers as a binary choice (e.g., "change or charity," "volunteerism or social justice work"), we limit avenues of inquiry. The Pathways framework was designed to expand options and spark curiosity in the hope that it enables students to become better advocates for the issues they choose to support.

As educators who, in the classroom, have considerable power and authority, the decision to take a stand or make a statement must always be understood as a choice between competing priorities: preserving the institution as a place of free and open discourse (critical inquiry) or uplifting the university as a forceful advocate for a just and sustainable world (advocacy). These two competing priorities represent a central polarity and must be managed. Because of its centrality to the college or university's mission, our commitment to critical inquiry must be viewed as paramount, but only insofar as it is a precondition of effective and morally defensible advocacy. Our commitment to either concept should only be compromised under extraordinary circumstances and for a very clearly understood set of reasons.

To effectively use the Pathways framework as a pedagogical tool, it is important to do what Parker Palmer suggests: bring our whole selves to the endeavor. The framework is most impactful when educators use it to model both critical inquiry and advocacy. This means demonstrating curiosity about the complex root causes of, and solutions to, our social challenges and showing them that the struggle of knowing the right pathway is an enduring part of the human condition. If it is difficult to model curiosity, critical inquiry, and advocacy, we should reflect on why it might be difficult. Doing so may open Parker Palmer's new frontier of good teaching—the inner landscape of a teacher's life—and contribute to our collective capacity to fulfill the dual mission of the university.

The Pathways framework does not provide the silver bullet for higher education to realize its role in cultivating a public good, nor the answer to the current state of democracy. Instead, the pathways offer a meaningful contribution and may serve as an aligning force for the many ways community engagement professionals are already addressing these issues. We hope readers will appreciate its potential for fostering meaningful exploration of the ways social change happens and for transforming individual, institutional, and field-wide practices in community engagement.

References

Cavagnaro, L. (2023). *Experiments in reflection.* Stanford d.school Library. https://dschool.stanford.edu/book-collections/experiments-in-reflection

Dolgon, C., Eatman, T. K., & Mitchell, T. D. (2017). The devil at the crossroads: Service learning and community engagement from here on out. In C. Dolgon,

T. D. Mitchell, & T. K. Eatman (Eds.), *The Cambridge handbook of service learning and community engagement* (pp. 527–533). Cambridge University Press. https://doi.org/10.1017/9781316650011.049

Fredrickson, B. L. (2001). The role of positive emotions in positive psychology: The broaden-and-build theory of positive emotions. *American Psychologist, 56*(3), 218–226.

Fry, R., Braga, D., & Parker, K. (2024, May 23). *Is college worth it?* Pew Research Center. https://www.pewresearch.org/social-trends/2024/05/23/is-college-worth-it-2/

Gotlieb, R. J., Hyde, E., Immordino-Yang, M. H., & Kaufman, S. B. (2019). Imagination is the seed of creativity. In J. C. Kaufman & R. J. Sternberg (Eds.), *The Cambridge handbook of creativity* (pp. 709–731). Cambridge University Press.

Graeber, D., & Wengrow, D. (2021). *The dawn of everything: A new history of humanity.* Penguin UK.

Hart, D., Richardson, C., & Wilkenfeld, B. (2011). Civic identity. In S. J. Schwartz, K. Luyckx, & V. L. Vinoles (Eds.), *Handbook of identity theory and research* (pp. 771–787). Springer.

Jones, J. M. (2022, July 5). *Confidence in U.S. institutions down; average at new low.* Gallup. https://news.gallup.com/poll/394283/confidence-institutions-down-average-new-low.aspx

Jones, J. M. (2024, July 8). *U.S confidence in higher education now closely divided.* Gallup. https://news.gallup.com/poll/646880/confidence-higher-education-closely-divided.aspx

Karwowski, M., Lebuda, I., & Beghetto, R. A. (2019). 19 creative self-beliefs. In J. C. Kaufman & R. J. Sternberg (Eds.), *The Cambridge handbook of creativity* (pp. 396–417). Cambridge University Press.

Levin, Y. (2024, August 15). *A new hope for saving the universities.* American Enterprise Institute. https://www.aei.org/op-eds/a-new-hope-for-saving-the-universities/

Lorde, A. (1983). The masters' tools will never dismantle the master's house'. In C. Moraga & G. Anzaldúa (Eds.), *This bridge called my back: Writings by radical women of color* (pp. 94–101). Kitchen Table Press.

Manville, B., & Ober, J. (2023). *The civic bargain: How democracy survives.* Princeton University Press.

McGonigal, J. (2022). *Imaginable: How to see the future coming and be ready for anything.* Random House.

Palmer, P. J. (1997). The heart of a teacher identity and integrity in teaching. *Change: The Magazine of Higher Learning, 29*(6), 14–21.

Pew Research Center. (2024, June 24). *Public trust in government: 1958-2024.* https://www.pewresearch.org/politics/2024/06/24/public-trust-in-government-1958-2024/

Sturm, S., Eatman, T., Saltmarsh, J., & Bush, A. (2011). *Full participation: Building the architecture for diversity and public engagement in higher education* [White paper]. Columbia University Law School, Center for Institutional and Social Change. http://Imaginingamerica.org/Wp-Content/Uploads/2011/10/Catalyst-Paper.pdf

Tomasi, J., & Khalid, A. (2024). The role of universities in the age of campus activism (Season 2, Episode 20). *Heterodox Out Loud* [Video Podcast]. https://heterodoxacademy.org/podcasts/s2-episode-20-the-role-of-universities-in-the-age-of-campus-activism

Editors

Sean P. Crossland, PhD, is the assistant professor and program director for the Masters of Higher Education Leadership program at Utah Valley University.

Thomas (Tom) Schnaubelt, PhD, is the assistant director of the Center for Revitalizing American Institutions at the Hoover Institution at Stanford University. He previously served as associate vice provost for education and executive director of the Haas Center for Public Service at Stanford.

Annabel Wong (she/her), MA/MPP, has been a member of the Pathways team since 2015. Her previous experiences include executing evaluation projects at Stanford University's Haas Center for Public Service and strategizing youth engagement at Plan Canada.

Contributors

Shamili Ajgaonkar, EdD, is a professor of biology and faculty chair for global education at the College of DuPage in Glen Ellyn, Illinois.

Aaliyah Baker, PhD, is a community-engaged scholar and faculty member in the Department of Educational Administration at the University of Dayton, School of Education and Health Sciences.

Melissa Bernard is the manager for professional development and programs at Georgetown University's Capitol Applied Learning Labs, where she plays a leading role in meeting students' cocurricular needs and providing career coaching as they live, learn, and intern in downtown Washington, DC.

Cassie Bingham serves as director of the UVU Center for Social Impact. She also serves as adjunct faculty, designing and teaching courses on social impact strategy, systems thinking for macro social work, and the evolutions of justice.

Agustin "Tino" Diaz, PhD, works as a manager for the ESG and Impact Office at Sorenson Communications where he leads research, project management, and data storytelling on various initiatives.

Vernette Doty directs the Community Engagement Center and the Margo F. Souza Student Leadership Centers at the University of California, Merced Campus.

Ryan W. Flynn is the high-impact practices director at the University of Illinois Springfield and is the former director of civic engagement and student leadership at Illinois College.

Breanna Lambert, LCSW, is the coordinator for skills workshops and mindfulness programs at the University of Utah. Breanna is also a dedicated therapist who specializes in working with populations that experience racial trauma.

Amanda Martin, MEd, is currently the assistant director of career services and student employment at Drake University in Des Moines, Iowa, and formerly served as the assistant director of community engaged learning.

Mike Moon serves as the associate director at the Utah Commission on Service and Volunteerism, which serves as the central coordinating body for service and volunteerism, including AmeriCorps and community engagement at the state level.

Lisa Morde is the associate director of civic engagement at Northeastern University in Boston, Massachusetts. She currently overseas a suite of co-curricular programs, including the Alliance of Civically Engaged Students and the Northeastern Votes Coalition of faculty, staff, and students.

Kemi A. Oyewole is a provost's postdoctoral fellow at the University of Pennsylvania Graduate School of Education. Her research explores the institutional and organizational conditions that shape the enactment of K–12 educational policy.

Katie L. Price, PhD, currently serves as senior associate director of the Lang Center for Civic and Social Responsibility at Swarthmore College. She specializes in engaged scholarship, particularly in the arts and humanities, contemporary literature and creative writing, and socially engaged practices.

Renee Sedlacek Lee, PhD, is a senior manager at Workiva, a leading software as a service company, where she plays a pivotal role in advancing sustainability and public affairs efforts. She previously served as director of community-engaged learning at Drake University, where she championed initiatives that bridged academic studies with meaningful community partnerships.

Nairuti Shastry (she/her) is the founder and principal of Nuance, a social impact consulting firm, through which she supports teams, organizations, and communities to both hospice the old and birth the new in pursuit of more just economic futures.

Ray Shiu, MA, serves as the deputy director of the Center for Social Justice (CSJ) at Georgetown University, where he is responsible for the overall management of CSJ's staff-run and student-run social justice community-based engagement, including student development, community and university outreach, and fiscal and administrative management.

Andrea Tafolla (she/her/ella), MS, works as the associate director of student leadership and community engagement at UC Merced, where she helps connect students and the larger Merced community through reciprocal partnerships in community service.

Luke Terra currently serves as the deputy director of the Haas Center for Public Service at Stanford University and serves as the resident fellow in Stanford's Public Service and Civic Engagement Theme House.

Joanne Tien, PhD, directs the RAISE Doctoral Fellowship Program at Stanford University, which supports doctoral students in connecting their research and scholarship to community engagement, social action, and positive impact.

Summer Barrick Valente, MPA, serves as a professional in residence in the Organizational Leadership Department at Utah Valley University's Woodbury School of Business, where she teaches in the Hospitality Management Program and other management courses.

Priscilla Villaseñor-Navarro is a former student fellow at the Center for Social Impact, where she currently works as a part-time coordinator for Utah Valley University's Student Leadership and Involvement Office.

Ally Wiseman is currently pursuing her master's degree in marine biology at the College of Charleston Grice Marine Laboratory, and she also has a teaching assistantship teaching intro biology labs.

Sarah C. Worley, PhD, is a professor of communication and director of community-engaged teaching and learning at Juniata College.

ACKNOWLEDGMENTS

Research Fellows:
Shamili Ajgoankar
Marissa Getts
Oliver "Gray" Jones
Renee Sedlacek Lee
Norma López
Mike Moon
Nairuti Shastry
Joseph Spiller
Joanne Tien

Peer Reviewers:
Elora Agsten
Sandra Bass
Renee Brown
Tara Carr-Lemke
Brianna Christy
Jessica Doak Flynn
Timothy Eatman
Tracy Finnegan
Daniel Hernandez
Hillary Kane
Debra Karp
Angie Kim
Stephanie N. Kurtzman
Kristina Lobo
Laura Martin
Nancy McHugh
Julie L. Plaut
Chrystal Stanley
Sarah Stoeckl
Sarita Tamayo-Moraga

Jonathon Westover
Andria Wisler
Kristen Wright

Community Practitioners:
Jill Adams
Deborah Adelman
Vanessa Alvey
Daniel Anello
Hannah M. Ashley
Joanna Cea
Julie Cencula Olberding
Theodoros Chronopoulos
Vira David-Rivera
Crystal Des-Ogugua
Leonora Dodge
Lina Dee Dostilio
Amy Dowley
Megan Downing
Tyler Dubois
Angelica Esquivel
Katie Evans
Katrina French
Susan Haarman
Eric Hartman
Rachel Humphrey
Tora Johnson
Hillary Kane
Rajiv Khanna
Martha A. Kirk
Heather Lord
Jennifer Magee

Earl Maneein
Dion McGill
Harold McNaron
Mandi McReynolds
Amanda Millerberg
Emily Moerer
Lauren Morgan
Christopher Nayve
Kristin Neeley
Mark Neikirk
Kristin Norris
Erin O'Keefe
Raymond Partolan
Deborah M. Pfliegel
Alison Powell
Debra Rowe
Lauren Sachs
Ari Sahagún
Sonia Sarkar
Jessamyn Shams-Lau
Kellea Shay Miller
Iyla Shornstein
Anna Smyth
Liza Springmeyer
Danielle Torain
Ayushi Vig
Katherine Waterford Darling
Anne Weiss
Lauren Wendling
Marq Withers

Student Focus Groups:
Bree Ank
Landon Ashlin
Makaiya Bedford
Nathan Carter
Savannah Clyde
Hannah M. Filizola Ruiz
Nachalah Gardiner
Elizabeth Germain
Ruth Hailemeskel
Stephanie Kiel
Marí Linares-Rigacci
Madison Luna
Bjorn Mustard
Kirby Nelson
Valentina Ramirez Barragán
Alexandra M. Ruiz Gaspar
Melanie Sadecki
Anshi Shastry
Arti Shastry
Corinne Sidebottom
Sydney Skemp
Andrea C. Smith
Rachel Sullivan
Kiona Wilson